Sinfree Makoni

AFRICAN APPLIED LINGUISTICS

**Selected Papers
Volume Two**
Including papers written in collaboration with
Busi Makoni, Ulrike Meinhof and Barbara Trudell

Edited by David Bade

**International Association for the Integrational Study of
Language and Communication**

This collection ©2020 by Sinfree Makoni.

Acknowledgements:

Introducing applied linguistics in Africa, ©2003 by Sinfree Makoni and Ulrike H. Meinhof. Originally published in AILA Review, 16(1), Jan 2003, 1-12.

Western perspectives in applied linguistics in Africa ©2004 Sinfree Makoni and Ulrike Meinhof, originally published in *AILA Review* 17(1),77-104.

The futility of being held captive by language policy issues in Applied Linguistics ©1993 originally published in *Per Linguam*, 9(2), 12-21.

Language and human rights discourses in Africa, ©2012 Originally published in *Journal of Multicultural Discourses*, 7(1), 1-20.

Complementary and conflicting discourses of linguistic diversity: implications for language planning, ©2006 by Sinfree Makoni and Barbara Trudell. Originally published in *Per Linguam* 22(2),*14-28.*

The consequences of a Chomskyan perspective on rules in second language acquisition 1994 ©originally published in *South African Journal of Linguistics* 12(3), 79-84.

English and Education in Anglophone Africa: Historical and Current Realities, ©2009 by Sinfree Makoni and Busi Makoni. Originally published in In M. Wong & S. Canagarajah (Eds.), *Christian and Critical English Language Educators in Dialogue: Pedagogical and Ethical Dilemmas*, pp.106-119. London: Routledge.

'I am starving with no hope to survive': Southern African Perspectives on Pedagogies of Globalization, ©2007 Sinfree Makoni and Busi Makoni. Originally published in *International Multilingual Research Journal,* 1(2), 105-118.

"They talk to us like children": language and intergenerational discourse in first-time encounters in an African township, ©1996 originally published in *Southern African Journal of Gerontology* 5(1), 9-14.

Aging in Africa, ©2008 originally published in *Journal of Cross-Cultural Gerontology,* 23, 199-209.

From Elderspeak to Gerontolinguistics : Sociolinguistic Myths, ©2017 originally published in *The Oxford Handbook of Language and Society* edited by Ofelia García, Nelson Flores, and Massimiliano Spotti, Oxford: Oxford University Press, 369-380.

International Association for the Integrational Study of Language and Communication

2015
David Bade, Rita Harris, Charlotte Conrad. *Roy Harris and Integrational Semiology 1956-2015: A bibliography.*

2020
Sinfree Makoni. *Language in Africa.* Selected papers vol. 1
Sinfree Makoni. *African Applied Linguistics.* Selected Papers, vol. 2
David Bade. *Efficiencies and Deficiencies: Essays on Cataloging and Communication in Libraries.*
David Bade. *Integrational Linguistics for Library & Information Science: Linguistics, Philosophy, Rhetoric and Technology*

In Preparation
Sinfree Makoni. *Linguistic Ideologies, Sociolinguistic Myths and Discourse Strategies in Africa* Selected Papers, Vol. 3
Sinfree Makoni. *Languages and Language Planning in South Africa and Zimbabwe.* Selected Papers, Vol. 4
Cristine Severo and Sinfree Makoni. *Language in Lusophonia: Perspectives from Bakhtin, Southern Theory and Integrational Linguistics.*

The International Association for the Integrational Study of Language and Communication

The IAISLC was founded in 1998. It is managed by an international Executive Committee, whose members are:

Adrian Pablé (University of Hong Kong), Secretary
David Bade (University of Chicago, retired)
Charlotte Conrad (Dubai)
Stephen J. Cowley (University of Southern Denmark)
Daniel R. Davis (University of Michigan)
Dorthe Duncker (University of Copenhagen)
Jesper Hermann (University of Copenhagen)
Christopher Hutton (University of Hong Kong)
Peter Jones (Sheffield Hallam University)
Nigel Love (University of Cape Town)
Sinfree Makoni (Penn State University)
Rukmini Bhaya Nair (Indian Institute of Technology)
Jon Orman (Brighton)
Talbot J. Taylor (College of William & Mary)
Michael Toolan (University of Birmingham)

Anyone wishing to join the Association can do so by email apable@hku.hk or by sending their name and address to the Secretary:

Dr Adrian Pablé
School of English
Run Run Shaw Tower
Centennial Campus
The University of Hong Kong
Hong Kong S.A.R

Contents

Editor's Preface 7

Applied Linguistics

I. *Introducing applied linguistics in Africa*
(with Ulrike Meinhof) 13

II. *Western perspectives in applied linguistics in Africa*
(with Ulrike Meinhof) 41

III. *The futility of being held captive by language policy issues in Applied Linguistics: an argument for implementation* 107

Language and State

IV. *Language and human rights discourses in Africa* 129

V. *Complementary and conflicting discourses of linguistic diversity: implications for language planning*
(with Barbara Trudell) 167

Language and Education

VI. *The consequences of a Chomskyan perspective on rules in second language acquisition* 197

VII. *English and education in anglophone Africa: historical and current realities* (with Busi Makoni) 215

VIII. *'I am starving with no hope to survive': Southern African perspectives on pedagogies of globalization*
(with Busi Makoni) 239

Gerontolinguistics

IX. *"They talk to us like children": language and intergenerational discourse in first-time encounters in an African township* 261

X. *Aging in South Africa* 281

XI. *From Elderspeak to Gerontolinguistics* 303

Editor's Preface
While the papers reprinted in the previous volume of Sinfree Makoni's selected essays *Language in Africa* were mostly written after his introduction to Roy Harris and Integrational Linguistics and focus primarily on theoretical issues, several of the papers reprinted in this second volume document the development of his ideas in the decade prior to that encounter with Harris. They chronicle a fascinating protest against theory in the face of a real world that contradicts it. In addition to general articles on Applied Linguistics as an academic discipline and a section on language rights, policy and planning, the editor has chosen papers representing two topics in Applied Linguistics which are not included in the other three volumes of these Selected Papers: language teaching and learning, and gerontolinguistics.

The two papers on language rights, planning and policy in the section "Language and State" represent but a small portion of Sinfree's publications on these topics. Most of his papers in this area focus on South Africa and Zimbabwe and are being collected and published separately in a subsequent volume.

The early paper on second language learning that opens the section "Language and Education" reveals the origins of theoretical dissent in a scholar and language teacher taking to heart his actual experiences with language teaching and language learners. Unlike the architect of The Standard Theory, whenever theory has been seen to conflict with the world of experience, Sinfree has always affirmed experience and sent theoretical prejudices packing. Even though Sinfree takes as his starting point the 'Principles and parameters' era of the 'Standard Theory' in his paper "The consequences of a Chomskyan perspective on rules in second language acquisition," by the end of his six pages he has already gone beyond those theoretical parameters. In his conclusion we read:

> I have argued that the degree of abstraction of the rules renders their relevance to language teaching doubtful. I have also argued that if the rules are to be useful for the purposes of language teaching, then some degree of 'deabstraction' is called for but at the same time some form of abstraction and idealization is inevitable in any language analysis. The deabstraction enables the analyst to reintroduce the learner's perceptions of the acceptability of her language. I have also argued that the issue of creativity overlooks the extent to which language use is formulaic and the conceptual problems of distinguishing between errors and creative innovations in language production was touched on. My conclusion is that Universal Grammar, as a way of doing linguistics, might have revealed a lot of interesting facts, but is of limited relevance for second language acquisition and teaching.

From all that I have read of his subsequent papers, this appears to have been Sinfree's farewell remarks to Chomsky and the 'Standard Theory.' His remarks on the conceptual problem of distinguishing between errors and creativity are especially noteworthy in light of his later research. The relation between variation and error is no less significant in the study of linguistic variation and standardization than it is in the mathematical theory of error, while the really significant linguistic creativity Sinfree found later and elsewhere, e.g. in the nursing homes, streets and taxi-cabs of Africa's urban centres.

In that same early paper we also find something of considerable interest: although not mentioned within the body of the paper, Deborah Cameron's 1994 paper "Putting our practice into theory" appears in the list of references, and there could be no more appropriate indication of the journey that Sinfree embarked upon at that moment than the title of that essay by one of Harris's students. It would be a decade before Sinfree began to read Roy Harris's writings, but at some point in 1994 the encounter had already taken place, unbeknownst to both participants.

A section on gerontolinguistics closes the volume. The three papers reprinted here date from 1996, 2008 and 2017 and represent some of his major publications in an area of research that he has pursued now for twenty five years.

David Bade
Rachel's Farm
8 July 2020

Applied Linguistics

I

Introducing Applied Linguistics in Africa (with Ulrike Meinhof)

The title, "Applied Linguistics in Africa", immediately raises a whole range of questions. Does it (a) refer to work by African scholars about an area of applied linguistics irrespective of the sociogeographical area it relates to? Does it (b) refer to work by scholars from any part of the world dealing with issues of applied linguistics in Africa itself? Or does it (c) imply work by African linguists about an applied linguistics issue within Africa? If the latter, what do we mean by an 'African linguist'. Is it someone who (d) lives and works in Africa? Or is it (e) someone of African origin? Or does Applied Linguistics in Africa refer (f) to a specific orientation to applied linguistics, which is uniquely African, speaking with an African 'voice'? These are complicated questions. Some restrictions are necessary if we are even to suggest useful perspectives. Accordingly, we have excluded work by African Applied Linguists on non-African material. And we have confined ourselves to Africa south of the Sahara. The socio-historical context of North Africa makes it a fascinating area, but it is radically different from the sub-

Saharan region and warrants separate attention. For the rest, we have been somewhat eclectic. All the papers included in this volume deal with an aspect of applied linguistics in an African country, and all of them are written by scholars of African descent as authors or co-authors. Most of the authors represented in this volume live and work in an African country and all feel a sociological and political affinity with Africa. What we hope to project is that applied linguistics in Africa, shaped by an intimate concern with the issues as they present themselves locally is every bit as ebullient, versatile and multifaceted as applied linguistics anywhere. Of course, there are considerable challenges ahead for African applied linguistics. In the words of Chinua Achebe, the famous Nigerian author and critic: 'It's morning yet on creation day'.

The current context of African applied linguistics has to be understood in relation to a long and varied history. Precolonial migration, trade down the centuries, the radical displacements of slavery, the growth of print literacy and the decline of oral culture, arbitrary territorial changes under colonialism, industrial exploitation of natural resources, and the unprecedented rapidity of migration and urbanization in the postcolonial period have brought language groups into contact and conflict, changing social and economic life and with it the shape, function and status of the languages within specific communities. This pattern is not unique to Africa. Nor is it uniform across Africa. But the detailed interweaving of the elements has produced tapestries of recognisably similar workmanship in most parts of the continent.

Around the 9th century, massive Bantu migrations from West Africa to central and southern Africa occurred. The migrations set a background against which a great deal of applied linguistics research has to be understood. The migrations brought Bantu clans into contact with Khoe-San peoples, the 'indigenous' peoples of the large areas of southern Africa they moved into and came to dominate. There was evidently some profitable contact, which has left a linguistic residue, but there was also major conflict as the agriculturalist and pastoralist Bantu clashed particularly with the hunter-gatherer San. A millenium later, another major Bantu migration, the Mfecane, saw mass movements northwards of Nguni clans, probably displaced by the Shakan revolution, and in their turn displacing other settled Bantu people.

In recent times, there have been major internal and international migrations prompted by economic and political pressures. In the face of political instability and civil war, with its attendant economic decline, there have been significant unstructured migrations, sometimes involving a three thousand-mile trek in search of security and a means of making a living. In most countries, a much larger and more common phenomenon in the globalising age has been a migration of rural people to the cities often into situations of dire poverty. The multi-layered history of migration has made research into language contact a major on-going theme in African applied linguistics, ranging from historical studies and explanations of grammatical and lexical forms, through to code-switching, the development of creoles and urban argots, and the phenomena of language growth, shift and decline —the latter a major concern in language planning.

In West Africa, the ancient empires of Ghana and Mali, and in East Africa the even older empire of Axum, perhaps echoed and interacted with larger forms of social organisation in the north such as ancient Egypt, Carthage and the 7th and 8th century Arab empire. South of these kingdoms and empires, social organisation was on a smaller scale. This changed in various ways. The complex history of slavery on the east coast, which involved Arabs, local Africans and Europeans, led to the development and spread of Swahili as a lingua franca and the emergence of a metropolitanisation of African identities as local groups of Africans began to identify with larger social realities. The later and more radically disruptive slave trade on the west coast also had major linguistic and social implications which are still felt today, not least in the pidgin languages of the region. In the south, the early 19th century Mfecane marked a major challenge to traditional patterns of social organisation. Prior to the Shakan revolution the clan was the main principle along which Bantu societies were organized. In founding the Zulu nation, King Shaka consciously broke with the traditions of the past. Clan organization was superceded by the demands of ethnicity and what readily became "nationality" along European lines in the contact with white settlers and colonial authorities almost immediately afterwards. Emergent colonialism crystallised the change. Blocks of dialects that had previously been in a continuum now represented critical identity markers. Each block became a separate language, a process of homogenisation much aided by developing reductive written forms.

The impact of colonialism in Africa is felt in two ways: the 'imposition' of colonial languages, and the redefined role of African languages. European colonial authorities adopted varying attitudes towards language in areas falling under their authority. The British and Dutch, while asserting their languages, effectively adopted a *laissez faire* attitude that led them to recognise local languages and local versions of 'metropolitan' languages. In British colonial contexts this meant recognition (though not encouragement) of local versions of English, and in areas under Dutch colonial rule in South Africa, this attitude contributed somewhat ambiguously to the formation of Afrikaans. The British and Dutch colonial policies were different from the French colonial policy which overrode local languages and attempted to 'erase' fromview African varieties of French whose impact ironically is more evident in France than in former French colonies in Africa today.

The general pattern in African education is for African 'languages' to be used as medium of instruction for the first three or four years. Thereafter there is a shift to the ex-colonial language of the region in question, most commonly English, French or Portuguese. Rarely are African 'languages' used as media of instruction beyond primary education. Unfortunately, even after the shift to French or English as medium of instruction most students do not receive much exposure to these languages outside the classroom. Because of their limited exposure to the language of instruction, most pupils have limited proficiency in English or French. Pedagogically, teachers find themselves having to code-switch into one of the 'indigenous' languages during their teaching (Ferguson 2000, Ferguson 2003). Given the educational disadvantages which attend learning through a language which is only partially understood, Ferguson makes a compelling case: in such circumstances applied linguists would be more effective when they investigate context-specific strategies which could minimise the educational disadvantages of learning in a 'foreign' medium. Despite the powerful arguments derived from psycholinguistic research which suggest that consolidation of a first language facilitates development of a second language, a shift to using 'indigenous' languages would not necessarily solve the educational problems. Cummins (1979,1984) and Williams (1996) are frequently cited to support the use of 'indigenous' languages as media of instruction in early primary education. However, the exigencies of the context cannot be ignored. Policy decisions delaying the introduction of ex-colonial languages as media of instruction in Africa are usually motivated by mundane and practical considerations rather than by research insights. All things being equal, there is a higher probability that at later stages in primary education the prospects of encountering teachers proficient in English or French are better than in the early stages.

Most applied linguists professionally experience 'indigenous' languages through the map and the list. There are two types of maps whose discursive registers are likely to shape the applied linguists experience of 'indigenous' languages in Africa. The first map owes its origins to the 'infamous blue pencils of imperial delegates' at the Congress of Berlin in the late 19th century, and its permanence to the decisions of African states to live permanently with those boundaries (Fardon and Furniss: 11). The second map is that of the linguist.

> ...each revision of this map tends to add to the number of named languages located in the virtual space of the diagram. Notoriously, this map fits ill with either the colonial or national maps. Some languages, often associated with past African imperial formations or with trading diasporas, are quite widely distributed on the map, others are so restructured that the map hardly allows space to inscribe their names. A higher level generalization of the language map groups languages into families. On this map we might note that in central and eastern and southern Africa, many of the languages are close cognates sharing a high proportion of lexical items and grammatical structures. In West Africa the distribution is far more fractured (Fardon and Furniss 1994: 11)

The second most frequent discursive register, which shapes the applied linguist's experiences of African languages, is the list. The languages are arranged ordinally in terms of the number of speakers or the number of speakers competent in them (see Themba Moyo's article in this volume). From an applied linguistic perspective, it is important to stress that the maps and lists are discursive registers, representations of Africa's linguistic complexity and not 'unmediated' realities. Bearing in mind that the maps and the lists are discursive registers is necessary when exploring the applications of the language 'facts' to language related problems.

This introductory essay sets the context for the ten articles that follow, not least by critiquing certain key activities and conceptualisations. Some 'applied linguistic activities' in Africa are examined specifically through the prism of African languages, as seen from a historical and a comparative contemporary viewpoint. We also explore the ways in which African languages are conceptualized and used in relation to paradigms such as World Englishes (WE), and to a lesser extent World French (WF). In deference to historical fact, a distinction is made between 'applied linguistic activities' on the one hand and 'applied linguistics' as a discipline on the other. The 'applied linguistic activities' we refer to either predate the formal inauguration of applied linguistics as a discipline, or have taken place outside its ambit. For example, the 'reduction' of African languages to writing, thereby 'creating' the languages from a set of dialects, was done outside applied linguistics 'proper'. On the other hand, current research in language planning, language and the law, and language and health has been conceptualized as part of applied linguistics. In the last section of the introduction, the articles contained in this volume are briefly surveyed.

Applied linguistics in contemporary Africa is practiced in an ambiguous context. On the one hand, the severe supremacism, material underresourcing, and internalized oppression characteristic of neocolonialism frequently mark its social, political and economic contexts. On the other hand, there is the promise and vitality of widespread multilingualism, projected in some discourses about Africa as a major resource. African applied linguistics is practised in social settings in which 'multilingualism' is the norm. Multilingualism is becoming much more widespread. For example, in Central and West Africa, the multilingualism includes a degree of expertise not only in a number of different African languages, but even in two or more ex-colonial languages, most frequently French and English. A fascinating aspect of applied linguistics in Africa is that some of its building blocks, African languages, are increasingly becoming objects of sustained criticism as deceptive constructions. Makoni, Smitherman, Ball and Spears (2003) argue that the notion of the 'indigenous' African languages is superimposed on the linguistic reality. It arises from and reinforces a colonial and foreign discourse about Africa, confirming the rightness of particular forms of social distinction or separation. Multilingualism in such contexts is seen as a plural variant of monolingualism, with the languages coordinated rather than in some vital relationship to one another. The multilingualism that is becoming more widespread is of the compound variety. This tension between the imposed and the organic, the top-down and the bottom-up, has had a major shaping influence on the evolution of applied linguistics in Africa. It is to an account of this evolution that we now turn.

Toward a history of applied linguistic activities in Africa
Selecting a starting point for any history is always an arbitrary procedure. Documenting the history of applied linguistic activities in Africa is no exception. One of the earliest activities, which today we would categorize as important in applied linguistics, is the codification and 'reduction' to writing of African languages. Swahili was initially written in an Arabic script around the 15th Century. The Arabic script was subsequently replaced by Roman script. 'When the Roman script was introduced at the inception of European colonial rule, it faced little resistance fromthe Arabic script, except in Arabophone Africa, where a longer and more

widespread tradition of writing, buttressed by the state, ensured the continuation of literacy in the Arabic script. In most other Afro-Islamic languages, including Fulfulde, Hausa, Kanuri,Mandinka, Nupe, Songhai and Kiswahili, the Arabic script has been giving way to the Roman script' (Mazrui and Mazrui 1998: 73). Another type of script which has been used in the writing of African languages is the syllabic alphabet for Vai, a language spoken in Liberia (West Africa). From the late 18th century and throughout the19th and much of the 20th, missionary imperatives led to grammar and spelling systems being 'developed' for African languages. That kind of work is currently being continued under the auspices of the Summer Institute of Linguistics (SIL) in different parts of Africa. Even if those involved in the codification and production of writing systems might not have defined what they were doing as applied linguistics, retrospectively we can argue that the production of the writing systems constituted applied linguistic activities of major significance in shaping sociolinguistic images of the African landscape. The production of writing systems for different languages was not a simple matter of writing down a language. It involved a process of inventing 'simplified' or standardised versions of African speech forms, mediating between a range of dialects, and losing vocabulary and social significance in the process.

    One of the reasons for the 'invention' of reduced versions of African languages was the limited range of terms the missionaries adopted for their purposes, the terms they excluded as improper, and the rest which they neglected out of limited interest in the full speech range of the people they had come to serve in more urgent ways. The missionaries often used a very small part of the stylistic range, partly because they had to write the language down early, when they had learned enough to get across certain quite basic messages. They were also people of the age of "progress", often impatient of the associative discourse so characteristic of oral cultures, and favouring linear reasoning styles. Willan (1984) describes some of the efforts of the first African novelist, Sol Plaatje, to extend the range of the Tswana language to include thousands of words which did not appear in the main dictionary of the language, to correct many errors in the dictionary, and to record and transcribe traditional oral forms as cultural reference points for Tswana children and others being taught the language formally. The end result of much well-intentioned linguistic work by missionaries seems often to have been reduced versions of African speech forms, which were then adopted by the colonial authorities because of the authority of the written word. The inadequate forms thus had political power with important social consequences. They were also labelled and stigmatised. For example, 'chibaba' is the name used to refer to the Shona associated with missionary and colonial interventions (Jeater 2001). In sum, the process of writing down African languages was in many cases the fumbling work of well-intentioned amateurs influenced by the spirit of the age. This fumbling work has had major consequences for applied linguistics, which now finds itself having to redescribe languages and the concept of a language, as well as negotiating the imperatives of finding common written forms of a range of related "languages" if they are going to sustain a flourishing print culture. The production of different orthographies for closely related 'languages'has had a substantial impact on the context within which subsequent generations of language analysts have operated in Africa. Attempts to 'harmonize' and 'unify' the different orthographies and reach agreement on a common core vocabulary have preoccupied the minds of many applied linguists in Africa as part of a broader strategy to redefine the linguistic boundaries of Africa (Prah 1998). The philosophical and political ideas underlying the codification of African languages has also had an impact on other areas falling under the rubric of applied linguistics, such as mother tongue literacies.

Literacy research in Africa has been the unwitting heir to 18/19th century Romantic notions about language, as seen for example in the influential writings of German thinkers on language and nation from Herder to Fichte, and the ways in which the relationship between language and ethnicity, language and nationhood, are compounded in these notions. Radical and politically astute approaches to the teaching of literacy are regularly and unfortunately constrained, if not undermined, by assumptions of what 'indigenous' African languages are. Mother tongue literacy work has focused on the literacy aspect without paying any systematic attention to the ways in which 'indigenous' African languages reached their written form. Accordingly, what constitutes 'mother tongues' in Africa is construed as unproblematic. A lack of sophisticated awareness about the politics and history of the notion of 'indigenous' languages means that literacy workers usually overlook the extent to which those languages presented as 'indigenous' languages are often versions very far from what is spoken. Such 'standardised indigenous' languages are then quite arbitrarily assumed to represent the mother tongues of the people concerned, when the people often have nothing like native speaker proficiency in them. There are other implications. Limited proficiency in one's supposed mother tongue has potentially vast negative implications for the success of education in that 'mother tongue'. This suggests that being educated through their supposed 'mother tongue' will not necessarily be beneficial to learners, and that 'mother tongue' education, vocally and persistently touted as a panacea for Africa's educational problems, is often highly problematic.

The development of African languages

Another theme that frequently recurs in research in African languages is the need to 'develop', elaborate and 'promote' the use of African languages so that they can serve new and scientific purposes. To that end, the production of dictionaries, the writing of grammar books, and the development of new terminology has become a productive area of research in African applied linguistics. Although some might argue that such activities are merely technical matters, their existence has nevertheless a much wider cultural and political impact. In this area African applied linguistics has had a very strong ideological dimension. Investigating and critiquing the very basis of the argument what constitutes a 'developed' or an 'undeveloped' language, Blommaert (1994, 1999) has forcefully articulated this in his writings about Swahili:

> The view of Kiswahili as an underdeveloped language in need of modernization is an allegory of a more general development attitude in Tanzania: that Tanzania is in need of development. The issue of development of African languages, where it has arisen as a debate, has tended to be discussed in terms of models of development of languages which should be followed. It raises questions whether it is meaningful to talk of an underdeveloped language. 'The idea of 'developing' Kiswahili—which is consistently defined as a 'developing' language by contrast to 'developed' languages such as English, French, or German—must be frustrating in the long run. An underdeveloped language can therefore never be developed since the developed languages themselves develop further. (Blommaert 1994: 218)

The construct of 'development' is an extremely powerful and emotive one, especially since the extent of the involvement of African local communities in the development of their own languages has been very limited. The development of African languages has always largely been done 'for' native speakers, and rarely 'with' them. Development of African languages will thus not necessarily result in the social advancement of Africans.

Discussion about the 'development' of African languages is directly linked with another important and prolific field in African applied linguistics: the area of language planning. Language planning studies have focused on the role and functions which African languages and ex-colonial languages, French, German, Portuguese, and German, occupy in postcolonial contexts— in education, parliamentary discourse, and the social lives of African communities. Recently, increased attention has been paid to the competition between French and English in West Africa (see the article by Tope Ominyi in this volume) or the displacement of Portuguese by English in former Lusophone countries such as Mozambique. There is increasing interest in an analysis of the discourses about language in language planning (Blommaert, 1999, Ridge 2001). An analysis of the discourses of language in language planning is important because it illuminates the overall ideological contexts in which language planning is taking place. Unfortunately, most of the language-planning discourses that have been analyzed are English-based, or are restricted to a few languages such as Swahili. Because the main staple of the analysis is in English and in discourses developed around European languages, there is almost inevitably an extension and transfer of Western assumptions about language and society to African contexts, legitimating the use of prefabricated solutions to African language problems. The main objective in African applied linguistics is to gain greater control over how problems are represented and constructed so as to avoid prevalent assumptions which are largely embedded in and mediated by English and reinforced by Western episteme and historicity—albeit in an increasingly transnational contexts (Escodor 1995). By changing the ways in and through which we construct ourselves and are represented we will be able, in effective practical terms, to avoid situations in which prefabricated solutions are applied without satisfactory definition of the problems.

An important corrective in African applied linguistics would be an analysis of 'discourses' about African languages in African languages. This would help us to understand the meanings and implications of sociolinguistic concepts, such as linguistic rights, multilingualism, and linguistic imperialism, from the perspective of African language speakers. When applied to highly complex and varied African contexts, these terms take on sometimes surprising meanings. Community understanding or misunderstanding (deliberate or otherwise) of the nature of language planning directly affects the success or failure of language policies and the distribution of human and material resources in support of them. Unless local communities themselves understand what is taking place and are actively involved in the implementation, no 'topdown' language policy can meet with lasting success (see the arguments in Themba Moyo's article). Discrepancies between assumed global norms in linguistics and local African perceptions are telling. For example, African language speakers generally distinguish between the version of their language that they use within the community, and the "standardised" version associated with formal education, which is thus marked as part of the colonial heritage even in postcolonial contexts. We also know that Africans generally make no clear distinctions between 'language' as a code and cultural practices. It is possible to be treated as a mother tongue speaker of a language in many African contexts even if one does not speak the relevant language with anything near native speaker fluency, but has mastered the cultural practices of the community.

This may mean in some cases converting to the religion of the community. The native/non-native distinction is thus culturally contingent: in many African contexts it reflects perceived cultural competence and not primarily linguistic expertise. Such factors need to be understood, and any language planning has to be sensitive to their significance.

Reconceptualising analytical categories in African applied linguistics

One of the major contributions which African applied linguistics can make is to contribute towards a reconceptualisation of some of the basic terms in applied linguistics such as 'language', 'style' etc. The continuous debates about the number of African languages reflect the problematic nature of the concept of a 'language' in the African sociolinguistic context. The problem is much deeper than the elusive distinctions between dialects and language; it reflects the uncertainty of what we are referring to when we are talking about 'language' in African contexts. The dividing up of a continuum into separate 'boxes' or discrete languages was an arbitrary procedure in Africa, as in other parts of the world. The main issue is that in Africa the decision about the separate categories was determined by outsiders without any reference to the socio-linguistic identities of the local communities. In African applied linguistics, as we have seen, the term 'indigenous' languages generally refers to the versions of the languages formalised by missionaries (and later by others) within the broad frame of the colonial enterprise. Linguistics was always a politically driven enterprise in Africa. After the African languages were decreed into existence, the function of linguistics in Africa was to produce and describe the prescribed African languages. As we have seen, Christianity has played a key role in African applied linguistics activities, but the religion, which is currently having a substantial impact, is not Christianity, but Islam.

There are more people converting to Islam than any other religion in Africa. Islam has a deep history in North Africa, some parts of West Africa and East and Southern Africa. Yet now, in ways, which have no recent precedent, Islam, is on the 'march'. There are more people converting to Islam than Christianity in Africa today. The increasing Islamic consciousness in many Africans poses significant challenges for the teaching of languages, particularly English. English, in an African Islamic perspective, might be construed as embodying values which are in conflict with Islamic values, and there 'is a great disparity between the objectives of teaching English and the ultimate aim of Muslim education' (Mohamed 1989: 33). Some of the problems and challenges of developing Islamic approaches to the teaching of English are being addressed in some Muslim countries, notably Malaysia (Casewit, 1985, Shafl 1983, Cooke 1998); but no systematic efforts have been carried out in Africa in spite of the increasing Islamisation of Africa. The heightened Islamic consciousness sweeping through Africa is a strong reason for applied linguists to give serious attention to the cultural politics of teaching languages in Africa. Ironically, proselytising for Islam is carried out through languages 'created' by Christian missionaries, so the exact meaning of 'indigenous' languages within an Islamic religious framework is still not clear.

African applied linguists not only 'mediate' but also actively intervene in the social lives of African communities, so the framework for thinking about their work must be brought into critical review. A new set of terms is desirable, or at the very least a radical reconceptualisation of existing ones. We feel that the sociolinguistic landscape in Africa can be more effectively analysed when we opt to use categories such as 'communitarian' languages. 'Communitarian' languages refer to 'languages' as defined by the users now across a variety of conventional boundaries. This would liberate our thinking about the languages from some of the restrictions and patterns of subordination implicit in the historically burdened term 'indigenous' languages. The distinction we are trying to propose here between 'indigenous' and 'communitarian' language/s is analogous to the one proposed by Hymes (1996) between a linguistic notion of language and an ethnographic notion of speech. 'Styles' have to be approached differently because they are given a different status in many African communities. The fact that 'styles' have a different status in many African communities leads us to approach the 'notion' of 'styles' differently. The conventional view in applied linguistics and sociolinguistics is that 'styles' are part of language however broadly or narrowly defined language is. In African sociolinguistics we are proposing a different orientation in which 'styles' are related to language and to 'communitarian languages' but not as constitutive elements. 'Styles', from the African perspective, are above 'language', and speakers may share the same stylistic inventories and stylistic space even though they have different 'communitarian' languages as mother tongues. Common stylistic spaces and inventories are a consequence of the frequent, intense and prolonged encounters between speakers that characterise city life in a rapidly urbanizing Africa. These stylistic inventories not only enable people to communicate with each other, but also allow people to express something about themselves to each other and the world. (Cook, 2002) "Resistance is clearly evident in the ways that black folks make language perform. ... Black folks, then, do not only perform language, but their language is made to perform, to work in the service of revising and altering the wor(l)d" (Walcott, 1997: 104). These stylistic inventories (expressive inventories) cannot be easily be reduced to linguistic rules! (Cook 2002).

African applied linguistics and World Englishes

In some circles in Africa there is still a tendency to define applied linguistics as English as a second language (ESL) (Young 2001). The conflation is understandable since the academic development of applied linguistics in Africa has been closely tied to the spread of ESL. With South African universities in mind, Young points out that 'one tragic and epochal event which more than any other factor, influenced the development ... of applied linguistics, language education, and related areas of study and intervention was the 1976 mass protest by black school students in Soweto, Johannesburg, against the apartheid government's policy of imposing Afrikaans as a medium of instruction' (Young 2001: 228). Historically, it is however important to consider, that the earliest applied linguistic activities in the British colonial period had to do with the provision and development of language learning materials in African languages for speakers of European origin, and not the provision of English to African language speakers (Jeater, 1993). However, while the provision of and teaching of African languages dominated early-applied linguistic activities, ESL later dominated applied linguistics as a discipline. Although early-applied linguistic activities were on African languages, subsequent research in African languages has tended to be narrowly linguistic in its orientation with a focus on theoretical aspects. This trend has gradually begun to shift with more applied interest in African languages, as some of the papers in this volume demonstrate.

One of the most widely used frameworks in an analysis of the spread and status of English in Africa is the World English paradigm (WE), which draws with some modification on the work of Kachru (1990). In Africa, researchers working within WE have focused and successfully demonstrated from their perspective the ways in which English in its spread has been 'indigenized' and appropriated by speakers of African languages. WE is a way of classifying different varieties of English. Inspite of the voluminous literature generated in terms of WE in Africa, English as a language has not replaced any African Language. English thus has not endangered African languages: it has been 'additive' and not 'replacive' (Mazrui and Mazrui 1998, Mufwene 2001; see also the contrastive arguments developed in *AILA Review* 13, 1999). By contrast, some African languages are increasingly endangered by the spread of urban vehicular languages (Mufwene 2001). There are also very few Black communities in Africa which use English as a primary means of communication. Because of that, labels such as Black South African English (Gough 1995) are anomalous and potentially misleading, unless the acquisitional context is borne in mind. For most African pupils, the educational setting is the primary domain in which they get most of their exposure to English, often delivered by teachers who in most cases are themselves second language learners of English. From the perspective of contexts in which English is acquired in Africa, it is important to stress that Black South African English is a second language phenomenon. A framework which would be most appropriate in addressing issues about the status of English in Africa is one which focuses on language spread and change within a sociohistorical context in which English is acquired largely as a second language (Brutt-Griffler, personal communication). Brutt-Griffler refers to her analytical framework as a World English framework.

From an African language perspective it has become self-evident that the construct of 'indigenous' African languages is itself open to serious contestation. If it is uncertain what constitutes 'indigenized' African languages, then conceptually it is not clear either what precisely is being 'indigenized' when reference is made to African English, (Schmied 1991, de Klerk 1995). What is required is a systematic analysis of African languages, the substrate languages underlying the use of English in Africa by non-mother tongue speakers. Such a counter analysis of the substrate African languages is necessary not only for African English, but for other contact languages which trace their roots back to African languages, such as African American Vernacular (Rickford 1987).

When the discourses of 'indigenous' languages and WE are juxtaposed, it becomes apparent that there is a strong underlying moralistic and romanticizing discourse common to them. Arguments for the use of 'indigenous' languages are equated with moral uprightness, while the use of English is practically necessary, but morally suscpicious. WE tries to resolve the moral dilemma through its notion of localization of English. To what extent WE has succeeded in resolving the moral dilemma through its use of the notion of localization is an open question.

African Applied Linguistics and French
There are two main discernible strands in the study of French in African applied linguistics. In 'Anglophone' West Africa, particularly in countries that share political boundaries with ex-French colonies such as Nigeria, and Anglophone Cameroon, French is normally acquired as a third language after the acquisition of English as a second language. Researchers into the acquisition of French have applied their minds to the psycholinguistic processes in the acquisition of French as a third language. The research has largely been psycholinguistic in nature, examining the cross-linguistic influences of (1) English on French and (2) the effects of French on English. In Francophone Africa the main thrust of the research into French has largely been of an educational and sociolinguistic nature. For example, the general status of French has shifted. French is increasingly becoming either a second or first language for most urban

African speakers (Aliodou 2003). The shift to a first or a second language has led to a need for a reappraisal of the ways French is taught in Africa, and who is professionally qualified to teach it.

Writing African applied linguistics

To date, there are very few academic texts in applied linguistics that have been written in 'indigenous' African languages. There is no debate similar to the one in African literature about the desirability or otherwise of using African languages as a medium for writing in the field. Although African languages have rarely been used as a medium through which African applied linguistics has been written, African applied linguistics has tended to be multilanguage in its form. By this we mean that even when the academic texts are written in either English or French, the data are drawn from African language linguistic and cultural contexts — hence texts combine analytical language in English or French with data quoted from many different African languages. This will be borne out in this volume which uses English for the purposes of accessibility across the global academic communities, but also includes data from 'indigenous' African languages, such as Shona, Chinyanja, Sesotho, Tswana and Malagasy.

Review of articles in this volume

Let us now turn to the articles included in this volume. They are based on research from different areas of Africa, West Africa, Central Africa, Southern Africa and the islands in the Indian Ocean, although we could not achieve a genuine geographical balance. They cover a range of sometimes interlinking but also separate areas of concern, including language planning, language and the judiciary, language use in everyday settings, language in education, language and cultural identity.

There are three articles on language planning issues in different African countries — Nigeria, Malawi, and South Africa — reflecting the transnational significance that this topic has within the African context. Tope Omonyi's article, 'Language, ideology and politics: A critical appraisal of French as second official language (FSOL) in Nigeria', addresses the changing nature of the relationships between English and French, relations which are continuously shifting. Tope Omonyi demonstrates the increasing importance of French inWest Africa, where French is being acquired in addition to English, and outlines the sociopolitical implications of the introduction of French in the political and cultural struggles between English and French over African cultural practices. Gibson Ferguson's paper, 'Classroom code-switching in postcolonial contexts, functions, attitides and policies' addresses the role of code-swthching in classrooms in post-colonial Africa. Gibson Ferguson argues that code-switching is a widespread phenomenon in multilingual, language contact settings in Africa, and indeed world-wide, yet it it is not infrequently regarded unfavourably by linguistically uninformed educational policy makers and teachers. He examines some of the assumptions about language which underly the construction of language and society in policy makers.

Themba Moyo's article, 'Democratization of indigenous languages in Africa', focuses on the roles of and relationship between 'indigenous' African languages. He demonstrates convincingly the ways in which Chinyanja was imposed on speakers of other African language under a political dictatorship in Malawi (a country in Central Africa). Ian Bekker's article: 'Using historical data to explain language attitudes: a South African case study' focuses on the social and political histories of the evolving relationships between Afrikaans, English and 'indigenous' African languages in South Africa. The social and historical account is an excellent example of how governmental institutional intervention attempted to change and purposefully manipulate the relationships between speakers of the different languages. It also shows how, historically, language has always been a source of sharp political contention in South Africa.

Constance Zulu's paper, "Supplemental instruction for at-risk students at an historically Black university in South Africa," addresses issues of equity and access in higher education. She explores the role which supplemental instruction might play in enabling students from disadvantaged backgrounds in South Africa to succeed in higher education. Her paper shows how applied linguistics might be able to mitigate the adverse effects of learning and being taught in a foreign language.

The articles by Pulie Thetela and Vivian de Klerk both focus on language and the law in South African contexts, but cover very different aspects and methodologies. Pulie Thetela's article, "Discourse, culture and the law: an analysis of crosstalk in southern African bilingual courtrooms", focuses on the role and effects of a special register, 'hlonipha', used by married women in southern Africa, and how this affects women's discourses in the law courts. The social conventions of 'hlonipha' forbid women to talk directly about sexuality. The lack of understanding in the courts of this taboo has potential adverse effects on the ability of women to secure justice in the law courts. Vivian de Klerk's article, "Language and the law: who has an upperhand? A corpus analysis of the Truth and Reconciliation Commission hearings in South Africa", deals more specifically with the accessibility of the language used in the proceedings of the Truth and Reconciliation Commission (TRC). Using corpus linguistics methods in analysing the documents and the hearings, she demonstrates the complexity of the language used in the TRC, rendering the TRC incomprehensible, at least to some. The nature of the language used in the TRC hearings, although enhancing the legal status of the Commission, defeats one of the basic goals of the TRC that was to render the truth accessible to most South Africans. Yisa Kehunde Yusuf's contribution, "Dysphemisms in the language of a Nigerian president", continues the theme in his analysis of language in the public space. He focuses on the speeches of the Nigerian president Obasanjo delivered in English. On the one hand, the paper falls readily within a tradition of Critical Discourse Analysis (CDA), on the other hand, it relates to the WE tradition in Africa. The paper analyses the linguistic and discoursal features of the speeches of Obasanjo, and how they encode his ideological orientation. It contributes towards a development of the WE debate by demonstrating how English is used in the political lives of the Nigerian elites when they address key issues affecting their lives.

The article by Pedzisai Mashiri: 'Managing face in urban public transport: public request strategies in commuter omnibus discourse in Harare, Zimbabwe' analyses the language used in the 'mini-buses': a common way of commuting in southern Africa. Building on pragmatic concepts from research on politeness, the paper analyzes everyday exchanges in Shona between the passengers and drivers. His work gives insight into the nature of language used by mobile speech communities. Speech communities have been defined in various ways, but the idea of mobile speech communities has not been an object of sustained sociolinguistic analysis. Pedzisai Mashiri's research is also valuable because it enhances our understanding of the role and functions of 'new' urban languages in urbanizing Africa.

The articles by Zafimahaleo Rasolofodrasosolo and Ulrike Meinhof, and Stanley Ridge, Sinfree Makoni and Elaine Ridge fall within the field of language and identity. Zafimahaleo Rasolofodrasosolo and Ulrike Meinhof focus on the discourses of and about popular Malagasy music. The article derives its vitality from the conviction that one of the defining features of any speech community is its music. In examining popular Malagasy music and its closeness to everyday social and political realities in Madagascar, they show its significance for the construction of cultural identity for Malagasy people in Madasgacar and abroad. The paper can accurately be defined as an analysis not of the language of music, but of what we would like to refer to as 'songified' talk, a genre which from a western perspective is a combination of talk and music. Technically, the article is a departure from usual practices of authoring papers in that one of the co-authors is an African musician, the other a European applied linguist. In their article, S. Ridge, S. Makoni and E. Ridge document and analyse the struggle of one woman to retain her sense of 'self' through her use of language during the onset and development of Alzheimer's disease. The article is a multidisciplinary analysis of the letters she wrote in her young adulthood, an academic text she produced at her prime, the semi-fictional correspondence she entered into with herself when she was in a nursing home, and her exchanges during a videotaped testing session. The analysis demonstrates the continuities and discontinuities in the ways she projects herself over a period of five decades. This study contributes towards an understanding of how issues about the 'self' and identity evolve and are maintained over a life course even when the person's social and cognitive abilities are being compromised by disease and ageing. Theoretically, the article tries to situate concepts such as the 'self', 'person' and retained capability within a Vygotskian orientation to health and ageing.

Concluding comments
In this introductory essay we have identified salient features of applied linguistics in Africa. The essay has sought to show that the recurring features in African applied linguistics are all related to serious efforts to address and shed in-

sight into local African situations. To quote from another article, applied linguistics in Africa is "likely to grow in importance as it explores the role of language in realizing the benefits of democracy in Africa and improving the lives of the people. Its contribution to international scholarship will be far greater for its detailed attention to local issues" (Ridge, Makoni and Ridge, 2001: 11).

Note
* The editors would like to thank Stan, Elaine Ridge, Janina Brutt-Griffler and the two reviewers for their comments and input at various stages of writing this introduction.

References
Barnard, F.M (1969), (ed.). *J. G. Herder on Social and Political Culture.* Cambridge: CUP.
Bamgbose, A. (1994). "Pride and prejudice in multilingualism" In R. Fardon and G. Furniss (eds), *African Language, Development and the State,* pp. 32–43. London: Routledge.
Bamgbose, A. et al. (eds). (1995), *New Englishes: A West African perspective.* Ibadan: Masuro.
Blommaert, J. (1999). *Language Ideological Debates.* Berlin: Mouton de Gruyter.
Canagarash, A. S. (2000). *Resisting Linguistic Imperialism in English Language Teaching.* Oxford: OUP.
Casewit, S.D (1985). "Teaching English as a foreign language in muslim countries" In *Muslim Education Quarterly* 2 (2): 4–16.
Cook, S. E. (2002). "Urban language in a rural setting: the case of Phokeng, South Africa" In G. Gmelch and W.P. Zenner (ed.), *Urban Life: Readings in Anthropology of the City* 4th edition, pp. 106–113. Prospect Heights: Waveland Press.
Cooke, D. (1998). "Ties that constrict: English as a Trojan

Horse" In A. Cumming, A. Gangne, and J. Dawson (eds), *Awareness: Proceedings of the 1987. TESL Ontario Conference,* pp.56–62. Toronto: TESL Ontario.

Fichte, J.G (1992). *Addresses to the German Nation.* (Translated by R.T.Jones and G.H.Turnbull). Chicago: University of Chicago Press.

Fichte, J. G. (1965) *Johann Gottlieb Fichte's sämtliche Werke.* I.H. Fichte (ed.), Berlin: Walter de Gruyter.

Hassana A. (2003). "Language policies and language education in Francophone Africa: A critique and call to action" in S.Makoni, G. Smitherman, A. Ball and A. Spears (eds), *Black Linguistics: Language, Society and Politics in Africa and the Americas.* London: Routledge.

Herder, J.G. (1987). "Ideen zur Philosophie der Geschichte der Menschheit. In his *Sämtliche Werke*, B. Suphan et al. (eds), Berlin: Weidmann.

Jeater, D. (1993). *Marriage, Perversion and Power: The Construction of Moral Discourse in Southern Rhodesia, 1894–1930.* Oxford: Clarendon Press.

Fardon, R and G. Furniss (eds.) (1994). *Language, Development and the State.* London: Routledge.

Graddol, D and U.H. Meinhof (eds). (1999). "English in a changing world" *AILA Review* 13.

Kachru, B. (1992). *The Other Tongue. English Across Cultures.* (2nd ed.). Urbana: University of Illinois Press.

Mazrui, A. and A.Mazrui. (1998). *The Power of Babel: Language in the African Experience.* Oxford :James Currey/Chicago: University of Chicago Press.

Mohammed NorWan Daud (1989). *The Concept of Knowledge in Islam and its Implications for Education in a Developing Country.* London: Mansell.

Phillipson, R. (1992). *Linguistic Imperialism,* Oxford: OUP.

Rickford, J. (1998). "The Creole origins of African American Vernacular English: Evidence from copula absence" In S. Mufwene et al. (eds), *African American English: Structure, history and use*, pp. 154–200. London: Routledge.

Schmied, J (1991). *English in Africa. An Introduction.* London: Longman.

Shafl, M. (1983), "Teaching English as a Foreign Language: The islamic approach. *Muslim Education Quarterly* 1 (1): 33–41.

Ridge, E, S. Makoni and S.G.M. Ridge. (2001). "Introduction" In *Freedom and Discipline: Essays in Applied Linguistics from Southern Africa*, pp. 5–11. New Delhi: Bahri.

Ridge, S.G.M. (2001). 'Discourse constraints on language policy in South Africa" In Ridge et al. (eds), *Freedom and Discipline: Essays in Applied Linguistics from Southern Africa*, pp. 15–30. New Delhi: Bahri.

Willan, B. (1984). "Sol T. Plaatje and Tswana literature: A preliminary survey" In L.White and T. Couzens (eds.), *Literature and Society in South Africa*, pp. 81–100. Pinelands, Cape: Maskew Miller Longman.

Young, D (2001). "Why 'applied language studies' and not applied linguistics? Aspects of the evolution of applied language studies in South Africa since the 1960's into the new millennium—a personal view" In E. Ridge, S. Makoni and S.G.M Ridge (eds), *Freedom and Discipline: Essays in Applied Linguistics from Southern Africa*, pp. 221–262. New Delhi: Bahri.

II

Western perspectives in applied linguistics in Africa
(with Ulrike Meinhof)

Abstract
The aim of this article is to analyze the nature of the historical and contemporary social contexts within which applied linguistics in Africa emerged, and is currently practiced. The article examines the challenges 'local' applied Linguistics in Africa is confronted with as it tries to amplify applied linguistic programs emanating from Europe and North America. The article argues that seemingly progressive applied linguistic projects interconnect in consolidating a western view of Africa in postcolonial Africa. In this way these projects end up mirroring the very theories which they seek to challenge.

Introduction
This article like many others since the 1970's (see Towa 1979; Hountondji 1977,1994; Mudimbe 1988; Masolo 1994) is a critique of western theories of African realities. Unlike earlier critiques which were mainly of religion, history and philosophy, this article addresses the field of applied linguistics. It critiques not only western theories but also emerging Africanist responses to the alleged eurocentricism of

some linguistic scholarship on Africa. (Mazrui and Mazrui 1998). The objective of the analysis is to create conditions which facilitate more independent production of knowledge about Africa in applied linguistics (Bates,Mudimbe and O'Barr 1993), and avoid the pitfalls of critiques of western theories from Africa which inadvertently have ended up mirroring the very theories which they are challenging.

The idea of focusing an article specifically on western perspectives on Africa raises a number of issues which demand immediate clarification: (i) the label 'western' in our title (ii) the apparent contradiction of viewing applied linguistics through western lenses while writing an article on Africa.

Said, in his book *Orientalism*, comments on the conceptualization of 'western' which is relevant to our overall argument when he writes:

> Labels purporting to name very large and complex realities are notoriously vague and at the same time unavoidable. If it is true that 'Islam' is an imprecise and ideologically loaded label, it is also true that the west and Christianity are just as problematic. Yet there is no easy way of avoiding these labels, since Muslims speak of Islam, Christians of Christianity, westerners of the west, Jews of Judaism, and all of them about all the others in ways that seem to be both convincing and exact. Instead of trying to propose ways of going round the labels, I think it is more immediately useful to admit at the outset that they exist and have long been in use as an integral part of cultural history rather than as objective classifications. (Said 1978: 86)

The second issue we want to address at the outset is a focus on western sources while addressing issues about applied linguistics in Africa. In a recent study Prah points to the dominance of western scholarship in African studies, however misconstrued, a situation which is markedly different from that in China, where sovereignty of Chinese scholarship on China is widely accepted (Prah 1998:25). In contemporary scholarship, the same holds true for the Japanese, for India and the Arab world who have created their own epistemologies for studying their own cultures and societies. Yet much of our systematic knowledge of African societies is derived from and continues to be produced by western sources.

> The real power of the west is not located in its economic muscle and technological might. Rather, it resides in its power to define. The west defines what is, for example, freedom, progress and civil behavior; law tradition and community; reason, mathematics and science; what is real and what it means to be human (what is applied linguistics and what is not—our addition) The non-western civilizations have simply to accept these definitions or to be defined out of existence. (Sardar 1999:44)

The historical and continuing 'hold' of western knowledge over Africa does not devalue the importance of clearly articulated arguments aimed at developing African perspectives on applied linguistics which have emerged over the years (see for example, Mazrui and Mazrui 1998; Robinson 1996; Webb and Kembo-Sure 1999). In as much as we are critical of western perspectives on applied linguistics in Africa we are also at the same time skeptical of the validity of ethnicising epistemologies in applied linguistics in Africa as an intellectually viable way of reacting to the 'dominance' of such western perspectives. The ethnicisation of epistemologies is typically expressed in the form of *African Voices*, *African Perspectives*, and we feel it forecloses rather than provides opportunities for continued debate. We therefore argue that some criteria for establishing 'local or regionally shared knowledge practices' are necessary (Crossman 2003; Canagarajah 2002).

In the article we explore ways in which diverse areas such as 'indigenous languages', the policies of the Summer Institute of Linguistics International (SILI) lexicography, orthography, New Englishes (NE), interconnect in consolidating a western view on Africa in the postcolonial period in spite of the seemingly progressive and egalitarian developments encaptured in them.

Historical contexts in which applied linguistics in Africa emerged

Because 'language' has always been a companion of imperialism and 'Empire' (Hardt and Negri 2000) it can be argued that there has always been one version or other of applied linguistics in Africa's colonial and neocolonial encounters with the west. Deliberately misreading Kaplan's (1980) argument that there is no site in which applied linguistics cannot play a role, we suggest, that there is no historical period of African colonial and postcolonial encounters with the west and where ethnic groups have been in contact within a polity, which did not include some version of applied linguistics. To understand the nature of these we propose a distinction between applied linguistics as a formal discipline and applied linguistic 'activities' (Makoni and Meinhof 2003: 4).

We construe applied linguistic activities to refer to applied linguistic projects such as lexicography or the development of language teaching materials to facilitate the acquisition of African languages. These were carried out in the late 19th and early 20th centuries in Africa either as part of mission linguistics, or as part of a concerted colonial policy of control and containment (Cohn 1996). These applied linguistic activities predated the emergence of applied linguistics as a formal discipline, which did not take place until the late 1950's and early 1960's. Historically, this much later 'inauguration' of applied linguistics 'proper' coincided with Africa's decolonization. The emergence of applied linguistics as an academic discipline in Africa was, in part, driven by the British concern about the 'quality' of English language teaching after the end of British colonial rule—as if the impending loss of explicit and formal British colonial control compelled the British to 'rediscover' the importance of English in postcolonial Africa. 'The British Empire was giving way to the empire of English' (Phillipson 1992: 1). The concern about the 'quality' of English language teaching after Africa's 'flag' independence is revealing because during the colonial period the British were less preoccupied with the teaching and learning of English particularly at primary school levels, but rather with the 'development' of what in our view is incorrectly described and conceptualized as a series of 'indigenous' languages. We shall return below to the implications this has for the prolific field of language planning in Africa.

The 'decolonization' of Africa and the Cold War period also resulted in a greater US involvement in Africa. Academically this contributed towards the establishment and 'flowering of what became known as African Studies in the US. African Studies is a western project, a way of explaining the other in the western mind' (Prah 1998: 31). Particularly in the USA a strand of African applied linguistics was subsequently subsumed within African Studies. However, the objective of this strand of applied linguistics in African Studies was not to create applied linguistic alternatives, but alternatives to applied linguistics.

If applied linguistic 'activities' were shaped by and contributed to shaping colonialism, applied linguistics as a discipline in Africa is still struggling to confront the 'hold' of what Hardt and Negri (2000) aptly refer to as 'Empire' because with political independence in Africa has come no freedom from the imperial grip (and local African dictatorship we hasten to add), but mediated command. The example par excellence is French West Africa which by way of a sophisticated and somewhat Machiavellan French strategy was divided into a dozen potentially functional, but in reality dysfunctional newly independent states. Nominally independent, these countries were dysfunctional from their inception because of their small populations and tiny national economies coupled with a convertible currency. These factors made these states 'poor countries with a currency of rich people' Charles De Gaulle quoted in Breton (2003: 207). With political systems which had no robust institutional past nor political structure (Breton 2003:206), the newly independent African countries, particularly former French countries became more rather than less dependent on France after they had attained independence. This created ideal conditions for Africa's neo-dependence or 'extraversion' (Crossman 2004: 40) as Africanists prefer to call it in economic terms as well as in the academic sector, especially as regards our own discipline. Applied linguistics in particular has not yet systematically confronted its own colonial legacy as other disciplines in Africa such as anthropology (Prah 1994: 95), which has shown considerable reflexivity under the pervasive influence of colonial and postcolonial theories. We therefore conclude our essay with some recommendations on how applied linguistics particularly in higher education might be 'developed' as a strategy to construct and initiate new and alternative futures in our discipline.

The inauguration of applied linguistics as an academic discipline was important because it occurred at an important historical juncture in Africa's decolonization process ushering in a new epistemological trend in language studies in Africa. While the main focus of applied linguistic activities in the colonial period had been the construction and 'development' of African languages for Europeans, applied linguistics as a discipline concentrated on the teaching and learning of European languages by Africans. This led in some parts of Africa, particularly South Africa, to a conceptualization of applied linguistics as synonymous with English language teaching (Young 2001). The trend of using indigenous languages as key sites of applied linguistics was to be continued by the Summer Institute of Linguistics International (SILI) and its domestic arm Wycliffe International (WI) previously known as Wycliffe Bible Translators. WI is generally responsible for the domestic 'fund' raising of the SILI in the US. According to its own stated mission, the goal of the SILI is to bring the 'word to Bible-less tribes' (Laitin 1992: 98). SILI was to be one of the key 'International Organizations' which was to subsequently shape and influence the direction of applied linguistics in Africa. Besides the SILI, there are other organizations which have contributed to the development of applied linguistics in Africa such as the Ford Foundation, the French sponsored Comité Linguistique Africaine à Dakar (CLAD), and the British Council (Laitin 1992: 98). Until recently AILA was not one of the major forces in the development of applied linguistics in Africa. There is only one AILA affiliated association in Africa, the Southern African Association of Applied Linguistics (SAALA) which in spite of the 'Southern African' nomenclature concentrates largely on applied linguistics in South Africa. SAALA was formed in 1980, during the period of academic boycott of South Africa when it was not strategic to use South Africa in the title of the association. There are, however, some other associations such as the Linguistic Society of Southern African Universities, the Linguistic Society of Nigeria and the English Studies of Nigeria which amongst other areas also engage in some applied linguistic research, but the influence of these associations pales in comparison to the historical and ongoing impact of SILI.

It is not our objective to provide a comprehensive summary of all applied linguistic activities in Africa. Given the diversity and range this would be an impossible undertaking. Our objectives are much more modest than that. We have three main aims: First to examine how western perspectives are embedded in seemingly progressive areas of applied linguistics in Africa. Secondly, to analyze the contradictions which emerge in African attempts at amplifying such projects. Thirdly, to discuss ethnicising epistemologies in Africa as a reaction to the dominance of the west in applied linguistics in Africa, and thus show their problematic nature.

Lexicography in applied linguistics in Africa
Christianity, lexicography, anthropology and more recently 'descriptive' linguistics particularly corpus linguistics, have been the key driving forces behind the development of Africa's modern day lexicography (Prinsloo and de Schruyver 2001, 2002).

Lexicography in Africa has its origins in word lists, 'Vocabulary-collecting was something visitors to the continent did' (Irvine 2001: 79) The earliest word lists were produced between 1643 and 1660 by Jesuit and Capuchian priests. Most of these early 'dictionaries' were bilingual and were produced for European language learners of African languages. For example, a quadrilingual dictionary of Italian, Latin, Spanish and kiKongo was published in 1650, predating by about a century the famous monolingual English dictionary by Samuel Johnson which was published in 1755 (Benson 2001). The dictionaries together with the language primers produced during the colonial period were targeted at Europeans. As other language teaching materials used to teach African languages, they are extremely revealing about the nature of European perspectives on Africans and their languages, and if seen from a contemporary African stand point are amenable to charges of eurocentrism. However, eurocentrism in this case should not be defined negatively, since such a critique suggests denigrating lexicographers for succeeding in their objectives. Not all 19th century lexicographers were Europeans, one notable exception was the Nigerian Samuel Ajayi Crowther who wrote a dictionary on his first language, Yoruba. He also worked on a range of other West African languages, notably Temne, Igbo, Nupe and Hausa (Irvine 2001: 77).

It is also important to stress that in the 19th century there was a much closer relationship between literary studies and the study of African languages in two key respects, in terms of the 'source material' which was used, and in what applied linguistics today might call the genre used in the 'linguistic' studies of African languages. The source material included proverbs which were seen as an important component of lexicography. Currently studies in proverbs are seen more as a key component of oral African literature than of applied linguistics in Africa. The dictionaries were also not only written for their linguistic sophistication but for their literary merits as well (Irvine 2001: 64).

The applied linguistic question worth posing is thus not so much whether the dictionaries and primers were Eurocentric as such, but rather focus on the effects of the eurocentrism when the dictionaries and primers were subsequently used in the provision of literacy in African education. Rather than targeting children's own cultural life dictionaries and language teaching materials were resources for the learning of African languages by Europeans as part of a strategy of containment. Underlying the policy of containment was the belief that one way to control people is to create European versions of African languages, and subsequently superimpose them when used as medium of instruction.

There have been extensive and on-going discussions on linguistic imperialism and the suppression of vernaculars (cf. Phillipson 1992; Davies 1996; Joseph 2004). Our perspective on this important topic is slightly different. Historical evidence shows that in African contexts, and particularly in British colonies, it was the victorious who were keen to learn the languages of the defeated rather than the other way round. Hence in such contexts linguistic imperialism is not to be seen as the imposition of a colonial language on the colonized but entails the imposition of a colonial version of an indigenous language on Africans. For example, in the Republic of the Congo, the colonial 'indigenous' variety associated with the state was referred to as the *kikongo ya leta* (The kikongo of the rock) and *kikongo ya matari* (The kikongo of the stone breaker) (Mufwene 2001:176). The chiShona associated with the state and missionaries in Zimbabwe was called *chibaba* the language of the missionaries (Chimhundu 1992). It is these versions which became the local vernaculars used as medium of instruction.

Our perspective of linguistic imperialism also entails a redefinition of expertise in African languages: in this case a shift from oral performance to textual analysis. As a rule, most of the analysts adept at textual analysis were either European professional linguists who typically had learnt African languages as second languages or they were western educated Africans. Thus the native speaker was displaced as a legitimate expert in his/her own language.

Currently, there is considerable interest and excitement in a more innovative production of African language dictionaries based on electronic corpora (Prinsloo and de Schryver 2001, 2002). The relative ease with which African corpora can now be established has led to a proliferation of corpus-based dictionaries often covering closely related languages/language varieties as is illustrated in the following lexical items:

Table 1. A comparative analysis of the Bemba/Lamba & Kaonde lexicon

English	*Bemba*	*Lamba*	*Kaonde*
All	Onse	Onsi	Onse
Animal	Nama	Nyama	Nyama
Ashes	To	Toi	To
Belly	Fumo	Kati	Vumo
Big	Kulu	Kulu	Katampe
Bone	Fupa	Fupa	Kupa

(Kashoki and Mann 1978: 82–93).

It is questionable whether it is justifiable to compile separate dictionaries for Bemba, Lamba, and Kaonde because of the considerable similarity in spite of the different labels. The converse does apply, that in some cases considerable diversity is masked by using a single language label. For exam-ple, there is both lexical and grammatical variability within Swahili. As illustrated in the following:

Table 2. A Comparative analysis of Ugandan kiSwahili and Tanzanian KiSwahili

KiSwahili (Uganda)	*Swahili (Tanzania)*	*English*
Bado	Mapema	Soon
Nguo za serikali	Sare	Uniform
Maktab	Ofisi	Office
Ndito	misicha...	Girl
Muro	chakula...	Food

(Mukama 2002: 67)

The differences also apply at a grammatical level. For example, Swahili in Uganda operates with 9–10 noun classes, while Swahili in Tanzania like any other Bantu languages has over 20 noun classes. Noun classes are the central organizing principle for the organization of Bantu languages. The presence of diversity within the same label does not preclude the possibility of compiling a single dictionary which accommodates that diversity. Research and dictionaries on African especially South African sign language (Penn and Reagan 1991, 1995, 2001; Reagan 1996) provide examples of how this can be achieved. In enumerating different types such as American sign language, British sign language, pidginized sign languages, they reflect the great diversity within sign languages. Penn and Reagan (1995) report that 98% of the words they compiled were represented by more than one sign. But the dictionary was compiled in such a way as to accommodate that range of diversity.

Rather than seeking to compile a dictionary for each variety which, as the above examples illustrate, might entail producing dictionaries which greatly overlap with one another, it should be feasible to compile a common dictionary, especially in situations of limited financial resources. To us the model to follow is not the development of one dictionary for each variety but a pluralistic one: the 'one dictionary = many varieties' model reflected in African sign language research and indeed in the dictionary of South African English which incorporates the different 'varieties' of South African English in its tradition. The South African lexicographical tradition started in 1913 under the auspices of Pettman (1913) cited in Bolton (2004), and continued to the present day with Branford (1987), and Silva's (1998) monumental *Dictionary of South African English on Historical Principles* (Bolton 2004: 381).

Sociolinguistics of urban vernaculars

In the sociolinguistic and psycholinguistic literature it is treated as established fact that in Africa code-switching and mixing are extremely widespread (McCormick 1995; Myers-Scotton 1993; Kamwangamalu 1998; Slabbert and Finlayson 2002). There are three discernible orientations towards code-switching and mixing research: psycholinguistic, sociolinguistic and linguistic. The objective of this section is not to review the voluminous literature on code-switching and mixing, but to examine the assumptions which form the basis of this literature, to investigate what it might tell us about the researcher's perceptions about Africa. From the perspective of an educated speaker it is plausible to assume that code-switching and mixing is the result of the speaker/ author's choice of linguistic material from different languages. This assumption is particularly valid for educated speakers who have been exposed to 'school language versions', since as a rule 'School language' is unmixed. However, whilst this may hold for educated speakers, it may not necessarily be true of non-educated speakers. For such speakers, unmixed forms are an exception, whereas the norm is a linguistic amalgam based on material from diverse languages as illustrated in the two extracts below.

The mixing may occur so frequently and so pervasively that it constitutes the norm for those speakers. The following two extracts illustrate the extent to which the mixing may be so intricately intertwined that it might be more plausible to describe it as a single code rather than a product of two or more separate codes. Thus what may be perceived analytically as bilingualism and a hybrid language from an analyst's perspective may indeed be a form of monolingualism from a noneducated language user's perspective. It is important to stress that when we call a language a hybrid we are making statements about its history, that it, is derived from many sources, but as we all know people do not necessarily inherit the history of their language when they are learning it!

> **Extract 1**
> Mi igioinki ki ndozala
> '(I'm on my way to the market') contains words from different languages: mi (I < Swahili mimi), gouink (go < English going), ki (LOC.,) French qui and ndozala (market < Lingala zando)
> (Goyavertz 1996: 125)

These mixed forms are not restricted to spoken medium only, but are apparent even in written discourse, and at times include different writing conventions as illustrated in the following extract from an electronic communication:

English in normal font, chiShona in italics, informal discourse in bold
Extract 2
Hi *sekuru* (uncle) compliments of the new year, I hope *makapinda mairi mushe mushe.* (you had a pleasant new year) Do you know how long the PR (permit res) is **gonna** take?

The short extract above seems to be an amalgam of different languages, and different styles and writing conventions. From the perspective of an educated analyst, it may be assumed that the author is astutely combining different styles and languages. But from the perspective of the language user, what a western educated linguist may construe as a mixture might simply be a single code albeit variable in the way in which it brings together 'elements' from different languages. To describe the codes as chiShona and English may be introducing distinctions which although available in the analysts mind are absent from the speaker's perspective.

Most of the speakers and writers of the linguistic amalgams do not necessarily have separate competence in the 'named' languages. But when they do not know the languages in the unmixed forms, is is not plausible to argue that they are combining material from different languages. The truth may be that for many African speakers whether in speech or writing it may now be impossible to separate African languages from different varieties of English. We may be witnessing a formation of a linguistic amalgam which is so complete that even for some educated speakers it may be difficult to identify the different 'varieties'. Nor are they strictly speaking 'street languages' restricted to urban areas since such mixes are even recorded in rural areas. It is the urban vernaculars which now constitute a threat to 'indigenous' African languages and not English. We refer to the linguistic amalgams as urban even though they are spoken in rural communities as well because they transcend physical location and stand in sharp contrast with indigenous (standardized) African languages deemed to be rural (Cook 2002: 108; Finlayson, Calteaux and Myers-Scotton 1998). Thus Urban and rural are not understood not as purely geographical locations only but as key aspects of an individual's identity, articulated in part through language. It is an open question whether it is appropriate to define the urban vernaculars as 'languages'. One possible way of defining them would be to regard them simply as 'expressive inventories, that not only enable people to communicate with each other, but also allow people to communicate something about themselves' (Cook: 2002: 111). These 'expressive inventories' pose a serious conceptual challenge to the neocolonial constructions of African languages which underpin most of the notions about language in language planning in Africa.

From a western perspective, the spread of the urban vernaculars such as Town Bemba in Zambia, Iscimatho in South Africa, Wolof in the Gambia and Senegal is of interest because although language loss is rare in Africa, it is the urban vernaculars and not ex-European languages such as French or English which constitute a threat to 'indigenous' African languages. In situations of economic collapse, 'petty' trading is one of the key professions, and it requires the command of urban vernaculars more so than either French or English, or 'indigenous' African languages. More importantly, English is closely tied to western models of modernization, Christian conversion and modernist social and capitalist development which since the late 1980s has come to represent a 'deadend for most suburban dwellers' (Devisch 1995, 1999).

While the endangerment of 'indigenous' languages may be read as potentially catastrophic by some linguists, from an Africanist perspective, the spread of the urban vernaculars reflects the extent to which African speakers are creatively adapting to new urban contexts. This underscores the importance of sociolinguistic frameworks which would be able to capture the nuances of the local contexts. An attrition framework may not be relevant (Mufwene 2001, 2002, 2004). The issue of language endangerment raises fundamental problems about the underlying notions of language, and the relative importance being attached to speakers as opposed to the languages themselves. We would like to argue that the endangerment of language does not necessarily mean the endangerment of the speakers of those languages. Indeed the creative adaptation by urban African speakers may enhance rather than reduce their chances of survival (Mufwene 2004).

In Africa according to Brenzinger (1998) 54 African languages are already extinct, and another 116 are at various stages of extinction. The statistics of the numbers of endangered languages raises issues which are extremely important in applied linguistics in Africa. It touches directly on the issue of enumerability/countability of languages in Africa.

We are not questioning either the statistics of the number of existing African languages nor the ones regarded as threatened or indeed the numbers of those regarded as likely to be extinct. What we seek to draw attention to is a much more fundamental problem. We are seeking to challenge the nature of the linguistic thinking, which makes it possible to think in terms of the enumerability of those languages in the first instance, and to foreground the role of enumerability as one of the modalities of governance. 'To census is an important gesture of power' (Hill 2002: 127).

Analytically, urban African vernaculars are comparable though not equivalent to creoles in so far as they arise in 'contexts of extreme domination (slavery, apartheid) and where one more or less dominant group presides over several subordinate groups. The new social contexts created by the political/economic formation, (e.g., urban centers and shantytowns rather than plantation) create new identities and ethnicities. Depending on the specific historical and social setting, urban vernaculars arise to express and complement these new identities, drawing from the linguistic landscape in different ways and gender-specific ways (Spears personal communication). For example, male urban vernaculars in South Africa draw more upon Afrikaans, than English, while the converse is true for young Black female South Africans (Cook 2002) analysis of 'street Se Tswana' in South Africa.

An analysis of language mixing in urban vernaculars provides an invaluable opportunity for understanding the nature of language contact in real time. Although we are not claiming that urban African vernaculars are creoles or pidgins as such, an analysis of the urban vernaculars sheds light on the processes which pidgins and creoles underwent because of the similarity in the basic processes of variation and simplification.

That urban vernaculars are being acquired as first and second languages pose important sociolinguistic questions with crucial educational implications. Is it always necessary to standardize languages if they are to be used and taught educationally? Without a standard variety what type of language teaching materials would be useful? We suggest that in that case such materials should reflect the heteroglossic (Bakhtin 1981) nature of African sociolinguistics; the materials should therefore be made up of diverse authentic texts. Although standardization might be useful in some contexts, it is possible that the absence of a single standard relieves users of urban African vernaculars of the intense pressures of a monolithic standard. If the urban vernaculars are subsequently standardized, one challenge is how to produce an orthography which allows variation within it. Issues about orthography have been at the core of a great deal of research into African languages, because of the inconsistencies within the orthography. At times the 'same' language may also have more than one orthography (Yanga 1980, 1998; Nyombe 1977). A solution might be to have a general agreement about the phonetic values of the letters, but no standard spelling for individual words. English followed a similar pattern for centuries one could encounter the same word on the same page, spelt differently.

African varieties of English—initiating an African response to new Englishes

The New Englishes (NE) paradigm has been extensively used by some of Africa's most prolific and talented applied linguists (Owusu-Ansah 1991;Kamwangamalu and Chisanga 1997; Arua Arua 2001; Dako 2001; Gough 1996; Wolf and Igboanuasi 2003; Letsholo 2000; Moyo and Kamwangamalu 2003) to analyse the ways in which phonologically, lexically, semantically, and pragmatically English has been adapted to Local African contexts in Nigeria, Cameroon, Ghana, Swaziland, South Africa, Zimbabwe, Botswana and more recently the Sudan. NE research has thus served as a counter to 'centrist' arguments about English. However, the main focus of our analysis is different. We explore the ideological implications of using NE within African contexts from the perspective of a majority of Africans with restricted, if any proficiency in English as a way of shedding light onto the status of English in Africa. A comparable ideological analysis of NE within non-western contexts has been carried out in Asia (Canagarajah 1999; Dasgupta 1993; Krishnasway and Burde 1998; Kandiah 1998). In New Englishes the sociolinguistics of landscape of Africa seems to be viewed through the prism of a national identity, and a national culture ('Leitkultur' (Nigerian English, South African English, Zambian English etc). Because the main prism is that of a nation state, the research overlooks the inescapable historical, economic and cultural inter-dependencies of contemporary Africa and the modern world. Such interconnections might shape the use of language particularly of English in Africa much more strongly than the nation state. It might therefore be useful for those working in the New Englishes paradigm in Africa to seriously consider developing paradigms where language in use is situated in transitional and transnational social networks. Such models have already begun to be developed in migration research in which the 'state' is conceptualized as an 'imagined community' (Anderson 1983), or through the 'narration of the nation' (Hall 1995). Unless such a conceptual shift is made away from a nation state towards more transitional networks, research in Englishes will find it difficult to account for the effects of Africa's voluntary and involuntary massive migration on language use. Because of the massive migration both within and across borders, speakers of Nigerian, Zambian, South African English rarely live in isolation from other nationalities.

There are three main types of English users in Africa:

i. monolingual English speakers, a majority of whom are white and 'settled' in South Africa.
ii. English/African language bilinguals with English as a second language (ESL).
iii. Trilingual speakers fluent in English/French or English/Portuguese and an African language. For these trilingual speakers, English is a foreign language. The trilingual speakers are largely but not exclusively in 'Lusophone' and 'Francophone' Africa.

Lanham andMacdonald (1979) distinguishes between three types of varieties of White South African English, also called General South African English: *conservative, respectable, and extreme.* Conservative is based on what White South Africans perceive to be Received Pronunciation *respectable* is a locally cultivated South African variety, associated with middle class South Africans. *Extreme* SAE is associated with lowly educated and low social class White South Africans (Gough 1996: xii). If the other types of English users in Africa, apart from the White South Africans are framed in terms of Kachru's (1986) and Graddol's (1996) concentric circles model of *inner*, and *outer* then the bilingual ESL group can be categorized as belonging to the *outer circle*. Such outer circle speakers are said to be *norm-dependent*. Trilingual speakers can be situated within the *expanding circle* (Kachru 1992: 2).

But how applicable is this model to Africa? If most speakers do not have access to native speakers of English in everyday encounters is it really feasible to claim that they are *norm-dependent*. Instead of using the construct of *norm-dependence* it may be more appropriate to refer to the use of English in such contexts as examples of what Pennycook describes as 'crucial acts of semiotic reconstruction' (Pennycook 2003). *Norm-dependency* also undermines what NE framework seeks to celebrate, namely the creativity of non-native speakers of English.

The NE framework purports to move 'from linguistic authoritarianism of the native speaker variety to a speech fellowship-specific realism' (Kachru 1995: 25), and thus ostensibly displaces the construct of the native speaker as central organizing principle. Yet norm-dependency reintroduces it by the backdoor. The Kachru framework in such a context appears to apply double standards. This ambivalence towards the epistemological role of English arises because English is defined through 'cross-referential or anaphoric meaning, which depends on the meaning of English in its native habitat'. (Dasgupta 1993:48), rather than being seen potentially independent, locally and contextually determined reference system 'the dictionary draws the reader's attention to semantic links between South African English with those found, for example, in the English of Britain, the United States, Jamaica, or Nigeria' (Silva: 1998:xv). There are also further problems with the applicability of the NE in Africa. There are no principled reasons why some linguistic forms are selected as typical of NE and other hybrid forms excluded. For example, it is not clear why Owusu-Ansah identifies some features as typical of Ghanaian English and excludes others. Similarly, there are no principled reasons why Gough (1996) selects the following features as typical instantiations of General South African English, African English, Colored English, South African Indian English:

General South African English
a. 'Busy' as a marker of the progressive: I'm busy cooking'
b. Reduplication of adverb 'now' as 'now-now', which denotes either 'immediately' or 'soon'.

African English
a. Use of indefinite article before certain 'non-count' nouns: 'He was carrying a luggage'.
b. Use of 'do' or 'did' in unemphasized statements and questions: 'I did tell him to come':Who did throw that? (Mesthrie 1993: 31)

'Coloured' English
a. Use of the dative of advantage": I'm gonna buy me a new car'
b. Retention of ordinary question order in indirect questions with the verb 'be': I don't know what's that' (Mesthrie 1989: 6).

Each of the above varieties is best construed as part of a continuum.

It is indeed possible that the above features represent the English used by different ethnic and racial groups in South Africa. It is, however, not clear what criteria were used to determine which linguistic features fall under each ethnic/racial category. Consequently, methodologically, NE reads like an elitist standardization of periphery Englishes relying on the 'prescriptive and elitist tendencies of center linguistics' which the framework wants to distance itself from (Canagarajah 1999: 180) another telling example of intellectual double standards! If the descriptions of the ethnic/racial Englishes cited above are largely linguistic, an alternative approach which is largely political emerged in what was referred to as 'People's English'. This perspective emphasizes the role which English played in shaping the identities of African users of English in South Africa during the apartheid 'People's English' is political because it represents a challenge to the current status of English in South Africa in which control of the language, access to the language, and the teaching of the language are entrenched within apartheid structures' (Norton Peirce1995: 108; see also Norton Peirce 1989). The objective of 'People's English was to wrestle the control of English from white South African native speakers. With the strategic advantage of hindsight a decade after the end of apartheid we can safely say 'People's English' failed to meet its political objectives, because English in South Africa is now firmly within the hands of white South African native speakers perhaps even more so than it was during the apartheid era.

Since the NE are describing the English used by formally educated Africans, some insights into African responses to notions about NE would be revealing. Educated African users of English find the categories' Nigerian' or 'Ghanaian English' sociolinguistically offensive as Kofi Sey, the founding father of Ghanain English Linguistics wrote, thus anticipating the discussion of NE in Africa:

> …Nothing disgusts an educated Ghanaian more than being told that the English he uses is anything but standard. The linguist may be able to isolate features of Ghanaian English and describe them. But once these are made known to him, the educated Ghanaian would strive to avoid them altogether. The surest way to kill Ghanaian English, if it really exists, is to discover it and make it known to him. (Sey 1973: 10)

One of the most powerful arguments advanced in support of the NE framework is its supposed inclusivity, underwritten by a heterogeneous philosophy and not the homogeneity typical of discourses of monolithic English emerging from Anglo-American centers. But from whose perspective is English heterogeneous or inclusive?

In comparison with or as a challenge to the monolithic and 'centrist' views of English in Anglo-American centers, the NE framework is clearly inclusive. But in the context of the language spoken and understood by the majority of Africans, it is clearly not inclusive at all. Even when the localized varieties of English are taken into account they clearly exclude a large majority of Africans who use pidgins and creoles (Mufwene 1998). Speakers who do not use English, that is the majority of Africans do not perceive any linguistic distinctions between British Standard English and Africanized adaptations of English. It is not possible to distinguish between types of what you do not know. In other words, for non-English users distinctions between British English and Africanized Englishes are rightly construed as part of the language games of professional elites.

English whether adapted or not remains an elitist code. Therefore, from the perspective of non-English speakers the homogeneity/heterogeneity distinction is not relevant. That NE, in contrast to popular French, should be so class marked is highly significant, and part of an important sociolinguistic process—particularly in South Africa as a caste-like social stratification is gradually replaced by social class. Paulston (personal communication 2004) points to a 'growing middle class of people of color and concurrently the growing number of private schools' where English is one of the, if not the primary, means of instruction. Belief in the neutrality of English will foreclose discussion in an important area of research at exactly the time when we need to focus on the complex interaction between social class and language. Pennycook (2003) takes this further in forging a connection between the apparent tolerance of different variations of NE with an already achieved world-wide dominance.

Applied linguistic concerns: The role of the non-native teacher
Given the amount of research which has been carried out on NE, and the contributions of non-native English teachers in

Africa, it is odd that there is very limited research which has focused on the role of the non-native teacher of English in the teaching and learning of English in Africa; yet the non-native teacher is increasingly becoming a focus of educational research in North American and European research (Kramsch 1993, 2002, 2004). Research into English in Africa also needs to examine much more systematically the nature of the relationship between the teaching of English and the use of English particularly in the workplace. Insights from such research will not only be useful linguistically, but might have an impact in terms of African governance as well. Some scholars (King 1986) attribute the slow functioning of African bureaucracy to the hesitation to commit ideas to paper in English!

Constructing indigeneity
Language planning in Africa is a rapidly expanding and contentious area. (Ridge 2001; Roy-Campbell 2003, 2002; Kamwangamalu 1998; Moyo 2003; Omoniyi 2003). One of the central concepts underlying language planning is the notion of 'indigenous languages'. The objective of this section is to examine how indigeneity is constructed. Our goal is not to provide an overview of language planning in Africa, especially since a number of excellent overviews already exists (cf. Fafunwa et al.1989; Bambgose 1976, 1991;Mazrui 2000). These texts should be read in conjunction with Robert Kaplan and Richard Baldauf's edited monographs on *Current Issues in language planning* which focus on individual African countries. To date monographs have been written on Botswana, South Africa (Nkonko Kamwangamalu), Tunisia, Ivory Coast (Paulin Djite), Malawi (Edrinnie Kayambazinthu), Nigeria. Monographs on other African countries are also being prepared.

The construct of *indigenous languages* is significant for two reasons. At a very general level, it involves 'local knowledge' (Geertz 1983), a vital ingredient in the growth of applied linguistics in Africa. At a more specific level, since one of the purported objectives of language planning is to ensure the survival of indigenous languages against the encroachment of dominant languages, the discussion is relevant to language planning. Our main objectives here are neither to suggest that applied linguistics in Africa should dispense with 'western' modern sciences, nor simply oppose local knowledge with western knowledge, but to initiate a discussion which would lead towards a construction of a more legitimate framework for understanding site specific applied linguistics and western applied linguistics. Seen from a different perspective, Western applied linguistics is in itself local from a different perspective.

The concept of indigenous languages been used extensively in academic discussions of language planning in Africa, usually with a focus on the technical, pedagogic, and economic contexts rather than on the conceptualization of the construct of indigenous languages itself (cf. Stroud 2002).

Although, the concept of indigenous has not been analyzed critically, it has even acquired a quasi-legal status in the Organization of African Unity (Organisation De l'Unité Africaine) Language Plan of Action and the 1996 Constitution of the Republic of South Africa.

In the Founding Provisions of the 1996 South African Constitution all the indigenous languages are official languages, but not all official languages are necessarily indigenous languages.

In spite of quasi-legal status of indigenous languages in these significant documents there are four questions which we seek to raise:

1. How valid is the binary distinction between *indigenous languages* and *ex-colonial languages*?

2. To what extent is the notion of the indigenous a postcolonial reaction to the legacy of colonialism, rather than a description of a pre-colonial state of affairs?
3. In what ways is the construct of the indigenous itself part of western nomenclature?
4. If you racialise and ethnicise epistemology through the use of constructs such as the indigenous are we not reinforcing colonial thinking?

The term *indigenous languages* is used uncritically in applied linguistics, even though the term indigenous is regarded as problematic in anthropology and political science. The term was used interchangeably with the so-called 'customary law', and 'traditional medicine'. The term gained wide currency after it was used extensively by Warren et al. in 'developmentalist' discourses. Mamdani demonstrates the problematic nature of the construct, when he writes:

> … The anthropologist considered the illiterate native a more reliable authority on customary law than the literate native, the authority was construed in terms of a primary source, to be sifted through, analyzed, its central contradictions smoothed over, its gaps and lapses filled in, all to arrive at a coherent, consistent, and comprehensive secondary formulation.
> (Mamdani 1996: 113)

Mamdani's analysis shows that indigenous knowledge systems (IKS) were seen by the colonialists not as true representatives of a pre-colonial past, but as products of their intervention. Hence, those accounts, whereby indigenous systems—including languages—become representative of a pre-colonial era, reflect a postcolonial orientation to colonialism rather than an accurate analysis of a pre-colonial social and historical state. Indigenous languages were created through a process of mediation which is irreversible. Breckenbridge and van de Veer's account of India resonates here very well with the African experience.

> The very languages that are called 'native' are products of an intricate dialectic between colonial projects of knowledge and the formation of group identities' (Breckenbridge and van de Veer 1993).

Notions about customary law, traditional medicine, ethnocosmology undermine the holism of indigenous knowledge. (Semali and Kinchele 1999: 21) Fortune, who played a key role in descriptions of Bantu languages, takes the argument further still when he observes that the separation of language from cultural practices as implied in structuralist descriptions of African languages is inconsistent with an African world view (Fortune 1977). Reformulating Fortune's argument we can say that the idea of African grammars having an ontological existence outside discourse and cultural practices is part of a tradition of African linguistic scholarship which in its preoccupation with grammar and linguistic structure 'often metaphorized as bringing grammar and structure to the languages' (Blommaert 1999: 178).

The 'complex dialectic' which Breckenbridge and van der Veer has in mind is analogous to Mamdani's 'secondary formulation'. Both 'complex dialectic' and 'secondary formulation' highlight the fact that the institutions may not be as 'natural/indigenous' to Africa as we may be inclined to believe. That the secondary formulation and by implication 'unnaturalness' was not restricted to customary law, and traditional medicine but extended to the so-called 'indigenous' languages as well can be illustrated by analyzing how European oriented meanings emerged in African vernaculars. A close analysis of 'indigenous' language raises issues about what is natural and what is not in 'indigenous languages'.

What is 'authentically' African in indigenous languages are the linguistic forms, the meanings of the words arose as a result of active social intervention. We demonstrate our point on the basis of linguistic evidence drawn from chi-Shona, a language used in Zimbabwe, and phonetic examples from Luwo, Lugbara and Ateso/Akarimojong spoken largely in Uganda.

In order to demonstrate how some of the European meanings of African words were created, distributed, circulated and legitimated—drawing on some of the work by Jeater & Hove (in press)—we focus on an analysis of the *Mashonaland Quarterly* (MQ). The MQ was launched in 1925 at Morgenster Mission. The mission station was run and administered by the Dutch Reformed Church. Geographically Morgenster is situated in south-central parts of Zimbabwe. The MQ is an ideal text to analyze because it was the first publication to be used by Europeans in then Rhodesia (now Zimbabwe) to communicate their world views to an African audience on issues about education, religion and how to carry out small scale farming. Since it was the first such publication, an analysis of the use of some of the lexical items will give us insights into how the meanings of some words were reconfigured rendering them amenable to control.

The term '*vanhu*' in chiShona for example, meant people, a generic word category not marked for race. After European intervention the term 'Vatema' emerged within the MQ and in subsequent publications on chiShona, to refer to 'Black people'. It replaced the generic *vanhu*: a creation of meanings for Europeans. The replacement of '*vanhu*' with '*vatema*' introduced racial distinctions which were absent in *indigenous* thoughts (Jeater and Hove in press). In a different noun class the root '*tema*' is '*nhema*' which means color '*nhema*' (black cow) and '*kutaura nhema*' (lies) creating a collocation in the MQ and subsequent standard chi-

Shona publications which links racial categorization with lies.

Although Africans were racially categorized, the Europeans did not use such categories to refer to themselves in African vernaculars. They simply referred to themselves in terms of their social status as 'bosses' or 'masters' using the word '*murungu*'. The term reflected social status and not racial categorization. Africans referred to Europeans as '*vasinamabvi*'—those without knees—meaning a people who couldn't bend to work on their knees, grinding, and digging, or as *mabvakure*. By sharp contrast to the racial categories about Africans central for the Europeans, there was no racial marking in African descriptions of either Europeans, nor in reference to themselves. (Jeater 2002; Jeater and Hove in press). Furthermore, Europeans frequently described Africans in the possessive: *wanhu wedu watema wari mu Afrika* (*our people who are in Africa*) (Jeater and Hove in press) Since European world views were embedded in the constructed vernaculars, the development of literacy in indigenous languages involved a shift away from an indigenous world perspective towards a European based one.

The introduction of European perspectives on African linguistic forms was not restricted to the lexicon only, it is also evident phonetically, for example in the superimposition of five vowels on Eastern Nilotic languages, and the absence of a standard orthography for Lwo, Lugbara and Ateso/Akarimojong (Walusimbi 2002: 15).

African scholars have argued quite forcefully for the use of 'indigenous' languages as medium of instruction highlighting the problematic nature of using so-called excolonial languages (Bamgbose 1976; Rubagumya 1998; Fafunwa et al. 1989).What has been absent from the debate is an analysis of the assumptions about language and education which form the basis of the construct of 'medium' in 'medium of instruction'. The notion of 'medium' seems to be based on a Lockean idea of communication and instruction through language as 'telementation' the transference of messages from one mind to another (Cameron 1990: 55; Makoni and Pennycook 2007). This is only possible if one accepts the idea of African languages as fixed codes. The construct of 'medium' of instruction also seems to reinforce the notion of instruction as consisting of a transference of information from the teacher to the student. The idea of medium of instruction thus reinforces a hierarchical relationship between teachers and students, and validates a one way flow of information. That the learning through and the teaching of English creates problems for learning in Africa is a well known fact. A logical but inaccurate inference to draw from such studies is, however, that the use of 'indigenous' languages as 'medium' of instruction of instruction will be a panacea to Africa's educational problems.

The lesson we can draw from the above analysis of *indigenous* languages is that there is a danger of falling prey falling prey to reductionist western binarism between excolonial and indigenous languages and thus to overlook the imprint of colonialism/European perspectives on indigenous languages. The use of the term indigenous may be politically correct, but it is a romantic, idealistic and ahistorical notion, subverting the efforts to address contemporary African language problems. Its use also highlights the dangers of an ethnicising and racializing epistemology which reinforces the very categories which the analyst is tying to escape from.

The notion of indigenous languages is founded on a conception of language as made up of discrete units, which Grace (forthcoming) refers to as 'Autonomous Text Languages' (AT), whose primary function is to serve as 'codes for expository prose' for communicating factual information by encoding and decoding propositions (Grace forthcoming). Such a conceptualization is problematic. The idea of indigenous languages as AT languages is a continuation of a long prescriptive tradition in western epistemology and cultural history. In other words, the notion of indigenous languages is an heir to western cultural history. It is a product of anthropological discourse about the 'other', which has analytically tried to supercede the discourses of racial and biological inferiority as a way of framing and conceptualizing differences. Clearly, indigeneity is a much more welcome concept for explaining difference than that of racial and biological inferiority. However, the discourses of indigeneity remain western constructs which do not successfully capture how indigenous people experience themselves. More importantly the discourses of indigeneity emerge from a series of unsuccessful 'development' discourses, and thus offer only an apparent escape from the evolutionary and scientific paradigms of applied linguistics. Epistemologically, Mufwene (2002: 393) reviewing Nettle and Romaine demonstrates that the use of indigenous is exemplified in sentences such as 'the greatest biolinguistic diversity is found in areas inhabited by indigenous peoples' (Nettle and Romaine 2000: ix, see also page, 13, 21, and 22 for what Mufwene calls 'semantic oddities' in the use of indigenous). Although the usage is odd, it is politically revealing because it 'erases' from view indigenous populations in Western Europe, creating the impression that Western Europe is one of those places without indigenous populations! (Mufwene 2002: 393).

From indigenous to endogenous
Although the significations of the concept of endogenisation have been explored (Devisch 1999; Crossman 2002; Crossman and Devisch 2002), the concept itself was coined by French-speaking West African scholars (Ki-Zerbo 1990; Houtondji 1977, 1995; Ela 1994,1994a,1998) in an effort to avoid some of the historical 'baggage' and misunderstand-

ings that have accrued to the term 'indigenous' and its derivatives in both French and English. In French the term has acquired bad connotations because of the wide spread use of the homonym 'indigent'. With the exception of econometrics, the term endogenous has not been used in the social sciences. It has however been used to good effect in botany revealing the key differences between the two terms i.e. indigenous and endogenous. Here 'indigenous' primarily refers to a species that is native to a particular topography while 'endogenous' denotes a plant's capacity to *develop on the basis of its own resources*, or 'growing or originating from within' (*Concise Oxford Dictionary* 9th Ed.) The major difference here is that topographical definition tends to portray the subject as static, its only descriptor being a quasipermanent link to a geographic locality or area, whereas the second allows for a more organic and dynamic understanding in that it evokes autonomously oriented growth' (Crossman 2004: 24).

Reflecting on endogeneity
The construct of endogeneity clearly has the advantage that it enables us to capture, hybridity, difference and mobility more effectively than indigeneity. In a sub-discipline of applied linguistics such as language planning in which scholarship and political activism merge it is important to be aware that hybridity, difference and mobility are not necessarily always liberating. For example, for refugees in Africa —(and Africa currently has the largest number of refugees in the world) a 'certain immobility, a fixed place to call home is an urgent need. 'In contexts of state terror and mystification, clinging to the primacy of the concept of truth can be a powerful and necessary form of resistance. The master narratives of the Enlightenment do not seem particularly repressive here, and the concept of truth is not fluid or unstable on the contrary' (Hardt and Negri 2000: 155). Hybridity is ano-

ther postmodern construct which has come under criticism in applied linguistics for not being grounded in material reality. This is frustrating because at a historical juncture when Third World scholars are celebrating their identities they quickly realize that Postmodern discourses deny them of their particularity (Canagarajah personal communication). It is crucial to extend Canagarajah's argument by stressing that as a notion hybridity is a metaphor originating from 'taxonomic biology'. It is founded on the presupposition that the offspring—the hybrid—is a heterogeneous mixture of relevant constituent parts. On the one hand, it is founded on the assumptions of purity/essentialism, on the other, purity itself is an epistemological construction because every pure form is a hybrid by one criteria or other (Bauman and Briggs 2003: 5).

Hybridity is the result of the appropriation which takes place in all contexts of cultural encounters. However, even though hybridity takes place in moments of cultural encounters, its usage is unfortunately restricted to describe the cultural appropriation by colonized subjects leading Lynn Mario de Souza to make the pertinent observation: 'So when a former colonized appropriates he is called a hybrid as if the former colonizing cultures and persons are above hybridity (Lynn Mario de Souza personal communication). 'We therefore conclude that hybridity, like indigeniety are two of the terms used in applied linguistics to consolidate the description of the 'Other'.

Educational research into the teaching of 'indigenous' languages either as L1, or L2 is still at an early stage, yet in spite of limited research two trends are emerging in Africa. First, in countries like Zimbabwe language teaching materials and syllabuses are designed for second language speakers to teach L1 speakers. In Nigeria, the opposite is the case, L2 speakers of Hausa, Igbo, and Yoruba typically use materials designed for L1 users. Perhaps the issue worth addressing here is whether within African contexts L1 and L2 distinctions are applicable or pedagogically of much relevance.

Even if such distinctions were valid, the scarcity of material resources makes the production of materials tergeted specifically at either L1 or L2 users of African languages unlikely. In such situations what is important is the training of teachers in methods of adapting their materials and 'methodologies' to suit the appropriate sociolinguistic situation.

African applied linguists are in an enviable position which enable them to create opportunities to formulate alternative ways of thinking, if they seriously take issues about African languages. Most applied linguists working in Africa have a real footing in at least two or more cultures. It is reasonable to expect from them an interest in examing the different ways in which knowledge about language is constructed in the communities they are affiliated to. It has been suggested that a large percentage of English metalanguage is constructed around the 'conduit' metaphor. If English is organized around a 'conduit' metaphor African languages are not necessarily organized around a similar metaphor. For example, most of the Hausa (spoken in west Africa) is constructed around ontological metaphors which provide ways of viewing it as events, emotions, ideas, touch, and smell.

Reflecting on research on African multlingualism at the level of the individual African sociolinguistics seems to find itself in an anomalous situation. On the one hand, it has argued quite vociferously against the continued use of so-called ex-colonial languages in education particularly English and French, because such policies marginalize African 'indigenous' languages. On the other hand, African sociolinguistic research into individual African multilingualism seems to be organized around the very same languages which are an object of sustained African critique. Although a majority of African individual multilingualism includes languages other than English and French, most of the studies nevertheless comprise either English or French and an African language. Wollf (2000) cites a sample of 20 studies which all follow this pattern. In other words, there was no study in which bilingualism consisted only of a combination of exclusively African languages, or of a bilingualism in which Africans spoke either a pidgin or a Creole and an 'indigenous' language. Yet arguably even such types of bilingualism are much more widespread than those which include an African language and either French English, or Portuguese (Lucko, Peter andWolf 2003).

Popular and standard French in Africa
In this section we examine issues relating to French in the so-called Francophone countries. In our discussion we are excluding the literature which is gradually developing which focuses on French in former British colonies (cf. Omoniyi 2003 for his account of French in Nigeria). Following Djite (1998) we maintain a distinction between SF — also called 'French French' in local Ivorian idiom and Popular French (PF). PF is a local simplified non-elite variety of SF. For example, the variety of PF in the Ivory Coast-one of the Francophone countries is referred to as Français de Moussa. It has a simplified verb system, is characterized by a general absence of articles, and has phonetic and prosodic features strongly influenced by African languages (Djite 2000: 35).

Table 3. Some examples of Popular French

Popular French	Standard French
C'est verse à Abidjan (*This is a common thing in Abidjan*)	C'est chose courante à Abidjan
Il'veunt mouiller mon pain (*He wants to get me into trouble*)	Il veut me créer des ennuis

Tout pres n'est pas loin près n'est pas loin	Maintenant
(*Let's do it here and now*)	
(Djite 2000: 34)	

Not only does PF adapt SF to local African contexts. It is also slowly becoming a linguistic pastiche drawing selectively from other languages in the Ivorian landscape such as English, and Dyula (the local lingua Franca) as apparent in expressions such as *Boro d' enjaillment*. *Enjaillment* is a PF adaptation of English enjoyment (Djite 2000: 35).

Typically PF is used as the language of non-elites. It is also used extensively in publications with a mass circulation such as popular drama, cartoons, and newspapers targeted at the lowly educated, even in a national daily newspaper such as Ivoire-Dimanche.

PF is predominantly a combination of Standard French, and local African languages, and at times it also includes elements from Standard English. PF is thus increasingly becoming a lexical pastiche and going beyond being a simple adaptation of SF only. Sociolinguistically, PF is unlike NE because the latter is an elite code for educated speakers, while PF is a 'code' widely used by lowly educated persons.

Paradoxically, the policy of legislating the use of French only as the medium of instruction from kindergarten to university has resulted in the spread of locally adapted versions of French, PF. By contrast, the British policy of introducing 'indigenous' languages and subsequently shifting to English has limited the spread of English, and restricted the use of NE to the educated class.

Wycliffe International (WI) and the Summer Institute of Linguistics International (SILI)

This section reviews some of the work carried out by the WI formerly Wycliffe Bible Translators (WBT) cum SIL. There are four main reasons for carefully reviewing the work by WI/SILI. First, the WI/SILI is one of the most expansive organizations involved in applied linguistics in Africa. Secondly, it has taken part in applied linguistics for a relatively long period of time, in some cases for over half a century. Thirdly, it has contributed directly towards shaping the nature of applied linguistics in Africa by creating administrative structures within which applied linguistics in Africa is conducted. Fourthly, although the work of the WI/SILI has been carefully reviewed in Latin America and the Pacific Region we are not aware of any such review in Africa. We therefore see this contribution as preliminary review of the work by an important player in applied linguistics in Africa.

The WI/SILI has had a dual identity since the WBT & SIL were institutionalized separately in the US in 1942. This dual identity of the WI/SILI has served the organization well. It enables WI/SILI personnel to 'play missionaries at home and linguists abroad' (Havalkof and Aaby 1981: 10). WBT/SIL was founded by Cameron Townsend. In 1934 he established camp Wycliffe in an abandoned farmhouse near Sulphur Springs Aarkansas in the United States and held the first summer course in linguistics for two students (Havalkof and Aaby 1981: 10). WBT is the domestic arm of the SILI tasked with the responsibility for raising funds within the US, while the SILI does the missionizing and applied linguistics abroad as it brings the 'Word to the Bibleless tribes' and to preserve languages.

Reviewing the impact of 'applied linguistics' of the WI/SILI is necessary because it is one of the biggest organizations working on language in Africa. In some countries it has worked on African languages for over half a century. In Cameroon it has been active since 1969, in Benin since 1981. Its activities in other parts of Africa are much more recent. For example, it initiated its activities in the Chad in 1989.

WI/SILI has worked in language development which they construe as translation, literacy, and the development of orthographies and the recording of local folklores. The range of its work is apparent when one takes a look at the bibliography of the 2002/3 SILI Africa Area report where it catalogues the list of activities which the SILI was engaged in. Below is an extract of the Africa Area Report cited below:

'Other literacy activities, events and milestones'

A primer workshop was held to train individuals and language teams to design effective basic primers for local languages. Fourteen Central Africans and one Congolese participated alongside several SILI members. Eight languages were represented. Booklets containing 10 lessons each were designed for CAR's Bogoto, Gbanu, Gbeya, Kaba, Manza, and Ngbugu languages (Area Report: 2002/3: 22)

WI/SILI established administrative centers which have played a key role in applied linguistics in Africa. For example, setting up the Ghana Institute of Languages in 1962, and in 1974 a Translation Center in Abidjan (the Ivory Coast). In the Central African Republic it has worked in close cooperation with the *Institut de Linguistique Appliquée* (ILA). In Mali it works closely with the *Institut des Langues Abdoulaye* (ILAB), and in Chad with the Linguistics department at the University of N'Djamena.

A review of the WI/SILI raises important issues which are not unique to Africa but which do seem to acquire special poignancy in Africa. Since a majority of American applied linguists working through the SILI are missionaries. This raises issues about the nature of the relationship between applied linguistics and religion particularly that of Christianity. To what extent do SILI or the local Africans perceive applied linguistics as a secular exercise? (Snow 2001). The relationship between applied linguistics and religion has not been systematically examined in Africa. Smith's writing about Peru in Latin America resonates with our African experiences: 'native peoples under the influence of the WI/SILI, have become fundamentalist Christians as they become literate. They are offered no choice'. Because of the impact of the WI/SILI, literacy and bilingualism have become intertwined with Christianity, difficult to separate from applied linguistics as a secular project. Bilingualism and literacy are therefore seen as ways of projecting Christian ways of thinking.

Another issue tied to the SILI is their impact on 'indigenous' languages particularly their objective to translate the Bible into all of the world's languages. There are two key issues which the work of the WI/SILI on indigenous languages raises. Firstly, SILI members are astute and highly motivated at learning African languages. Their learning of the vernaculars has, perhaps rightly, been characterized as motivated by the desire not 'to learn the meaning of things, but to acquire the means of transmitting their own message.' The learning of African languages in such contexts results in a sophisticated use of vernaculars to articulate profoundly European modes of thought. The idea of translating the Bible into all of African languages however commendable it might be, is based on the assumption that there are a definite number of discrete languages in Africa—an issue which is quite controversial in African linguistics. Philosophically, the orientation towards African languages on which the translation of African languages into all of Africa's languages is based on a descriptive 'tradition which focuses on linguistic structure rather than linguistic praxis' (Blommaert 1999: 178).

Christian English teachers: The need for 'prayerful thoughts'

If the focus of the SILI was on 'indigenous languages' the main focus of the Christian English Teachers (CET) as might be expected is on English. English has been conceptualized in a number of different ways. In this section we focus on a way of conceptualizing English which does not yet have wide currency in applied linguistics, namely English as a missionary language (EML) (cf. Pennycook and Coutard-Marin 2003). It is intriguing that in spite of the magnitude of the EML project it has not been the focus of systematic study in applied linguistics—perhaps because it is a type of English which is more widely spread in non-western contexts than in Anglo-American communities. Nonwestern perspectives or the perspectives of the 'other' easily reveals the connection between English and religion, particularly Christianity in this case. Christian English Teachers (CETS) explicitly state that English is not only a western language but a Christian language as well.

The framing of English as a Christian language is particularly important because it brings English Language Teaching directly into potential 'conflict' with Islam. Because of the link between Christianity and English the African student who associates English with conversion to Christianity is not completely wrong, because it is indeed the type of connection which CETS and EML would like language learners/converts to make. In other words, the distinction between religious conversion and linguistic categories on which some, if not most, of western applied linguistic research is predicated may be difficult to sustain both theoretically and in practice in non-western contexts.

Concluding remarks
In the concluding section we propose some strategies which may be pursued to consolidate applied linguistics in Africa. Some of the problems confronting this project are typical of the African academy, while others may be peculiar to applied linguistics as a discipline. Hence some of the strategies we are proposing are generally applicable to the African

academy, while others may be much more specifically relevant to applied linguistics only.

One of the suggestions we proposed recently to the AILA Executive to enhance the development of Applied Linguistics in Africa was to encourage the formation of more national and regional associations in Africa. On the face of it such a recommendation seems reasonable because to date the Southern African Association of Applied Linguistics in Africa (SAALA) is the only AILA affiliated association in the entire African continent. However, efforts to set up 'newer' national or regional applied linguistics associations in the rest of Africa have to date not been successful, and are unfortunately unlikely to succeed in the foreseeable future. Most of African countries with the exception of Nigeria, and South Africa do not have a 'critical mass' of applied linguists to make the formation of national or regional associations of applied linguistics a viable alternative.

The formation of Applied Linguistics Associations are also likely to fail because they will be faced with an acute shortage of financial and material resources necessary for a successful administration of the Associations—a problem which would not be unique to Applied Linguistic Associations, but one which they would share with the African academy generally. For national and regional associations to function successfully they will have to depend to a large degree on the 'generosity' of the African nation/state. Unfortunately, African state authorities have not been forthcoming in their financial support of the academy 'Regarding African scholarship more as a threat than a constructive stake holder. They have thrown African scholarship to the winds. So off we go, riding into the sunset, looking for kinder masters and honorable or dishonorable patrons' (Prah 1998: 28).

A more modest but perhaps more feasible strategy standing a better chance of succeeding is the strengthening of already existing academic networks through the exchange of external examiners and shared doctoral supervision. Facilitating more intellectual exchanges between African applied linguists within Africa would enhance South to South cooperation which could be complemented by well structured North to South cooperation. Unfortunately, the success of North to South 'collaboration' has been varied and has been subjected to severe criticism by some Northern European scholars for enhancing rather than reducing African dependence on the North (Devisch 2004: 15; Gaillard, Krishna and Waast 1997; Yesufu 1973).

The African academy generally, and applied linguistics in Africa in particular has not escaped the criticism,—perhaps rightly so—, of being psychologically and academically unduly dependent upon Northern scholarship. Mazrui and others have argued that rather than being a source of development, the African university has played a key role as an agent of neo-dependency by perpetuating academic and cultural dependency upon the North. 'African universities have been the highest transmitters ofWestern culture in African societies' (Mazrui 1992: 105).

The key strategy which has been proposed to overcome African academic and cultural dependency on the North is what is referred to in African studies as the effort to domesticate the modern project, what has been felicitously described by Chakrabarty an Asian scholar (1992) as provincialising' the west. By this we mean efforts to bridge the gap between the contexts in which some of the applied linguistic ideas are generated and the contexts in which they are subsequently applied in Africa. The mediation is a common practice in applied linguistics but it becomes even more so in Africa because the theoretical ideas which underpin our work in Africa are not typically produced with Africa in mind. This is not to say that ideas generated elsewhere are not relevant to applied linguistics in Africa but that their relevance has to be demonstrated rather than assumed.

Applied linguistics in Africa has to constantly distinguish between that which is globally current and that which is locally relevant if it is to be a problem-oriented discipline. Unfortunately in some cases that which is locally relevant might be regarded as outdated in other regions in which applied linguistics is practiced. This creates pressures for applied linguists in Africa which scholars in other regions might not necessarily feel: a need to constantly refer to some work which is globally current, even if it is not immediately relevant, so as to protect the 'quality' of their work in the eyes of their 'western' colleagues. Although there is a growing interest in the development of local versions of applied Linguistics in Africa, the 'prestigious' journals in Applied Linguistics and indeed in most disciplines are published in English and 'from western locations' (Cangarajah 2002: 254). In such contexts, and irrespective of subject matter and methodology, African scholars are underprivileged in relation to western colleages especially when quality of scholarship is assessed in terms of frequency of publishing in internationally refereed journals (Crossman 2004).

There are more publications in internationally refereed journals by western scholars on Africa than by African scholars themselves! The 'domestication of modernity' does not, however, exclude the use of western sources but proposes that they cannot remain the centre of gravity of knowledge of Africa. They should be complemented by (Prah 1998: 27) drawing parallels between African applied linguistics and utilizing other non-western sources from other 'Third World' communities such as India, Latin America and indeed even immigrant communities in North America and Europe (Spivak 1987).

The 'domestication of modernity' also has an important methodological dimension. It requires that African applied linguistics be both 'local' and national before it can become fully international. It cannot proceed in the opposite direction i.e. from being international to the local. This should not be construed to mean that African applied linguistics should not be concerned with international readership. It simply means that applied linguistics in Africa can only arrive at internationalism through the local. If local applied linguistics has sufficient 'cognitives cold' it will soon register internationally (Prah 1998; Ki-Zerbo 1990; Ngugi wa Thiongo 1993).

Failure to achieve this has adverse effects not only on the type of African scholarship but on staff retention because African institutions ions in a single minded pursuit of excellence have trained researchers with little stamina to address issues about development which ostensibly they should be spearheading (Mamdani 1993: 15).

'Domestication of modernity' unless handled circumspectly has serious pitfalls. It seems to encourage a proliferation of academic material claiming to be presenting 'African perspectives' or African Voices'. Such approaches although clearly welcome create the impression that academic authority is determined by cultural affiliation. When expertise is determined solely or largely by cultural affiliation we run the danger of losing an invaluable opportunity to develop a reflexive relationship between applied linguistics and African constituencies—something which should be a hallmark of applied linguistics in Africa.

The development of applied linguistics in Africa has also been adversely affected by the scarcity of academic materials with an African focus. Serious efforts to address this lack of resources is gradually being redressed in that there is some progress in the development of academic materials with African perspectives. For example, the following is a list of some of the notable publications seeking explicitly to develop African perspectives:

– Spencer (1971a) *Colonial Language Policies and their legacies*

- Spencer (1971b) *The English Language in West Africa*
- Mazrui (1975) *The Political Sociology of the English language: an African experience*
- Adegbija E (1994) *Language attitudes in Sub-Saharan Africa.*
- Robinson (1986) *Language use in a rural development: an African perspective.*
- Mazrui and Mazrui (1998) *The Power of Babel. Language Governance in the African experience.*
- Webb and Kembo-Sure (1999) *African voices: an introduction to the languages and linguistics of Africa.*

Some of the publications not only focus on Africa but seek to compare African experiences with the experiences of other ethnic minorities particularly in North America. A recent example, of such scholarship is Makoni, et al. (2003) *Black Linguistics, a study of the social, political and linguistic problems of languages in Africa and the Americas.*

Most of these Africa based materials have the explicit objective of developing 'African-oriented training programs' because as Webb and Kembo-Sure aptly observe:

> most 'introductory textbooks in linguistics are (understandably, we suppose) shaped by North American or British/European perspectives... while students of linguistics in Africa need, in addition to the knowledge, insights, and skills, relevant to Africa'. (Webb and Kembo-Sure 1999: x)

Initiatives for the development of Africa based materials is progressing not only in Africa but outside Africa as well. For example, Kaplan and Baldauf have initiated a series of monographs as part of the journal of *Current Issues in Language Planning*. Although focusing on language planning these publications provide useful and up to date information on different aspects of the social, political, linguistic and educational aspects of African countries. Monographs on Botswana, South Africa (Kamwangamalu 2000), Malawi (Kayambazinthu 1998; Côte d'Ivoire (Djite, 2000), Tunisia have already been published and a number of monographs on other African countries may be prepared in the future. These monographs update and complement earlier publications reporting on research funded by the Ford Foundation on Language in Africa in the 60s and 70s, for example, John Spencer's article 'Colonial language Policies and their legacies' in the edited collection by Thomas Sebeok: *Current Trends Linguistics*. More recently, a special issue focusing on Applied Linguistics in Africa, *AILA Review* (16) was published (Makoni and Meinhof 2003).

The production of academic materials and syllabi on African applied linguistics should beconstrued as part of a broader strategy of Africanization or contextualization. In this article we construe Africanization as a strategy to 'domesticate modernity'. Because Africa is socially, and politically and geographically diverse we do not anticipate Africanization to take the 'same formand expression' across Africa (Crossman 2003: 23). This means that a version of applied linguistics might emerge in North Africa which would be different from that in southern Africa.

It is important to reflect on whether it is always and necessarily desirable or indeed feasible to develop African perspectives in applied linguistics and what epistemological objectives which we are seeking to achieve in doing so. Because so much of applied linguistics is based on English scholarship the relevance of assumptions about what constitutes 'language', being 'human' learning cannot be uncritically accepted. The following are some examples of English linguistic scholarship which have to be carefully scrutinized in applied linguistics in Africa:

1. the belief in distinct word classes
2. the belief in the possibility of using the same descriptive labels for all languages
3. the belief in the separability of language from so-called non-linguistic phenomena
4. the belief in the existence of separate languages.
(Mühlhausler 1996: 328)

The development of applied linguistics in Africa demands not only a critical evaluation of western versions of applied linguistics, but more importantly a careful and systematic reflexivity clearly articulated by Sole (1997: 215) when he writes:

> In my opinion black 'post-colonial' intellectuals cannot accept tenure as spokespeople for their community without the constant interrogation of their own positions demanded by their own poststructuralist predilections. What is most striking about the approaches of both white and black critics of this ilk, though, is a tendency to use post-structuralists techniques when scrutinizing the 'oppressor', but to slide back into positivism and liberal humanism when faced with the products of the 'oppressed'.

Expressed differently, the development of African applied linguistics is not likely to succeed as long as 'the historical construction of what constitutes 'language' remains unquestioned' (Heryanto 2007). It is also not likely that African applied linguistics will succeed unless it takes full cognizance of the implications arising from the fact that applied linguistics is a western cultural construct, which means that some of the assumptions it makes about language, 'humanity', 'learning' might need to be questioned.

'Domestication of modernity' has stronger chances of succeeding at this historical juncture because parallel reforms are taking place in Europe and America to an extent not possible until postmodernism, and the hiatus between so-called empirical and interpretive traditions in western scholarship (Wallerstein 2001) In spite of these changes, we should not underestimate the material and psychological pressures on scholars on Africa because of the sheer weight of the modernistic western paradigm.

Whatever is the ultimate outcome of efforts to develop African perspectives on applied linguistics, there is no shortage of interest in the discussion both within and outside the academy. A constituency demonstrating (surprisingly) special interest in the Africanization of the academy are radical non-formally educated African feminists. Their interests are different from those of the African intellectual. They are interested not so much in the impact of African scholarship on the west, but the impact of western scholarship on Africans.

It is appropriate to bring this article to a close by giving the final say to an African writer keenly interested in the impact of western scholarship on Africans, the poet Okot p'Bitek, from his *Song of Lawino*:

There is no single true son left
The entire village
Has fallen into the hands of war captives and slaves!
Perhaps one of our boys
Escaped with his life!
Perhaps he is hiding in the bush
Waiting for the sun to set
But will he come
Before the next morning?
Will he arrive in time?
Bile burns my inside!
I feel like vomiting
For all our young men

Were finished in the forest,
Their manhood was finished in the class-rooms,
Their testicles
were smashed
With large books!

References

Adegbija, E. (1994). *Language Attitudes in Sub-Saharan Africa.* Clevedon: Multilingual Matters.

Ajayi, J., L. Goma and G. Johnson. (1996). *The African Experience with Higher Education.* London: James Currey.

Anderson, B. (1983). *Imagined Communities: Reflections on the Origins and Spread of Nationalism.* London: Verso.

Arua, Arua. (2001). "Swazi English" In E. Ridge, S.Makoni and S.G. Ridge (eds), *Freedom and Discipline: Essays in Applied Linguistics from Southern Africa*, pp.129–138. New Delhi: Bahri.

Bakhtin, M. (1934/1981). *The Dialogic Imagination.* Edited by Michael Holquist. Austin, TX: University of Texas Press.

Bamgbose, A. (1976). *Mother Tongue Education: the West African Experience.* London: Hodder and Stoughton.

Bamgbose, A. (1991). *Language and the Nation: the Language Question in Sub-Saharan Africa.* Edinburgh: University Press.

Bates, R. H., V.Y.Mudimbe and J.F.O'Barr (eds) (1993). *Africa and the Disciplines: the Contributions of Research on Africa to the Social Sciences.* Chicago: University of Chicago Press.

Bauman, R. and C. Briggs. (2003). *Voices of Modernity: Language Ideologies and the Politics of Inequality.* Cambridge: Cambridge University Press.

Benson, P. (2001). *Ethnocentrism and the English*

Dictionary. London and New York: Routledge.
Bolton, K. (2004). "World Englishes" In A. Davies and C. Elder (eds), *The Handbook of Applied Linguistics*, pp 387–396. Malden: Basil Blackwell.
Blommaert, J. (1999). "Reconstructing the sociolinguistic image of Africa: Grassroots writing in Shaba Congo" *Text* 19 (2): 175–200.
Branford,W. (1987). *The South African Pocket Oxford Dictionary*. Cape Town: Oxford University Press.
Breckenbridge, C. and P. van de Veer (eds) (1993). *Orientalism and its Postcolonial Predicament: Perspectives from South Asia*. Philadelphia: University of Pennsylvania Press.
Brenzinger, M. (ed.) (1998). *Endangered Languages in Africa*. Cologne: Rudinger Koppe Verlag.
Breton, R. (2003). "Sub-Saharan Africa" In Jacques Maurais and Michael A. Morris *(eds.) Languages in a Globalizing World*. (pp. 203-216) Cambridge: Cambridge University Press.
Cameron, D. (1990). "Demythologizing sociolinguistics, why language does not reflect reality" In J. E. Joseph and T. J. Taylor (ed.), *Ideologies of Language*, pp. 79–93. London and New York: Routledge.
Canagarajah, A. S. (1999). "On EFL teachers, awareness and agency" *ELT journal* 53(3): 207–214.
Canagarajah, A. S. (2002). "Celebrating local knowledge on Language and Education" *Journal of Language, Identity, and Education* 1(4): 243–261.
Chakrabaty, D. (1992). "Postcoloniality and the artifice of history" *Representations* 37:1–26.
Chimhundu, H. (1992). "Early missionaries and the ethnolinguistic factor during the invention of tribalism in Zimbabwe" *Journal of African History* 33: 87–109.
Cohn, B. (1996). *Colonialism and its Forms of Knowledge:*

The British in India. Princeton: Princeton University Press.

Cook, S. E. (2002). "Urban language in a rural setting: the case of Phokeng, South Africa" In G. Gmelch and W.P. Zenner (ed.), *Urban Life: Readings in Anthropology of the City* 4th edition, pp. 106–113. Prospect Heights: Waveland Press.

Crossman, P. (1999). *Endogenisation and African Universities. Initiatives and Issues in the Quest for Plurality in the Human Sciences.* Belgian Administration for development Cooperation.

Crossman, P. (2002). *Teaching Endogenous Knowledge: Issues, Approaches. Teaching Aids.* DAE, Sovenga: University of the North. Pretoria: Cindek, University of Pretoria. Leuven: ARC, Kuleuven.

Crossman, P. (2003). "Endogenous knowledge: an anthropological perspective" In C. Odora-Hoppers (ed.), *Towards a Philosophy of Articulation: IKS and the Integration of Knowledge Systems*, pp. 30–45. Cape Town: New Africa Education Publisher.

Crossman, P. (2004). "Perceptions of Africanisation or endogenisation at African universities: issues and recommendations" In P. Zeleza and A. Olukoshi (eds), *African Universities in the Twentieth-First Century: Knowledge and Society.* Volume 11, pp. 24–42. Dakar: CODESRIA.

Crossman, P. and R. Devisch. (2002). "Universiteiten in Zuid-Saharisch Afrika in de 21 seeuw" *Mededelingen der Zittingen van de Koninklije Academie voor OvrzeeWetenschappen – Bulletin des séances de 'l Academie royale des sciences d'Outre-Mer* 45: 443–463.

Dako, K. (2001). "Ghanaianisms: towards a semantic and a formal classification" *English World Wide* 22(1): 23–53.

Dasgupta, P. (1993). *The Otherness of English: India's Auntie Tongue Syndrome*. New Delhi: Sage Publications.

de Schruyter and D. J. Prinsloo. (2000). "The compilation of electronic corpora with special reference to African languages" *Southern African Linguistics and Applied Language Studies* 18(2): 89–100.

deKlerk, V and D. Gough. (2002). "Black South African English" InMesthrie, R. (ed.), *Language in South Africa*, pp. 356–38. Cambridge: Cambridge University Press.

Devisch, R (1995). "Frenzy, violence, and ethical renewal in Kinshasa" *Public Culture* 7:593–629.

Devisch, R. (1999). "Universiteiten in Zuid Saharisch Afrika in de 21 ste eeuw" *Koninklijke Academie voor Overzeese Wetenschappen – Bulletin des séances de l' Académie royale des sciences d'Outre-Mer* 45:443–463.

Devisch, R. (2004) "Endogenous knowledge practices: cultures and sciences: some anthropological perspectives" In F. Nahavandi (ed.) *Repenser le development et la cooperation internationale* p 109–134. Paris, Karthala.

Djite, P. (1998). "Correcting Errors in Language Classification: Monolingual Nuclei andMultilingual Satellites" *Language Problems and Language Planning*. 12(1): 1–14.

Djite, P. (2000). "Language Planning in Cote d'Ivoire: Non scholea sed vitae discimus. We do not study for academia, but for real life" *Current Issues in Language Planning* 1(1): 13–46.

Ela, J-M. (1994). *Restituer l' histoire aux societes Africaines: prouvoir les sciences socials en Afrique Noire*. Paris: Harmattan.

Ela, J-M. (1994a). *Afrique: l'irruption des pauvres : société contre ingérence, pouvoir et argent.* Paris: l'Harmattan.

Ela, M.-M. (1997). "L'avenir de l'Afrique: enjeux théoriques, stratégiques et politiques", *Alternatives Sud*, vol. 4(1), p. 101-120.

Ela, J-M. (1998). *Innovations sociales et renaissance de l'Afrique noire.* Paris: Harmattan.

Fafunwa, B. A., I.Macauley, J. Ii and J. A. Sokoya. (1989). *Education in the Mother Tongue: the Primary Education Research Project (1970–1978).* Ibadan: University Press. Ltd.

Ferrant, J. and L. Alfonso. (1997). "Strategic planning at African universities: how relevant are Northern models?" *Higher Education Policy* 10:23–30.

Finlayson, R., K. Calteaux and C.Myers-Scotton (1998). "Orderly mixing and accommodation in South African code-switching" *Journal of Sociolinguistics* 2(3): 395–420.

Fortune, G. (1977). *Shona Grammatical Constructions. Part II.* PhD dissertation, University of Rhodesia.

Gaillard, J.,V.Krishna and R.Waast (eds) (1997). *Scientific Communities in the Developing World.* NewDelhi: Sage.

Geertz, C. (1983). *Local Knowledge: Further Essays in Interpretive Anthropology.* New York: Basic Books.

Gough, D. (1996). "The English of black South Africans" In V. De Klerk (ed.), *Focus on South Africa* (Varieties of English Around the World, volume 15), pp.53-77. Amsterdam: John Benjamins.

Goyvaerts, D. L. (1996). "Kibalele: form and function of a secret language in Bukavu (Zaire). *Journal of Pragmatics* 25: 123–143.

Grace, G. (2007). Collateral damage from Linguistics? *Ethnolinguistic Notes* Series 4, Number 21
http://www.ling.hawaii.edu/faculty/grace/elniv21.html

Graddol, D. (1996). "And is it English?" *English World*

Wide 17:153–74.

Hall, S. and Gay, P. (1995). *Questions of Cultural Identity*. Thousand Oaks: Sage Publications.

Hardt, M. and A. Negri. (2000). *Empire*. Cambridge, Massachusetts: Harvard University Press.

Havalkof, S. and P. Aaby (eds) (1981). *Is God an American? An Anthropological Perspective on the Missionary Work of the Summer Institute of Linguistics*. London: Survival International.

Heryanto, A. (2007). "Then there were languages: Bahasa Indonesia was one among many" In Makoni, S. and A. Pennycook (eds), *Disinventing and Reconstituting Languages,* pp.42-61. Clevedon: Multilingual Matters.

Hill, J. (2002). "Expert Rhetorics" in advocacy for endangered languages: who is listening, and what do they hear? *Journal of Linguistic Anthropology* 12 (2):120–133.

Hountondji P. (1977). *Sur la 'philosophie africaine': critique de 'l ethnophilosphie*. Paris: Maspero.

Hountondji, P. (ed.) (1994). *Les saviors endogens: pistes pour une recherché*. Paris: Karthala.

Hountondji, P. (1995). "Producing knowledge in Africa today" *African Studies Review*. 38(3):1–10.

Irvine, J. (1995). "The family romance of colonial linguistics: gender and family in 19th century representations of African languages. *Pragmatics: Quarterly publication of the International Pragmatics Association* 5:139–153.

Irvine, J. (2001). "Genres of conquest: from literature to science in colonial African linguistics" In K. Knoblauch and H. Kotthoff (eds), *Verbal Art Across Cultures: the Aesthetics and Proto-aesthetics of Communication*, pp. 63–89. Tübingen: Gunter Narr Verlag.

Jeater, D. (2002) "Speaking like a native" *Journal of African History* 43: 449–468.

Jeater, D. and C. Hove (unpublished). "And the God was made word: exploring the limitations of translation and power in the 1920's."

Joseph, J. (2004). 'Language and Politics'. In A. Davies and C. Elder (eds), *The Handbook of Applied Linguistics*, pp. 347–367. Malden: Blackwell.

Kachru, B.B. (1986). *The Alchemy of English: The Spread, Functions and Models of Non-native Englishes.* Oxford: Pergamon.

Kachru, B.B. (1992). "Teaching world Englishes" In Kachru, B.B. (ed.), *The Other tongue: English Across Cultures,* pp.353–366. Urbana: University of Illinois Press (2nd edition).

Kachru, B.B. (1995). "English as an Asian Language" In M.L. S. Bautista (ed.), *English is an Asian Language: the Philippine Context.*, pp. 1–25. Manila: The Macquarie Library.

Kamwangamalu, N. (1998). "Identities of English and codeswitching in post-apartheid South Africa" *Multilingua* 17(2/3): 277–296.

Kamwangamalu, N. (2000). "The language planning situation in South Africa" *Current Issues in Language Planning* 2(4): 361–445.

Kamwangamalu, N. and T. Chisanga. (1997). "Owning the other tongue: the English language in Southern Africa" *Journal of Multilingual and Multicultural Development* 18 (2): 89–99.

Kandiah, T. (1998). "Epiphanies of the deathless native users' manifold avatars: A postcolonial perspective on the native-speaker" In Singh, R. (ed.), *The Native Speaker: Multilingual Perspectives*, pp.79–110. New Delhi: Sage Publications.

Kaplan, R. (1980). "On the scope of linguistics, applied and non" In R.B. Kaplan (ed.), *On the Scope of Applied Linguistics*, pp 76–86. Rowley, MA: Newbury House.

Kashoki, M.E. and M. Mann. (1978). "A general sketch of the Bantu languages of Zambia" In S. Ohannessain and M.E. Kashoki (eds), *Languages in Zambia*, pp. 9–46. London: International Africa Institute.

Kayambazinthu, E. (1998). The language planning situation in Malawi. *Journal of Multilingual and Multicultural Development* 19 (5&6): 369–400.

King, K. (1986). "Concluding comments" In A. Davies (ed.), *Language in Education in Africa*. Centre for African Studies, University of Edinburgh.

Ki-Zerbo, J. (ed.) (1990). *Educate or Perish: Africa's Impasse and Prospects*. Dakar: Unesco-Unicef.

Kramsch, C. (1993). *Context and Culture in Language Teaching*. Oxford: Oxford University Press.

Kramsch, C. (ed.) (2002). *Language Acquisition and Language Socialization: Ecological Perspectives*. London: Continuum.

Kramsch, C. (2004). "Language, thought and culture" In Davies, A. and C. Elder (eds), *The Handbook of Applied Linguistics,* pp. 235–262. Malden: Basil Blackwell.

Krishnaswamy, N. and A. Burde. (1998). *The Politics of Indians' English: Linguistic Colonialism and the Expanding English Empire*. Delhi: Oxford University Press.

Laitin, D. (1992). *Language Repertoires and State Construction in Africa*. Cambridge: Cambridge University Press.

Lanham, L.W. and C. A. Macdonald. (1979). *The Standard in South African English and its Social History*. Heildelberg: Julius Groos.

Lanham, L.W. (1985). "The perception and evaluation of

varieties of South Africa English in South Africa society" In S. Greenbaum (ed.), *The English Language Today*. Oxford: Oxford University Press.

Letsholo, R. (2000). "English in Botswana: a sociolinguistic description" In. S.Makoni and N. Kamwangamalu (eds), *Language and Institutions in Africa*, pp.161–179. Cape Town: Centre for the Advanced Studies of African Societies.

Lucko, P., L. Peter and H-G.Wolf (eds) (2003). *Studies in African Varieties of English*. Frankfurt: Peter Lang.

Makoni, S. and U. Meinhof. (2003). "Introducing Applied Linguistics in Africa" *AILA Review* 16, pp. 1–12. Amsterdam: John Benjamins.

Makoni, S. and Pennycok (eds) (2007). *Disinventing and Reconstituting Languages*, Clevedon: Multilingual Matters.

Makoni, S., G. Smitherman, A. Spears, and A. Ball (eds) (2003). *Black Linguistics: the Social, Linguistic and Political Problems of Languages in Africa and the Americas*. London: Routledge.

Mamdani, M. (1993). "University crisis and reform: a reflection on the African experience" *Review of the African Political Economy*. 5(8):7–19.

Mamdani, M. (1996). *Citizen and Subject: Contemporary Africa and the Legacy of Late Colonialism*. Princeton: Princeton University Press.

Masolo, D. (1994). *African Philosophy in Search of Identity*. Bloomington: Indiana University.

Mazrui, A (1975). *The Political Sociology of the English Language: an African Perspective*. The Hague: Mouton.

Mazrui, A. (2000). "The mirror of Africanity: reflections on scholarship and identity" In T. Falola (ed.), *Tradition and Change in Africa, essays of J.F. Ade Ajayi*. Trenton, NJ: African World Press.

Mazrui, A. and A. Mazrui. (1998). *The Power of Babel: Language and Governance in the African Experience*. Chicago: University of Chicago Press.

McCormick, K. (1995). "Code-switching, code-mixing and convergence in Cape Town. In R. Mesthrie (ed.), *Language and Social History*, pp. 193–208. Cape Town: David Phillips.

Mesthrie, R. (1989). "The origins of Fanagalo" *Journal of Pidgin and Creole Languages* 4(2):211–40.

Mesthrie, R. (ed.) (1993). *Language and Social History*. Cape Town: David Phillips.

Moyo, T. and N. Kamwangamalu. (2003). "Some characteristic features of Englishes in Lesotho, Malawi and Swaziland, *Per Linguam* 19(1&2): 39-54.

Moyo, T. (2003). "The democratization of indigenous languages: the case of Malawi" *AILA Review* 16: 26–38.

Mudimbe, V. (1988). *The Invention of Africa: Gnosis, Philosophy, and the Order of Knowledge*. Bloomington: Indiana University Press.

Mufwene, S. (1998). "Jargons, pidgins, creoles and koines. What are they?" In Spears and D. Winford (eds), *The Structure and Status of Pidgins and Creoles*, pp. 35–70. Amsterdam: John Benjamins.

Mufwene, S. (2001). *The Ecology of Language Evolution*. Cambridge: Cambridge University Press.

Mufwene, S. (2002). "Colonisation, globalisation, and the future of languages in the twenty-first century" *MOST Journal of Multicultural Societies* 4(2): 165–197.

Mufwene, S. (2004). "Multilingualism in linguistic history: creolization and indigenization" In T. Bhatia and W. Ritchie (eds), *The Handbook of Bilingualism* Malden: Blackwell.

Mühlhäusler, P. (1996). *Linguistic Ecology: Language*

Change and Linguistic Imperialism in the Pacific Region. London: Routledge.

Mukama, R. (2002). "The use of Swahili as a (male) code in the security sector" In K. Glanz and O. Benge (eds), *Exploring Multilingual Community Literacies: Workshop at the Ugandan German Cultural Society*. pp. 65-72 Hamburg: Sonderforshungsbereich 538. (*Arbeiten zur Mehrsprachigkeit*, Band 41)

Myers-Scotton, C. (1993). *Social Motivations for Code-Switching*. Oxford: Oxford University Press.

Nettle, D and S. Romaine. (2000). *Vanishing Voices: the Extinction of the World's Languages*. Oxford: Oxford University Press.

Norton Peirce, B. (1989). "Toward a pedagogy of possibility in the teaching of English internationally: People's English in South Africa" *TESOL Quarterly* 23:401–420.

Norton Peirce, B. (1995). "Social Identity, investment, and language learning" *TESOL Quarterly* 23: 410–420.

Ngugi wa Thiong, O. (1993). *Moving the Centre: the Struggle for Cultural Freedom*. London: James Currey.

Nyombe, B.G.V. (1977). "Survival or extinction: the fate of the indigenous languages of the Southern Sudan" *International Journal of the Sociology of Language* 125: 90-130.

Omoniyi, T. (2003). "Language ideology and politics: a critical appraisal of French as second official language in Nigeria" *AILA Review* 16, pp. 13–26.

Owusu-Ansah, L. (1991). "Is it or is it not an interlanguage? A head on confrontation with non-native English" *Edinburgh Working Papers in Applied Linguistics* 2:119–116.

Penn, C. and T. Reagan. (1995). "On the other hand: implications of the study of South African sign language of the deaf in South Africa" *South African Journal of Education* 15:92–96.

Penn, C. and T. Reagan. (1991). "Toward a national policy for deaf education in South Africa" *South African Journal of Communication Disorders* 38:19–24.

Penn, C. and T. Reagan. (2001). "Linguistic social and cultural perspectives on Sign Language in South Africa" In E. Ridge, S. Makoni, and S.G. Ridge (eds), *Freedom and Discipline: Essays in Applied Linguistics from Southern Africa*, pp. 49–65. New Delhi: Bahri.

Pennycook, A. (2003). "Turning English inside out" *Indian Journal of Applied Linguistics* 28(2): 25–35.

Pennycook, A. and S. Coutand-Marin. (2003). "Teaching English as a missionary Language" *Discourse Studies in the Cultural Politics of Education* 17(3) 337–353.

Pettman, R. C. (1913). *Africanerisms. A Glossary of South African Words and Phrases and Their Names.* Green and Company. London: Longmans.

Phillipson, R. (1992). *Linguistic Imperialism.* Oxford: Oxford University Press.

Prah, K. (1994). *Beyond the Color Line: Pan-Africanist Disputations: Selected Sketches, Letters, Papers and Reviews.* Trenton, NJ and Asmara, Eritrea: Africa World Press.

Prah, K. (1998). "African scholars and Africanist scholarship" *CODESRIA.* 3:425–431.

Prinsloo D. and G-M. de Schryver. (2001). "Taking dictionaries for Bantu languages in the New Millenium, with special reference to Kiswahili, Sepedi and isiZulu" In J.S. Mdee and H.J.M. Mwansoko (eds), *Makala ya Kongamano la kimataifa*, pp. 188–215. Dar es Salaam: TUKI Chuo Kikuru cha.

Prinsloo, D. and G-M. de Schryver. (2002). "Designing a measurement instrument for the relative length of alphabetical stretches in dictionaires, with special reference to Afrikaans and English" In A. Braasch and C. Povlsen (eds), *Proceedings of the Tenth EURALEX International Congress*. EURALEX 2002, Copenhagen, Denmark, August 13–17, 4:583–494.

Reagan, T. (1995). "Neither easy to understand nor pleasing to see: the development of manual sign codes as language activity" *Language Problems and Language Planning* 19:133–150.

Reagan, T. (1996). "Bilingualism and the culture of the deaf" *South African medical journal.Suid-Afrikaaanse mediese tydskrif* 86: 797–799.

Reagan, T. (2001). "The promotion of linguistic diversity in multilingual settings: policy and reality in postapartheid South Africa" *Language Problems and Language Planning* 25:51–71.

Ridge, S. (2001). "Discourse constraints on language policy in South Africa" In E. Ridge, S. Makoni and S.G. Ridge (eds), *Freedom and Discipline: Essays in Applied Linguistics from Southern Africa*, pp. 15–30. New Delhi: Bahri.

Robinson, C. (1996). *Language Use in Rural Development: an African Perspective*. Berlin: Mouton de Gruyter.

Roy-Campbell, Z.M. (2003). "Promoting African languages as conveyors of knowledge in educational institutions" In S.Makoni, G. Smitherman, A. Spears and A. Ball (eds), *Black Linguistics: Language, Society, and Politics in Africa and the Americas*, pp. 83–103. London/New York: Routledge.

Roy-Campbell, Z.M. (2001). *Empowerment Through Language: the African Experience, Tanzania and Beyond*. Trenton, NJ: Africa World Press.

Rubagumya, C. (eds) (1998). *Teaching and Researching Language in African Classrooms*. Clevedon: Multilingual Matters.

Said, E. (1978). *Orientalism*. New York: Pantheon.

Sardar Z. (1999). "Development and the locations of Eurocentrcism" In R. Munck and D.O. Hearn (eds), *Critical Development Theory*, pp. 44–62. London: Zed.

Sardar Z. (1977). *Science, Technology and Development in the Muslim World*. London: Croom Helm.

Seidlhofer, B. (2003). *Controversies in Applied Linguistics*. Oxford: Oxford University Press.

Semali L. and J. Kincheloe (eds) (1999). *What is Indigenous Knowledge: Voices from the Academy?* New York: Garland Press.

Sebeok, T. (1971). *Current Trends in Linguistics*. The Hague: Mouton.

Sey, K. (1973). *Ghanaian English: an Exploratory Survey*. London: Macmillan.

Silva, P. (1998). *A Dictionary of South African English on Historical Principles*. Oxford: Oxford University Press.

Slabbert, S. and R. Finlayson. (2002). "Code-switching in South African townships" In R. Mesthrie (ed.), *Language in South Africa*, pp.216–235. Cambridge: Cambridge University Press.

Snow, D. (2001). *English Teaching as Christian Mission*. Scottdale, Penn: Herald Press.

Sole, K. (1997). "South Africa passes the posts" *Alternation* 4:116–151.

Spencer, J., (1971a). "Colonial language policies and their legacies" In Sebeok, T. A. (ed.), *Linguistics in Sub-Saharan Africa* (Current Trends in Linguistics, 7), pp. 537–547. Paris-La Haye, Mouton.

Spencer, J. (1971b). *The English Language in West Africa*.

London: Longman.
Spivak, G. (1987). *In Other Worlds: Essays in Cultural Politics.* London: Routledge.
Stroud, C. (2002). "Framing Bourdieu socioculturally: alternative forms of legitimacy in postcolonial Mozambique" *Multilingua* 21:247–273.
Summer Institute of Linguistics International Annual Reports 99–02. Dallas, TX: SIL International. Available at: www.sil.org, accessed July 2004.
Towa, M. (1979). *L'idée d'une philosophie négro-africaine.* Yaonde, Clé.
Wallerstein, I. (2001). *Unthinking Social Science: the Limits of 19th Century Paradigms.* Philadelphia: Temple University Press.
Walusimbi, L. (2002). "Multilingual Literacy in Uganda" In Glanz and Okot P. Benge (eds), *Exploring Multilingual Community literacies.* pp. 8-12. Hamburg: Sonderforschungsbereich 538. (Mehrsprachigkeit Band 41)
Webb, V. and Kembo-Sure (eds) (1999). *African Voices: an Introduction to the Languages and Linguistics of Africa.* Cape Town: Oxford University Press.
Wolff, H.E. (2000). *Pre-school Child Multilingualism and its Educational Implications in the African Context.* PRAESA Occasional Papers 4.
Wolf, H-G. (2003). "The contextualization of common core terms in West Africa: evidence from computer corpora" In P. Lucko, L. Peter, and H-G. Wolf (eds), *Studies in African Varieties of English*, pp 3–21. Frankfurt: Peter Lang.
Wolf, H-G. and H. Igboannusi. (2003). "Semantic Dislocation in Nigerian English. In P. Lucko, L. Peter and H-G. Wolf (eds), *Studies in African Varieties of English.*, pp. 69–83. Berlin: Peter Lang.
Yanga, T. (1980). *A Sociolinguistic Identification of*

Lingala. Ph.D.thesis, University of Texas, Austin.

Yanga, T. (1998). "Harmonisation, standardization and the emergence of state Languages: a case from Zaire" In K. Prah (ed.), *Between Distinction and Extinction: the Harmonization and Standardization of African Languages*, pp. 173–187. Johannesburgh, South Africa: Witwatersrand University Press.

Yesufu, T. (ed.) (1973). *Creating the African University: Emerging Issues in the 1970's*. Ibadan: Oxford University Press.

Young, D. (2001). "Why Applied Language Studies and not Applied Linguistics?: aspects of the evolution of Applied Language Studies in South Africa since the 1960's into the new millennium: a personal view" In E. Ridge, S.Makoni and S.G. Ridge (eds), *Freedom and Discipline: Essays in Applied Linguistics from Southern Africa*, pp. 149–170. New Delhi: Bahri.

III

The futility of being held captive by language policy issues in Applied Linguistics: An argument for implementation

Abstract
Some South African Applied Linguists and political language activists are currently operating in a policy mode. This paper argues that the continued interest in and preoccupation with language policy issues arises from an interplay of two factors:

(I) Overconfidence in the role that a new language policy could play in effecting change particularly in education
(2) Overconfidence in the beneficial impact of innovations.

The paper also argues that trust in the effectiveness of language policy is misplaced because many language problems cannot readily be solved by planning unless detailed attention is paid to what is necessary for policy to be implemented and evaluated. The paper concludes by proposing how such detailed implementation could be carried out.

Introduction
This paper is divided into three parts. The first evaluates the continued interest in language policy issues in South African Applied Linguistics. The second part tries to provide an explanation for the continued interest in language policy, arguing that language policy is one of the fads in Applied Linguistics.

The third part of the paper makes a case for attention to issues of implementation by arguing that what should be central in policy formulation is the degree of implementability of the policy and not its political popularity or marketability.

Determining the popularity of language policy issues in South African Applied Linguistics

"There are fashions in these matters as in everything else" (Lyons 1992: 262).

Our concerns in Applied Linguistics, as in other areas of education, may be influenced much more strongly by fashion than we are prepared to admit. The impact of fashion on Applied Linguistics is not necessarily always a bad thing. What is bad, however, is that fashion can become so tyrannical that as Davies (1977: 1, restated in Davies 1993: 14) points out we become "reluctant to submit our guess work to the *rigour* of hypothesis and experimentation" because we fear our ideas are more valid politically than intellectually.

It is certainly more fashionable to investigate some areas of Applied Linguistics than others. For example, studying language policy issues may be regarded as more fashionable than investigating the reading problems of second language users. The former has a higher political surrender value then the latter, even though our rational selves might make us feel that concentrating our investigatory efforts on reading problems may be a more economic way of using our intellectual resources than debating the possible language options future governments might follow. Decisions about language policies are essentially "political" (Whiteley 1974; Treffgarne 1986).

The recently announced eleven languages policy is an excellent example of how decisions about language policy are primarily political, settled in a "court of politics" in which input from Applied Linguists is at best minimal.

One way of assessing the popularity of some areas of academic enquiry is through investigating topics which are the subjects of 'talk' at local and international conferences. An analysis of such talk would form part of what I would call an *ethnography of conferencelogy*—a heavily underresearched area. The limited research into an ethnography of conferencelogy holds some interest because I suspect most academics would agree that, funds permitting, conferencing plays an integral role in our intellectual life. One advantage of conducting an ethnography of conferences is that all papers read at conferences do not necessarily find their way into print. Thus, conferencelogy may be a more reliable and valid index of the popularity of a topic than simply listing items in a bibliographical essay.

Conferences play a dual role in generating and sustaining interest in some academic areas. The selected topics are felt to be of sufficient interest among academics, or more cynically, the selected topics are ones which some academics feel should be of interest to the intellectual community.

As conferences can reflect prevailing intellectual interests and help set agendas, it is worth examining recent conferences that devoted time to language policy issues.

The fifth conference of the Association of South African Applied Linguistics (SAALA) was held at the University of Cape Town in 1986. One of the themes of the conference was language planning in education. Twelve papers were selected and finally appeared in a collection edited by D. Young (1987).

An analysis of the conference documents shows that 6 out of a total of 43 presentations focused on language planning at the 1989 Conference which was held at the University of Witwatersrand. But in the book which emanated from the conference, edited by K. Herbert (1992), the language planning and policy sections had become numerically dominant. One can only speculate on what transpired between the conference and the final publication of the book. But, whatever the case, it seems clear that language planning and policy are popular concerns, which are seen as worthy to be "embalmed" in print, perhaps even more so during the printing stage than during the conference itself.

In 1992, language planning again featured prominently at a conference held at the University of Cape Town organised under the auspices of SAALA. The physical presence of C. Kennedy and the satellite link with J.W. Tollefson in the U.S.A. highlighted the importance of language planning at that conference. Both Tollefson and Kennedy are well known in Applied Linguistic circles because of their work in language planning. Tollefson had recently published a book entitled *Planning Language, Planning Inequality*.

The 1993 conferences held at the Universities of Pretoria and the Witwatersrand had special sessions which addressed issues on language planning. Like the 1992 conference at the University of Cape Town, language policy issues were given a high profile by the physical presence of prominent scholars in language policy in the field - M. E. Kashoki and E.G. Bokamba. Even more recently in September 1993, a conference held at the University of Lesotho and organised by LICCA devoted a considerable amount of time to issues of language policy. Bamgbose who had recently published a book on language planning entitled *Language and the Nation: The Language Question in Subsaharan*

Africa was scheduled to attend the conference, again emphasizing the importance attached to language planning issues.

This view on the current popularity of debates about language policy in South African Applied Linguistics is not new. A similar argument was made earlier by Du Plessis (1987: 17) when he argued that "the language policy and planning issue is in some way one of the fads of South African Linguistics. Whether it is due to blow over soon still has to be seen, taking the seriousness of the South African situation into account." I regard my argument here as an extension of Du Plessis's.

Is it necessary for language planning to attract so much attention?

This part of the paper begins by situating interest in language planning in an international context. Interest in language planning is not a peculiar characteristic of South African Applied Linguistics; it is an area of interest which has been revived in British Applied Linguistics. For example, the title of the 1991 annual meeting of the British Association of Applied Linguistics (BAAL) was *Language and Nation*, suggesting that there might be more similarities between former Eastern Europe and Third World conditions in South Africa than most people are prepared to admit in public (see Phillipson and Skutnabb-Kamgas 1994). The revival of interest in issues in language planning at BAAL could be attributed to the political events in former Eastern Europe.

The overwhelmingly contemporary perspective on planning in South African Applied Linguistics is odd. Rarely are detailed historical accounts of pre-colonial language policies given because of an excessive concern with current issues. On those few occasions when language analysts demonstrate a sharp and welcome sense of historical consciousness, the history of language policies is traced back either as far as colonial times or the arrival of missionaries, whichever is the earlier (Phillipson 1992; Wardhaugh 1987). This view on language policy is unduly modernistic because it forcefully creates an impression by default that issues about language policy were non-existent prior to the arrival of Europeans in Africa. Such a view is inaccurate. It overlooks the extent to which issues about language policy are intricately interwoven into the history of precolonial African formations. Laitin (1992) cites interesting evidence of a contrast between the language policies of nomadic and agricultural based African formations in East Africa.

What is language planning?
There are a number of different ways in which language planning could be defined (see for example Cooper 1992; Laitin 1992). The most widely known and oft-quoted definition of language planning is, however, the one proposed by Jernudd and das Gupta (1971) who describe language planning thus: "The term language planning refers to an organised pursuit of solutions to language problems typically at national level". This should not be construed as implying that language planning does not occur at lower levels than the state and in other areas as well, for example corpus and acquisitional planning. The aspect about language planning which is most germane to my current argument is its futuristic nature. Language planning is futuristic because it involves having to make decisions between competing alternatives and provides the intellectual with unique opportunities to be both prophet and academician. The argument is expressed forcefully by Appel (1993: 231):

> When intellectuals use academic knowledge to develop policy they present themselves as prophets, censuring society and mentoring it towards the future. Here is another difference between academic theory and policy; academic theory is principally aimed at

explaining the past and the present; extrapolations into the future, as economics shows, are notoriously unreliable, while policy work looks into the future.

If one of the pre-conditions for the continued popularity of language planning in South Africa is an unstable political environment, my guess is that language planning is unlikely to continue being popular in South Africa for some time to come. To quote Du Plessis once more, "as a fad it is likely to blow over soon". However, the conditions which engender its popularity seem to have been reinforced rather than weakened with the passage of time.

In a stable world of complete equilibrium, where each day is very much like the one before it and the other one to come, and where all members of society are satisfied with their condition, language planning would be unlikely (Cooper 1989: 165).

If planning is futuristic, it is not surprising that it is not only language which is being planned. Planning is taking place in a number of diverse areas including, but not restricted to, housing, education, health etc. It can be argued that language planning belongs to a cluster of activities which are all primarily concerned with strategies of manipulation, either part of redress or as a subtle way of sustaining existing inequalities.

In some circles because of an exaggerated belief in the power of policy to bring about educational change, a shift in language policy is hailed as "a panacea to a particular educational problem", but as Treffergarne (1986: 143) warns while discussing his French West African experience, the policy may be 'scapegoated' if the educational policy goes sour or even worsens. Appel (1993: 233) cautions about South Africa in a rhetorical form: "Is it difficult to imagine that when policies fail to solve educational problems, terror and dogmatism will prevail?"

Language policies may be scapegoated or give rise to dogmatism not only because they have not been successfully implemented, but because of the way they have been conceptualised. One of the consequences of language planning belonging to a repertoire of other planning activities is the tendency to compare planning language with planning other areas of human experience, notably economics. Although the comparison is inevitable and may be illuminating, it overlooks the fact that language, unlike other resources such as economics, is symbolic, i.e. it is value loaded.

Restating the position in Jernudd (1971) that it is unnecessarily simplistic for language planners to believe that language is easily amenable to planning, Laitin (1991: 151) notes that. "language planners seem to be unaware of the fate of their brethren in urban and economic planning where lofty goals have long been subverted by grim reality". Cynically, I would add that language planning, although seemingly futuristic, is an attempt to redress current educational problems using anachronistic models drawn from disciplines such as economics.

In the third and final part of this paper, I argue that discussions about the various policy options are futile unless they address issues of implementation. Policies in themselves do not bring about change, but the way they are implemented could bring about change. "Detailed implementation is the essence of change" (Ferguson 1993). It is therefore unfortunate that language specialists have so far been more preoccupied with policy options than addressing issues on implementation.

What is implementation?
Because implementation is concerned with strategies of translating ideas into action, it is an exercise in continuous experimentation and not a delivery date. It is unnecessarily simp-

listic to regard implementation as consisting of putting pre-defined ideas into action. In some cases a more robust and flexible policy may be a by-product and not a precursor of exercises in implementation.

If the aim of any policy implementation is to achieve certain goals, it becomes necessary to build into the implementation exercise a mechanism for determining whether the policy has realised its intended goals.

In other words: a policy has to be evaluated.

There are two main problems for language education policy in restricting evaluation to the end of the implementation exercise.

First, given the uncertainty about the "gestation period" of language (Berretta 1992), it is difficult to know when the summative evaluation should begin. Secondly, when an evaluation is restricted to the end of a programme (assuming the end point can be identified), the evaluation loses its power to influence the policy currently in operation. The alternative is for the policy to be shadowed by its own evaluation. Concurrent evaluation has the merits of shadowing and consequently forming the development of the policy, hence potentially pre-empting problems which might arise during the implementation, but were not foreseen at the beginning of the programme, It is, however, naive to assume that all problems of implementation can be seen in advance (Ferguson 1993).

In the South African context a more radical proposal has to be made. The evaluation which has to take the form of some fact-finding "mission" may have to be carried out. The aim of the fact finding will be to assess the degree to which the situation is sensitive to innovation. Makoni (1993) elaborates on this type of evaluation.

Educationally, an evaluation preceding implementation provides information about what the situation was like before the language policy was implemented. For the applied linguist the type of evaluation provides opportunities for a gathering of baseline data which enables comparisons to be made with the situation developing after implementation.

> Interest in this aspect of language education is increasing and more systematic attempts at describing the status quo ante, rather than relying on or referring to anecdotal or assertive accounts of the situation, are being developed. (Anderson 1985: 287).

The aim of investigating the status quo ante is to try and test the degree of fit between the nature of the context and the ideas to be implemented. Investigations into the degree of fit between ideas and context can be followed by a pilot project. Unfortunately pilot projects, although desirable, do not guarantee successful dissemination. Because of the special circumstances of pilot projects, their implementation is "doomed to success" as Crossley (quoted in Ferguson 1993) puts it. The morale of the "tale" is that implementation is a complicated process and may have to be carried out on a piecemeal basis, and even this does not guarantee its success.

Implementation at state level
There are a number of institutions which can be involved in language policy implementation including governments. In my view Davies (1986: 6) argues correctly that governments rarely make or are able to make overall decisions. What often happens is that policies are partially implemented and indeed partially interpreted because in some cases governments may lack the necessary political, human and material resources to implement the policy. Implementation also requires contingency resources because resources required to carry out routine system-maintenance may have to be expanded or reorganised to cater for innovation. Any language

educational policy has to compete for resources with other areas of human experience which are also engaged in their own planning. Whether a government is to allocate the necessary resources to language education depends on the priorities which are set by that government.

I strongly feel that in situations of diminishing resources and keen competition from more deserving areas such as health, housing, etc., language education is not likely to be regarded as a top priority, irrespective of what we as applied linguists might like to believe. If language education is not regarded as a top priority, resources allocated to it may not be sufficient for a full implementation of the policy, and implementation of language educational policies normally requires considerable resources. For example, if all the eleven officially recognised South African languages were to function as media of instruction, materials would have to be provided in each of the individual languages. Provision of these materials is very expensive and requires a high degree of expertise. Hard economic realities mean that governments rely heavily on commercial publishers. Unfortunately, because "economies of scale" dictate that publishers invest in instructional materials for languages with relatively large number of speakers, it means that languages with relatively few speakers such as Pedi, Venda, etc. may not receive fair treatment.

The issue of resources for implementing media of instruction requires that the issue of what constitutes a language for instructional purpose must be addressed. It is relatively easy to determine what constitutes a language for instructional purposes in speech communities in which communities are. prepared to overlook dialectal diversity. Unfortunately, this is not always the case because "minor dialectal variations may be viewed locally as so significant that the exclusion of one variety from an educational role may constitute an affront to the particular group" (Ferguson 1988).

Conceptual clarity

Implementation of a policy requires some form of conceptual clarity on the part of those who are to implement the policy. Arguments about the desirability of each child receiving instruction in its mother tongue, which are questionable on cognitive grounds (see Makoni 1993), run into problems over what constitutes the mother tongue, first on linguistic grounds and secondly on sociolinguistic criteria.

Linguistically, the concept of mother tongue has been questioned on the basis of the way it avoids issues of dual first language shift, cases of language loss, language standardisation, etc. Can a child who speaks a non-standardised dialect at home, receiving instruction in a standardised dialect, be said to be benefiting from mother tongue instruction? Can you claim to be a mother tongue speaker of all the different dialects of your language? It is presumptuous for me to claim to be a mother tongue speaker of the various dialects of Shona if the variety of language which I speak may be classified as a dialect of Shona. How can I. be a mother tongue speaker of dialects which I do not know? Furthermore, since we all attend school in a "non-home code", can anyone be said to have attended school in his or her mother tongue? An even more powerful argument would question the entire basis of the notion of a mother tongue by arguing that, since there is a considerable amount of individual variation between speakers of the same mother tongue because "all grammars leak", the only language one can be a mother tongue speaker of is one's idiolect (Davies 1986).

Perhaps Paikeday (1985) is right in his dramatic claim that "the Native speaker is dead". To implement a policy in which students are said to learn through their mother tongue may be seen then as a serious attempt at implementing a fictitious and highly idealised construct.

In the South African context, sociolinguistically the implementation of mother tongue education, if I may call it that, is complicated less by the heterogeneity which is characteristic of urban centres such as Johannesburg, as is frequently claimed (see Nelissa and Van der Berg 1993), than by the presence of urban argots which may be the mother tongue of many urban-dwellers. These urban argots or "antilanguages", as Halliday (1992) would call them, are rarely counted. For example, in the recently announced eleven languages policy for South Africa the urban argots were not included when the number of African languages were given, perhaps because they are not standardised. Street (1992) puts it neatly when he writes, "A major problem with this strategy is the artificiality of the concept of mother tongue. Young children living in urban townships may find themselves living next door to Nguni speakers, across the road from Sesotho speakers, whilst their parents derive variously from Xhosa or other language groups. Their everyday 'first language', then, may be some sort of urban Creole ... such children when they enter school have a 'mother tongue' designated for them and have to spend three or four years learning through it even though it is as alien as English" (Street 1992: 34). The degree of African multilingualism is clearly being constrained by the Creolisation of urban African linguistic mixtures suggesting that African urban centers may not be as multilingual as is frequently claimed.

Even if the resources were available and the conceptual issues surrounding mother tongue proficiency had been resolved, the implementability of the policy would finally depend on the language teacher's proficiency in the language designated and her expertise to initiate and sustain change- as Davies (1986: 2) puts it:

> The key issues are how well trained the teachers are and in particular how good their proficiency is in the

medium of instruction and what goes on at the local level within a school, within a classroom everyday.

The use of each of the official languages as media of instruction in initial education also has practical implications in the organisation and deployment of teachers. It means the calculation of teachers has to be conducted on a local linguistic level and not on a global level. This means that discrepancies in the availability of staff between various regions cannot in the short-term be addressed by drafting teachers from one region to another. For example, an undersupply of teachers from Venda cannot be redressed by recruiting from another region.

The impression I have so far created is that language policy can be implemented if certain conditions which I will restate are met:

(1) A government is willing and able to provide the necessary resources.
(2) Some clarity is reached on basic terms such as mother tongue.
(3) Teachers with the .necessary commitment and expertise to explore the implications of the policy on a day-to-day basis are trained.

Closely related to the third condition would be the implementation of a policy as part of the so-called grassroots movement. A bottom-up process is an attractive way of initiating change, particularly in situations in which a government is perceived as illegitimate in the eyes of members of the community. Bottom-up strategies are preferred by Western agencies and leftwing academics (see Alexander 1992). Each strategy, however, has its own strength and weaknesses. The advantage of a top-down approach is that the state provides the necessary human and material resources which may be required to facilitate the implementation of the policy, hence increasing the chances of a long-term survival and institutionalisation of the change the policy seeks to bring about.

I am not as optimistic as Alexander (1992) and White (1992) that grassroots involvement necessarily makes decisions about implementation more democratic and that decentralisation necessarily improves the quality of decision making. The disadvantages of a bottom-up implementation strategy is that the policy is easily subverted in the name of rendering it more context-sensitive. Conversely, a top-down strategy is more difficult to subvert, but unfortunately the policy may not be rendered easily implementable because it is not adequately sensitive to the ideals and aspirations of the communities in which it has to take effect. In reality what is required is a mixture of top-down and bottom-down strategies with local initiatives exerting upward-pressures on national policies and national policies imposing downward pressure —so that local initiatives can reflect national policies.

But whether the strategies are going to be more top-down than bottom-up depends on the degree to which the institutions are coupled, with loosely coupled states likely to opt for more bottom-up than top-down implementation and more tightly coupled systems opting for more top-down and bottom-up strategies.

Subversion and resistance to language policy implementation

Resistance to a policy may not necessarily be a bad thing, just as supporting any innovation is not necessarily always a good thing. Most language policies invite opposition particularly if the policy is seen as detrimental to the interests of the group. Successful language policy implementation may need to take into account the views of the resisters. Attempts to take into account the views of resisters may lead to a reconceptualisation of a policy.

Klein (1967: 36) feels that resisters are best described as defenders. Implementation of language policy may be more successful if the positions of the defenders are taken into account. Resisters of a policy should be distinguished from saboteurs. Policy saboteurs are those who, on the one hand, are articulating arguments in support of a policy, but are undermining it by their activities; a situation which emerges as Laitin (1992) puts it when "public and private interests are in conflict, resulting in a private subversion of public good".

The classic example of saboteurs is that of Tanzanian bureaucrats, who.on the, one hand publicly supported Swahilisation, and on the other hand, set up private schools in which English remained the medium of instruction.

Conclusion

In this paper I have sought to provide some limited evidence concerning the popularity of language policy issues. I have argued that an attempt to explain the popularity of language policies may shed insight into the way language policy is conceptualised. The final part of the paper has sought to demonstrate that unless adequate attention is paid to issues of implementation, the preoccupation with policy issues in Applied Linguistics is unwarranted.

References

Alderson, J.C. (1992). "Guidelines for the evaluation of language education" In Beretta, A. and J.C. Alderson (eds), *Evaluating Second Language Education*. New York: Cambridge University Press.

Alexander, N. (1992). "Language policy from the grassroots" In K. Herbert (ed.), *Language in Society in Africa*. Johannesburg: University of the Witwatersrand Press.

Appel, S. (1993). "Chalk and cheese" *Reflections of Educational Policy*, Vol 14(2): 229-239.

Beretta, A and Alderson, JC (eds). 1992. *Evaluating Second Language Education*. New York: Cambridge University Press.

Cooper, L. (1992). *Language Planning and Social Change*. Cambridge: Cambridge University Press.

Davies, A. (1977). "Introduction" in Allen, J. P. B. and A. Davies (eds.) *Testing and Experimental Methods* (Edinburgh Course in Applied Linguistics. Volume 4) Oxford: Oxford University Press.

Davies, A. (1986). "Introduction" in A. Davies (ed.), *Language in Education in Africa: proceedings of a seminar held in the Centre of African Studies, University of Edinburgh, 29 and 30 November, 1985, 141-170*. Edinburgh: Center of African Studies, University of Edinburgh. (University of Edinburgh Working Papers)

Davies, A (ed.). (1993). *Speculation and Empiricism in Applied Linguistics*. University of Edinburgh Working Papers in Applied Linguistics, 4(14).

Du Plessis, LJ. (1987). "Language planning: promoter of ideologies" In D. Young (ed.). *The planning and medium in education*. Rondebosch: The Language and Education Unit and SAALA.

Ferguson, G. (1993). "Implementing innovation in language education" *University of Edinburgh Working Papers in Applied Linguistics*, 4: 27- 40.

Halliday, M.A.K. (1992). *Language a Social Semiotic*. London: Edward Arnold.

Herbert, K (ed.). (1992). *Language in Society in Africa*. Johannesburg: University of the Witwatersrand Press.

Jemudd, B. and J. das Gupta (1977). "Towards a theory of

language planning" In J. Rubin and B. Jemudd, *Can language be planned?* Hawaii: University of Hawaii. Press..

Kashoki, M.E. (1982). "Rural and urban multilingualism in Zambia: some trends" *International Journal of the Sociology of Language*, 34: 137-166.

Kennedy, C. (ed.). 1989. *Language Planning and English Language Teaching*. New York: Prentice Hall.

Laitin, D. (1992). *Language Repertoires and State Construction in Africa*. Cambridge: Cambridge University Press.

Lyons, J. (1992). *Language and Linguistics*. Cambridge: Cambridge University Press.

Makoni, S.B. (1993). "Mother tongue education: a literature review and proposed research design" *South African Journal of African Languages* 13(3): 89-94.

Paikeday, T.M. (1985). *The Native Speaker is Dead.* Toronto and New York: Paikeday Publishers.

Phillipson, R and T Skutnabb-Kangas (1994). *English, Panacea or Pandemic?* Sociolinguistic special issue of *English Only*.

Rubin, J. and B. Jemudd (ed.) (1977). *Can Language Be Planned?* Hawaii: University of Hawaii. Press.

Spencer, J.C. (ed.) (1971). *Language in West Africa.* London: Longman.

Tollefson, J.W. (1989). "The role of language planning in second language acquisition" In C. Kennedy (ed.), *Language Planning and English Language Teaching*. New York: Prentice Hall.

Treffgarne, C. (1986). "Language policy in francophone Africa: scapegoat or panacea?" In A. Davies (ed.), *Language in Education in Africa: proceedings of a seminar held in the Centre of African Studies, University of Edinburgh, 29 and 30 November, 1985*, pp.141-170. Edinburgh: Center of African Studies,

University of Edinburgh. (University or Edinburg Working Papers)

Whitely, W. (1974). "Language policies of independent African states" in J.A. Fishman (ed.), *Advances in Language Planning*. pp. 177-190. The Hague: Mouton.

Young, D (ed.) (1987). *The Planning and Medium in Education*. Rondebosch: The Language and Education Unit and SAALA.

Language and State

IV

Language and human rights discourses in Africa: Lessons from the African experience

Abstract
In this article, we investigate the question of who benefits from language minority research by analyzing the discourses of language rights and human rights jointly, because language rights are perforce part of human rights. We argue that some 'small' minority languages flourish and others fail unless speakers of these languages articulate their voices and needs. We also explore how human rights discourses relate to traditional practices. The interests of local communities and the involvement of linguists do not enhance the status of minority communities unless linguists traverse the gap between academic discourses on rights and vernacular discourses on similar topics. African linguists are themselves in a double bind: on the one hand, they seek to promote the interests of local communities and, on the other hand, they have to meet their professional obligations. They are not able to address the material needs of local communities because advocating language and human rights cannot resolve Africa's intractable problems. In addition, epistemologically, African scholarship is not sufficiently contextualized to be relevant to complex, labile, and polyvalent contexts. The defining epistemological trope contributing to the crises in African scholarship on rights and other sociolinguistic topics is 'theoretical extraversion': African linguists construe their professional work as a space to test Western

constructs rather than to develop endogenous knowledge practices, a situation that is difficult to overcome.

> But it is indeed an awful feeling among minorities to have lost one's traditions and embraced those of the dominant population only to find oneself not (totally) accepted by the same population, discovering oneself in a no-man's land, so to speak. Many of us who have operated professionally and often socially exclusively in the economic dominant language have indeed found themselves short changed socially and often professionally—alas, sometimes even in our homelands—when native speakers of European languages receive selective advantage. Unfortunately, the alternatives proposed by Linguists are not realistic ones for us, because the economic underpinnings necessary for the success of these alternatives have typically been omitted. (Mufwene 2010: 927)

Prolegomena
This paper builds on the work of Edwards (2006), who posed the question of who stands to benefit from language minority research. Drawing on examples from different parts of the world, Edwards concludes that if local communities in different regions of the world benefit from minority language research, the benefits are minimal and fleeting. In this article, we pose the same question. Drawing on examples primarily from southern Africa, we analyze Tonga, a language/ethnic group in northwestern Zimbabwe and southern Zambia. Further examples are drawn from southern, southeastern, and northern Africa, particularly the Dinka.

Introduction
In this article, we analyze both language rights (LR) and human rights (HR) discourse because LR is perforce a part of HR. The article has two main objectives. First, we critic-

ally examine the nature and suitability of notions about rights and language underpinning both HR and LR frameworks. Second, we attempt to capture how people experience HR and LR discourses in order to develop the perspectives of laypersons on these discourses. LR and HR discourses have been developed by professional communities, typically excluding those who might be directly impacted by changes in policy, including the elderly, the young, and women. Unfortunately, eliding and displacing the discourses of the less powerful prioritize etic perspectives (frequently articulated by institutions much more powerful than local communities).

In plurilingual societies, LR are complicated by a number of sociolinguistic factors, such as (a) 'fuzziness of language boundaries, (b) fluidity in language identity, (c) identity claims versus language communication, (d) complementarily of intra-group and inter-group communication' (Khubchandani 1997: 87), and (e) 'echo' systems. The term 'echo systems' refers to the mobility and density of the population, as well as inter-group and intra-group communication. It is conceivable that some of what may be regarded as languages may better be conceptualized as communication amalgams, 'stylistic inventories,' or linguistic ensembles that defy easy categorization. The rise of this 'new' urban multilingualism presents numerous challenges for LR because these linguistic ensembles are constantly in flux, are predominantly oral, exist in diversified linguistic environments, and are often street languages. As a result, they avoid the limitations inherent in the construct language (Cook 2009) and render it extremely difficult to attribute rights to them.

Urban sociolinguistics has shown that plurilingualism is the norm. Globalization processes and their impact on migration and free movement of people have led to diversified environments that pose serious challenges for LR. It follows then that the idea of language occupying a minority status is of questionable validity, even though this idea has been extensively used in the sociolinguistics of LR. Central to LR are notions of community, identity, and language, which are presented as natural phenomena, yet, in a critical perspective, languages are viewed as social constructs (Heller 2007). In addition, the notion of languages as separate, discrete entities and 'countable institutions' (Makoni and Pennycook 2007: 2) is not central to critical linguistics, making categorizations of individuals based on their 'ethnicity' or 'language' (Blackledge et al. 2008) difficult to sustain. The difficulty in categorization is accentuated by 'the messiness of actual usage' (Heller 2007: 13) and the difficulties of maintaining a 'correlational relationship' between language and ethnicity in multidimensional social spaces.

Analytical framework
Our analysis of LR is largely informed by critical perspectives on language, partially drawing upon integrational linguistics (Harris 2009). Integrational linguistics construes language as]presupposing communication.' Communication is treated as embedded in situations of people, time, and space, which rely heavily on contextual factors. The main thrust in such an approach is how laypeople integrate their social experiences. In integrational linguistics, language is not a code, 'a fixed plan' (Harris 2008; Hutton 2010) of 'hermetically sealed units' (Harris 2008; Hutton 2010; Makoni 1998: 244). From an integrational perspective, the process of naming languages is complicated because it assumes that languages are external entities and not socially constructed. Even if this idea is endorsed, it is still necessary to identify and enumerate the number of speakers of a language, which is difficult if the notion of what constitutes language evaporates and is further complicated by the fact that different individuals may not have identical understand-

ings of the 'same' language. From a layperson's perspective, even when speakers claim that they are using the 'same' language, the 'speakers' may not necessarily agree on the characteristics and boundaries of that language. For example, what a speaker may understand as 'chiShona' today may not necessarily be the same subsequently. This dynamism between speakers and language is overlooked unless a layperson's perspective is taken into account when counting speakers of a language (Harris 2008). The dynamic and constantly changing relationship between speakers and language renders the issue of LR much more complicated than might be initially assumed.

Centering our analysis on emic and lay perspectives, this article addresses the following questions related to LR and HR discourses:

1. How are HR discourses construed in local African contexts, and how do they relate to traditional cultural practices?
2. How are LR discursively framed?
3. How effective are LR as social instruments of change?
4. In what ways is the Linguistic Citizenship (LC) framework successful in overcoming the limitations of LR?
5. Who wins in minority language research?
(Edwards 2006: 4)

Results
How are HR discourses construed in local African contexts, and how do they relate to traditional practices?
From an Africanist layperson's perspective, tension between human dignities (i.e., *ubuntu* which means the essence of humanity) and HR is often encapsulated in the expression *umuntu ngumuntu ngabantu* (in Nguni languages): 'no man is an island.' They also feel that these discourses are arti-

culated in an idiom not readily accessible to them, hence the lack of extensive and robust knowledge of popular understandings of HR. In essence, HR discourses are complicated by the challenges of 'translating rights-talk' into vernaculars. In *chiNyanja* spoken across four countries (Malawi, Zambia, Mozambique, and so widely in Zimbabwe that it has influenced urban *chiShona*, a language spoken in Malawi; Makoni, Makoni, and Rosenberg 2010), HR are translated as *ufulu wachibadwidwe* or the freedom with which one is born (Englund 2001). This terminology demonstrates that even if HR are construed as universal, their interpretation can only be locally instantiated through the use of local vernaculars, hence the importance of language in HR and the need for a culturally embedded translation that is cognisant of the original intentions of HR discourses.

How are LR discursively framed?
LR are constructed differently. In macrocontexts, language is projected as a commodified form of cultural capital. It is an entity which can be owned by a people (*ethnos*) and exists independently of state recognition. From such a juridical perspective, rights discourses intended to be characterized by demands for equality, transparency, and explicitness which are treated from a lay perspective as vague, complementing, and contrary to cultural practices: a vagueness consistent with a communication perspective of integrationism.

Some language activists, as in the case of the *Tonga* in Zimbabwe, strongly object to being referred to as a 'minority language' group and prefer instead to be labeled as an 'indigenous' language (Makoni and Pennycook 2007). The objection to the term 'minority language' is also shared by the *Shangani* in southwestern Zimbabwe. However, unlike the *Tonga*, *Shangani* speakers prefer the expression 'community language.' Even though the use of this term is consistent with the interests of the *Shangani*, it does not fully resolve their problems as speakers of a minority language seeking to acquire official recognition. In fact, the term is not part of the Zimbabwean government's official discourses about languages. Thus, although useful as a marker of group identity, the term is self-discriminatory because the group is marginalizing itself through its own discourses, thereby highlighting the limitations of micro-ethnic nationalism as a corrective strategy for speakers of minority languages. Most importantly, these views reflect fundamental differences between etic and emic perspectives.

How effective are LR as instruments of change?
Put simply, LR are ineffective as instruments of social change unless embedded in the history and experiences of lay individuals as articulated in integrationism combined with other strategies, a fact Edwards (2006: 7) forcefully articulates when he comments on efforts by language activists to maintain language:

> One does not cure measles by covering up the spots; one cannot maintain a language by dealing with language alone. A logical approach to language maintenance, and the halting of decline and shift, is to unpick the social fabric that has evolved and then reweave it in a new pattern . . . this is theoretically possible (as with revolutionary upheavals) it is a considerable understatement to say this is a difficult and delicate undertaking.

In what ways is the Linguistic Citizenship (LC) framework successful in overcoming the limitations of LR?
Even though the idea of language in LC is consistent with integrational linguistics, it does not succeed in overcoming the limitations of LC because the idea of citizenship in LC is

based on a Western-centric, binary distinction between those who are citizens and those who are not citizens thus discriminating against the very people it is seeking to serve.

Who wins in minority language research?
Everyone loses, including communities and African scholars (who may be the same people) because African scholarship has to satisfy the delicate challenges of meeting both the requirements of advocacy and of some views of scholarship. Furthermore, contemporary African social problems are not easily amenable to intervention of LR and HR.

Human rights trajectories
The origins of HR can be traced back to the history of Western cultures (see Plato [BC 427-BC348], Aquinas [1225-1274], Groitius [1583-1645], Kant [1724-1804], and a series of legal documents and treaties such as the American Declaration of Independence; see Shi-xu 2012). Nevertheless, our entry point into the analysis of HR discourses is based on the 1948 formal *Universal Declaration of Human Rights* (UDHR). However, HR discourses in both Europe and Africa have a much longer historical trajectory preceding their formal inauguration in 1948. In Europe, LR have "a long history from the theory of natural rights through divine rights to the agreements made in social contract between autonomous and rationale moral agents" (Hellsten 2004: 62). African roots of HR are assumed to go as far back as precolonial Africa. Whether it is historically accurate to trace the HR origins in Africa to this point is insignificant. What is important is the significance of the mythical genesis of HR. The invented genesis is socially significant because activists use it to enhance the moral legitimacy of upholding rights and conversely accentuating the social consequences of HR violation.

HR are bifurcated into civil and political rights (negative rights), on the one hand, and economic and social/cultural rights (positive rights), on the other. Even though HR are bifurcated, they are conceptually interdependent. The objective of negative rights is to protect individual civil rights from state encroachment. Under the positive rights regimen, governments are compelled to provide social services such as health and education to their citizens. Positive rights also have implications for how individuals relate to each other, a phenomenon termed 'horizontal effects' (Hellsten 2004: 74). Arguably, 'rights of language' and 'right to language' (Mazrui 2007: 59) include freedom of expression and distinctions on the right to use whatever language variety one prefers because language practices in the private domain are not regulated by public institutions. The challenge in practice is that the distinction between the private and public domains is ambiguous.

Even though LR is a framework for the institutional support of minority languages, the framework does not necessarily promote the social and political interests of minority language speakers. Furthermore, not all members of minority groups are equally disadvantaged by being members of minority languages, as Mufwene (2010: 915) asks: "Is it really true that speakers of languages other than the major ones are all disadvantaged because they happen not to have sufficient proficiency in the widely used language?" If this were true, it would be difficult to account for the fact that members of the present economic and/political elite in Sub-Saharan Africa are not all native speakers of the majority languages they use professionally or of European languages that are emblematic of their power. In fact, the proficiency of large proportions of these elite groups leaves much to be desired, at least by 'native' speaker standards.

Promotion of minority languages may accentuate social divisions, particularly in a climate of ethnic-based political parties (Edwards 2003). Social class differences are further complicated by the possibility of 'polyphonic voices' (Hultton 2001: 5). Furthermore, minority communities do not orient to LR in the same way. In Zimbabwe, promotion of LR projects is complicated by the tension between minorities, as the case of the *Sotho* and *Shangani* demonstrates.

LR movements tend to focus on an essentialized, language-centered view that, although readily amenable to language promotion campaigns and bureaucratic strategies, is ill suited to plurilingualistic contexts characterized by non-standard and unplanned languages (Pattanayak 2000) and failure to account for the high degree of linguistic dexterity in multi-ethnic communication. Governments typically concede to the demands of minority language campaigns when they feel that the campaigns do not constitute a threat to their existence and are not directly associated with oppositional politics. Even when governments concede to demands by minority speakers, they may find that they have spent more time and energy on the promotion of minority languages than the benefits that accrue to speakers of minority languages themselves. In isolation, the promotion of minority LR is not an adequate strategy of redress, and its social effectiveness has been exaggerated (Edwards 2003). Therefore, if one of the objectives of the promotion of rights is to seek redress *and* alleviate poverty, it will be necessary to combine rights discourses with other social redress strategies.

Basically, a language-centered perspective tends to attribute rights to languages and not people, as Fardon and Furniss (1984) noted regarding Africa. While a language-centered universe might be useful for the purposes of linguistic analysis, it may paradoxically lead to discrimination against migrants and refugees. Such discrimination is unfortunate and clearly an important issue. For example, more than a third of the approximately nine million Zimbabweans live outside Zimbabwe, with a majority being in South Africa. Ascribing rights to language thus deprives them of any opportunity to have their rights recognized.

In this article, we trace the trajectories of HR in Africa, depict their current status, and analyze Africanists' responses to HR discourses which we construe to culturally differentiated and competitive (Shi-xu 2005). The article highlights the point that commitment to HR can be understood within a context of a number of powerful forces, including market economy and multiparty democracy. English is an important component of market economy, so while a promotion of indigenous languages is an important component of LR and, *ipso facto*, HR, the promotion of market economy creates a tension between HR and market economy. The latter is aided by 'big' languages such as English, while the primary focus of HR is minority languages. This creates tension between HR discourses and commercial contexts.

The argument developed in this article is that even though HR are framed as international legal discourses, they are local and site-specific. In other words, they can only be interpreted in given situations and are mediated by cultural and linguistic factors and by individual proclivities. Because HR and LR discourses are socially embedded, they may be interpreted in multiple ways by communities and ethnically based associations since their cultural frame of reference might not necessarily correspond with that of language advocates or with what is promoted by powerful actors such as non-governmental organizations (NGOs), churches, and governments. The relationship between language and ethnicity is extremely complicated and, at times, depends on the interaction between local and international discourses of identity. In their efforts to advocate the HR and LR of minorities, HR activists may flatten and calcify identities that were previously variable. For example, in international discourses, African and Arab are polar opposites. Yet in Darfur, the same individual can be defined as both African and Arab. While the global 'war on terror' and powerful international HR activism has traumatically transformed these identities, Darfurians have no difficulty with multiple identities. The case of Darfur demonstrates how well-intentioned international and LR activism can radically transform the identities of the very same people whose identities they seek to promote.

According to Edwards (2003: 352), "Discussions of language rights often focus on minority groups." The main objective is ostensibly to protect minority languages that are threatened with extinction (Batibo 2005; Nettle and Romaine 2000). In some rare cases, linguists acting in collaboration with local religious organizations are able to maintain the so-called threatened languages. For example, Batibo (2010) reports on a project funded by the Dutch Reformed Church, the Kuru Development Trust, which helped the Naro develop self-sustaining economic systems, rendering it possible for their languages to be maintained. In an economic climate in which resources are reduced, the possibility of securing assistance such as that allocated to the Naro may be rare. Ironically, some small languages may still be able to survive, if not flourish, not because they are supported by massive aid but because of the nature and quality of their intra-community relationships. It is because of the quality of the relationships that languages such as *Fengu* in South Western Zimbabwe and *Barwe* in Northern Zimbabwe are able to survive, even though their speakers are few.

This line of research is driven by a strong commitment to social activism aiming to 'preserve' languages. In this line of research, projections about the number of endangered languages are part of an intellectual trope of highly emotive discourses (Heller 2007). The language endangerment discourses are drawn from an ecological discourse that assumes that since the loss of species is expected to have adverse effects, the loss of language will have adverse effects as well. Yet it is not obvious how loss of languages will necessarily have negative effects since languages are cultural and not natural species. In essence, the loss of languages should not have the same adverse effects as the loss of species.

In addressing these issues, the article is organized as follows: in setting the scene for the entire article, we situate the conceptualization of HR in an African context and present some Africanists' responses to HR discourses. This is followed by a discussion of mother tongue education and LR. The third part is a discussion of the implications of LR on intra-language variation. Evidence is presented from a recently concluded court case in South Africa that suggests that providing individuals with a 'wrong' variety of their mother tongue constitutes an infringement of LR. The final section of the article deals with the rather elusive concept of LC, and the argument is advanced that even if LC has a framework that is better tuned to plurilingual contexts, its effectiveness is hampered by the fact that it is still caught up in an old fashioned paradigm of citizenship in jurisprudence.

Human rights discourses

HR discourses can be mobilized by both the powerful and powerless, the right and the left, the religious and the agnostic (Hardt and Negri 2000). Paradoxically, LR discourses may, at times, create conditions that justify their violation. LR can, on the one hand, be used to provide institutional support to minorities and, at the same time, provide a rationale for language-based discrimination. An excellent example of how HR discourses may be mobilized to serve conflicting objectives is apparent in colonial struggles wherein colonialism was justified using the discourses of HR. Similarly, African liberation movements used HR discourses to challenge colonial governments (Mazrui 2004). The degree to which HR discourses can be mobilized by the powerful to the detriment of the less powerful is articulated forcefully by Minogue (cited in Edwards 2003: 555):

> Your average demagogue now loves rights; they have become devices for taking control of subjects who can easily be persuaded that being given a right is always a benefit. In fact, it is a device for creating a static and servile society.

One of the primary objectives of HR is to enhance a pluralistic view of the world. Fortunately, it is not only the state that has assumed the responsibility of protecting languages but also transnational actors such as NGOs. At times, NGOs not only advocate for protection of minority languages but also directly shape the nature of the language policies of some countries.

However, powerful NGO discourses marginalize other discourses like a "dead end, a particular understanding of human dignity" (Englund 2000: 380). By promoting a specific view of conceptualizing HR, NGOs are sanctioning very specific ways of understanding HR that are culturally embedded but articulated under the guise of internationalism. The rigorous promotion of HR by transnational actors such as NGOs displaces local understandings of HR, rendering it difficult for such discourses to be readily embedded and appropriated in local African contexts. Ironically, the NGOs that are extremely powerful advocates of LR and HR are 'hegemonic.' Their advocacy rarely considers the communities' understanding and framework of what constitutes HR. In spite of the overwhelming influence of the NGOs, their impact on language policies and LR research, and the demand they make on governments to be accountable in terms of languages, the NGOs rarely feel obliged to be accountable to the constituencies they serve. Unfortunately, the roles that such NGOs play in shaping the intellectual contacts with which discussions about minority languages take place have not been subjected to critique. According to Englund (2000: 584):

> The preoccupation of these NGOs directly implicated in LR issues rarely critically analyze whether LR talk may limit our understanding of social, political and educational problems. NGOs have embraced the discourse of rights with such enthusiasm that it is becoming the only language persons in public office are able to speak.

Nonetheless, HR discourses that NGOs enthusiastically spread are predicated on the notion of 'stand alone' individuals. This is consistent with Udogu's (2004) observation that the fundamental discourse regarding HR rests on the character of a human being.

Two major philosophical reactions to HR exist in Africa: universalists and relativists (Bhebhe and Ranger 2001a; Makoni and Trudell 2009; Zeleza 2004). For universalists, every individual has inalienable rights arising from the simple fact of being human. While African scholars endorse the idea that each individual has inalienable rights, they are skeptical of the idea of an individual forming the basis of individual rights. The idea of a 'stand alone' or autonomous 'individual' underlying HR philosophies is incompatible with Africanists' understanding of the role and obligations of the individual in African communities (Hellsten 2004). From an African perspective, spirituality is an integral part of being human and, indeed, there may be no distinction between spirituality and human beings as social individuals (Cobbah 1987). In African communities, groups are made up of interdependent individuals, which renders a firm distinction between individual and group rights questionable. On the other hand, relativists are also critical of HR discourses. Relativists feel that the discourse of rights masks social and economic differences and serves the material interests of the state and the powerful. In addition, relativists are also critical of the universalistic notion of history. Relativists feel that the promotion of HR is more a reflection of African states' desire to be 'aid worthy' than a serious commitment to upholding HR. African countries may, on the one hand, develop a progressive HR regimen while, on the other hand, still retain a very conservative social agenda (Bhebhe and Ranger 2001b). In spite of the relativists' skepticism and critique, the majority of African countries have some form of HR provisions written into their constitutions.

A large number of institutions have been established in Africa, such as the Pan African Commission on Human and People's Rights. the Ethiopian HRCouncil, the Nigerian Legal Research and Resources Development Centre, Roseau African pour le development of Senegal, the HR Commission in South Africa, and the Commission for the Promotion and Protection of Religious and Linguistic Community Rights in South Africa, to name but a few. Given the differences in how HR are framed, it can be argued that advocacy of HR is an extremely powerful way to change what African societies understand about being human.

Even though we have outlined Africanists' responses to HR and LR in this section, it is conceivable that even within Africa there might be substantial differences between Francophone, Anglophone, and Lusophone countries. If HR are universal, it is logical to assume that there will be similarities across different regions of Africa in spite of their different colonial histories.

Human rights discourses: Focusing on language rights
LR are, to a large degree, based on language ecology (Nettle and Romaine 2000; Skutnabb-Kangas 2000). According to

LR, dominant groups may deprive less politically powerful groups of opportunities to exercise their LR. Politically weaker groups lose their languages when they shift to a dominant language, a process which, for most immigrants, occurs over three generations (May 1999; Mazrui 2007). In this regard, the identities of communities are radically changed by the loss of language. As a result of language loss, it is argued that communities are deprived of a unique source of knowledge tied to the individual language. In order to preempt such loss, the state acts as a powerful mechanism for the protection of minority languages. However, dilemmas are created for language activists if speakers of the languages are voluntarily shifting from one language to another because they may feel the language does not serve their social, cultural, and economic interests.

Language preservation is oriented toward the past because it is only those aspects of language and culture that are deemed to be part of the past or tradition that are supposed to merit preservation. Such preservation is complicated because the past is fluid and is always in a state of becoming. Preservation, therefore, radically changes language and culture by freezing what was inchoate. Even though "memories of the past may be best kept in libraries in and museums ... linguists must clearly articulate ways in which indigenous populations can live in both the past and the present without considering the past as an unnecessary burden" (Mufwene 2010: 914). Tradition is, to some extent, a site of tension between HR and ethno-nationalists, with the former arguing that it falls within HR and the latter arguing that it is not within the purview of HR. As Hellsten (2004: 79) points out:

> Part of the problem is that the protection of tradition does not always make a clear distinction between the normatively valuable, rather abstract elements of the

tradition, such as equality, solidarity and tolerance, and the undesirable, actual practices embraced by the same tradition.

According to Mazrui (2007), the focus of LR is to promote access to language and cultural practices. However, these rights are often articulated in a European idiom congruent with the conceptualization of the North's framing and understanding of rights (Hellsten 2004). The 'idiom' used to frame rights, irrespective of what these rights are, renders them inaccessible to lowly literate Africans who might benefit from such rights. Englund (2000: 584) corroborates the problem of accessibility of rights discourses when he comments thus: "Some NGO activists, urban-based graduates more attuned to donor fashions than to social situations in rural areas, were perplexed by the apparent irrelevance of their message on the ground..."

One of the most powerful and recurring dimensions of LR is the importance of the right to use one's mother tongue as a medium of instruction because it is an important way of protecting the interests of speakers of minority languages. However, many scholars point out that the term 'mother tongue' is elusive. What constitutes a mother tongue is not always defined by members of the respective communities but, rather, by powerful agencies such as the state. The state's view of a mother tongue may not necessarily be shared by individual members of the different communities. The implementation of LR is further complicated by the fact that individual members of communities may experience language differently, as Khubchandani (2002: 32) points out: "In a plural society a speaker's declaration about his/her mother tongue is purely individual, mostly based on the considerations of his/her social identification and group loyalty, rather than the speech he/she uses for primary communication." Khubchandani (1997: 93) also points out that the number of mother tongues for the Bahri group "increased between 1951 and 1961 by 14,611 percent." The fluctuation in the number of mother tongues varies because of the challenges of converting cultural phenomena into an object. The fluctuation reflects the high degree of subjectivity which "adopts an objective stance in reporting the results" (Khubchandani 1997: 71).

This "dissonance between the declared mother tongue and actual home usage" (Smolicz and Radzik 2004: 520) exists in certain areas of *Binga* in Zimbabwe wherein *Tonga* speakers have at times identified themselves as *Ndebele* speakers and at other times as *Shona* speakers. In view of the multiple and sometimes conflicting ways in which a mother tongue is understood in postcolonial contexts, when a state promotes mother tongue education or upholds the LR of minorities, its activities amount to a "systematization and simplification of linguistic reality, and [reflect] the elite's attempt—consonant with numerous parallel attempts through history—to dictate behavior (here, linguistic behavior) to the restless lower classes" (Toolan 2009: 17). The inconsistency with which states may define what they mean by 'mother tongues' complicates the implementation of LR.

It is, therefore, plausible to assume that the promotion of standardized minority languages is a simplification of a complex reality and a subtle imposition of a specific version of reality. When based on the promotion of standardized varieties of minority languages, LR get caught up in the same paradigm they seek to escape and, thus, deprive minorities of their 'voice.' Education is a powerful mechanism for reproduction of social class differences, for dominant classes and the elites, but access to education by the less privileged, even if the medium of instruction is through an identified 'mother tongue,' is not able to successfully challenge social hierarchies. In fact, it may have the opposite effect of reinforcing them.

Nonetheless, the dissonance evident in the delineation of what constitutes a mother tongue is also evident in the delineation of ethnic identities. In other situations, speakers of the same language might be affiliated with different ethnic groups, as in the case of the *Lomwe* who shifted from *chiLomwe* to *chiTumbuka* (Kayambazithu 1989). The *Lomwe* voluntarily shifted to *chiTumbuka* because they felt that the use of *chiLomwe* would reinforce the negative images some ethnicities had of the *Lomwe*. *Lomwe* speakers' decision to learn and use *chiTumbuka* was not a consequence of the 'hegemony' of the *Tumbuka*. In other words, it is possible for the weaker people to opt to voluntarily learn the language of the dominant group. However, this is inconsistent with a conventional notion of 'linguistic imperialism' (Phillipson 1992). The converse is also true: the conquering group might voluntarily learn the language of the ethnicity it has conquered. For example, the *Ngoni* in Malawi have learned *chiTumbuka* even though, historically, the *Ngoni* are known to have defeated the *Tumbuka*. In spite of the imagined linguistic and intellectual loss, the *Ngoni*'s choice to deliberately shift to *chiTumbuka* has to be respected because choice is part of HR. Similarly, British colonialists appropriated African languages as part of an overall conquering strategy.

In Malawi, for instance, as in many other African countries, there has been a proliferation of linguistically and ethnically-based associations that reflect a heightened sense of group consciousness (Englund 2000) that was also reinforced by the development of ethnic-based political parties. The dynamics within the associations varied considerably and changed constantly. For example, at times, the *Tumbuka* and *Tonga* identified themselves as a single group, but the *Tonga* eventually identified themselves as distinct from the

Tumbuka, demonstrating how individuals may move from one ethnic group to another and showing the "amorphous nature of individual and group identities" (Englund 2000: 18). Similarly, the *Fengu* (*Xhosa* in Zimbabwe) are on the periphery of Zimbabwean society but are a dominant ethno-political association in South Africa. If the case of the *Tumbuka* and the *Tonga* is one of ethnic splintering; then the case of the *Runyakitara* in Uganda is exactly the opposite, it is in fact a case of ethnic integration wherein the *Nyoro* (or *Runyoro*), *Chiga* (or *Rukiga*), *Nyankore* (or *Runyankore*) and *Toora* (*Rutooro*) merged in order to create a more powerful ethnic group that may perhaps counter the dominance of the Luganda (Bernstein 1996). In essence, the case of the *Tumbuka* and *Tonga* demonstrates that groups are not static entities, "and the periphery of yesterday may become the center tomorrow; minorities here may be majorities there" (Edwards 2003: 552).

Sociologically, some of the minorities may neither recognize nor accept the 'official' names used to refer to them, as the case of the *Nuer* and *Dinka* in the Sudan reflects. In response to his rhetorical question "Who are really the *Dinka* and *Nuer*?" Southall (1976: 463) responds, "The *Nuer* is not *Nuer* and the *Dinka* are not *Dinka*," preferring instead the terms '*Jieng*' or '*Naatg*,' which simply means 'we are people.' The complexities outlined above are apparent if we are cognizant of the communities' views of themselves (i.e., an emic perspective). Typically the main thrust of Liberalism is on individual rights and not group rights. Kymlicka (2001) argues that individual rights as construed within a liberal tradition are compatible with group rights.

Language rights and intra-language variation
A canonical view in LR is that speakers are discriminated against when their language is not accorded a particular status. LR debates are, therefore, based on the premise that

existing policies entail the selection of either language X or language Y. Hence, variation within each language is deemed insignificant. However, Wee (2005) takes the stance that speakers of Singapore English (Singlish) are potentially discriminated against because of a policy that powerfully promotes Standard English and discounts other language varieties such as Singlish. The controversy regarding which variety to use in formal domains also surfaces in parts of Africa, hence the relevance of intra-language variation to LR. For example, whether to use Standard or colloquial Arabic in the writing of Egyptian fiction has been debated for many decades. Colloquial Arabic is characterized as mixed and corrupt, while Standard Arabic is referred to by 'language defenders' (Suleiman 2004) as authentic and pure. The linguistic characterization has moral overtones as well because the moral integrity of the users is judged according to language use. Those who use mixed varieties are viewed as somewhat corrupt.

If intra-language variation is accepted as a potential source of discrimination, then speakers of non-standard varieties can claim to be discriminated against when a standard variety of their language is the only entity accorded LR. The issue of intralanguage variation is also potentially relevant to Africa, given the substantial differences between the varieties used in urban centers and standardized African languages. The emergence of urban varieties across Africa (Makoni et al. 2007) will produce languages without rights, if policy holders do not recognize the 'new' rights (Wee 2005).

The South African case *Nkosi v. Vermark* made the issue of intra-language variation a substantive legal and LR issue. Nkosi, the plaintiff, lodged a case against a Durban-based English multi-racial school in South Africa, arguing that her son had been unfairly discriminated against. Her son, an *isiZulu* first language speaker, had been taught in what she derogatorily termed 'kitchen Zulu' (in her view, this was the variety meant for second language learners), even though *isiZulu* was ostensibly his mother tongue. The issue before the court was, therefore, not that Nkosi's son was not being offered *isiZulu* but, rather, that he was being taught a wrong *variety* of *isiZulu*. Nkosi went on to claim that her son was discriminated against because Afrikaans, mother tongue speakers of English, were offered their respective languages at mother tongue level. Nkosi argued that being taught in what she called 'kitchen (*isi*)Zulu' adversely affected her son's development of proficiency in *isiZulu*. She further stated that the practice was dehumanizing and deprived her son of the proficiency necessary for him to be able to "appreciate the full values of novels, drama and poetry".

The *Nkosi v. Vermark* case provides a twist on issues regarding intra-language variation and possibilities of unfair discrimination. It is one of the few cases in which a mother tongue speaker argued that being taught in a different variety of the mother tongue constitutes a form of discrimination and, therefore, an infringement of LR. The arguments were founded on the assumption that a clear boundary between first and second languages and, by extension, *isiZulu* and other languages exists and can be determined. Linguistically, the distinctions between first and second language and between full and partial proficiency are difficult to ascertain and sustain in complex plurilingual communities.

Although the court ruled in favor of Nkosi, her arguments were not linguistically compelling. The assertion that one cannot reach full proficiency in his or her mother tongue when taught in a different variety of the same language is difficult to sustain. It assumes that full mother tongue proficiency can only be achieved through classroom teaching using the standard variety of the language. It also assumes that full appreciation of literary works in the mother tongue can be achieved through classroom instruction. From a critical perspective, most individuals will ultimately be able to mobilize the linguistic and semiotic resources needed to carry out repeated activities in their social lives. We are refraining from discussing individual proficiency in terms of mother tongue 'competence' because the idea of native speaker norms is implausible in situations in which such a great diversity of human experiences exists. Furthermore, Nkosi's argument that mother tongue speakers are 'dehumanized' when taught in an intra-language variety is epistemologically difficult to understand. The Nkosi v. Vermack case reflects an important ideological discussion in African sociolinguistics and the controversy about the appropriate varieties to be used as medium of instruction (Cook 2009; Meeuwis 1999). This important debate is often erased from view because of the focus on the status of African languages as opposed to that of European languages.

LR as instruments of social change

The contradiction is that LR and the promotion of minority languages can be more readily carried out when language is regarded as a monolithic, rigid structure and motivated by a monolingual perspective, a position that a critical linguistics paradigm rejects. This conceptualization of language is increasingly being categorized as a 'fiction' (Haugen 1966: 325), a myth that might have been useful in the past but is increasingly questioned (Harris 2010; Hutton 2002; Makoni and Pennycook 2007). The LR paradigm, therefore, seeks to introduce social justice by applying a 'fiction' and by stressing differences between ethnicities while social differences within ethnicities are overlooked. The ineffectiveness of LR is also evident in 'narrative inequality' (Englund 2004: 527). Surprisingly, this has not been an object of critique by mainstream sociolinguistics of LR.

However, a relatively large number of NGOs play an important role by providing legal assistance to African citizens. Unfortunately, differences in communicative resources between lawyers and clients create inequalities that are reflected in differences in communicative resources. The lawyers are able to astutely strip the narratives of the clients and situate them into a legal framework that they control. It is important to analyze how differences in communicative resources may deprive clients of the redress they seek. This reflects the importance of situating rights talk in a context of communicative resources rather than in macro-sociological contexts (May 2000).

Linguistic citizenship
Given some of the problems identified above that affect LR, Stroud and Heugh (2004) propose an alternative framework of linguistic citizenship. They argue that the notion of language underpinning LR is inconsistent with complex plurilingual societies and that the idea of languages as bounded, autonomous systems with uniform constructs (Heller 2007) is not feasible in such contexts. Ideas reinforced by grammars, dictionaries, etc., have to be replaced by the idea of languages as communicative and symbolic resources. The position taken by Stroud (2000) and Stroud and Heugh (2004) has two potential implications. If languages are construed as communicative resources that circulate, albeit unequally, in social networks and are shaped by individual experiences, it becomes difficult to retain the idea of LR. It means, practically, that each individual has variable linguistic resources that may indeed change according to the nature of the individual's experiences. This idea resonates with a critical perspective in which the emphasis is on individual and variable resources. Inasmuch as the LR issue operates with a restricted notion of language and the idea of HR, linguistic citizenship is also limited by its unsophisticated notion of citizenship. The relationship between language and citizenship is extremely complicated and varies from state to

state. The examples cited earlier in the paper on Zimbabwe/ Zambia *chiTonga* and *chiTumbuka*, Malawi, and indeed the *Nkosi v. Vermack* case, demonstrate the weakness of linking ethnicity to nation-state with language. There is no African country in which proficiency in language is a pre-condition for citizenship.

  The case of the *Nubians v. Kenya* is an excellent example of the complexity of citizenship issues in Africa. It also shows how such cases are handled in African legal systems, thus providing a legal view of linguistic citizenship. The *Nubians* alleged that they were being discriminated against because they were deprived of their Kenyan citizenship, which rendered them, de facto, stateless since they were now neither Sudanese nor Kenyans. The Nubians claimed that they should be eligible for Kenyan citizenship on the basis of birth more so than on descent. They challenged the criteria set by the Kenyan government that they produce their grandparents' identity documents to establish eligibility for Kenyan citizenship, viewing this requirement as a disingenuous strategy by the Kenyan government to deprive them of their rights since most of them are unable to produce such proof. Implicit in the arguments about the case of the *Nubians* is that they were being denied their citizenship on the basis of ethno-linguistic reasons. The *Nubians* were denied citizenship because of the colonial border that effectively created two nation-states out of people who had hitherto migrated freely across the African plains in search of pastures for their animals. Thus, in terms of citizenship, the *Nubians* on the Kenyan side are still seen as belonging to the group on the Sudanese side.

  In essence, to argue that language use in plurilingual Africa is determined by some 'citizenship' is to adhere to the Western-centric perspective of sociolinguistics: a state in which the 'nation' or citizenship determines language use and or vice-versa. The arbitrary nature in which nation-state borders or citizenship were created makes it difficult to apply the notion of LC to Africa's complex multilingual contexts. Citizenship is critically important for determining whether an individual can legitimately be expected to lay claim to rights. For example, if individuals are not regarded as citizens, their claim to LR is weakened. They are denationalized, disempowered, criminalized, and deprived of the necessary resources they should be able to access. Issues about citizenship are, therefore, critically important for understanding the factors that may facilitate or constrain opportunities for people to exercise their rights not only linguistically but socially and educationally as well.

Like LR and HR, LC is based on rights, obligations, and privileges that accrue to one who is a member of a nation-state. But the rights, obligations, and privileges are not natural or neutral but are structurally determined and enforced by regulations enacted by the elite. The idea of a nation-state of citizens bounded by geographical boundaries was created by colonialists in order to exercise control over the newly created citizens. As Appadurai (2001) has argued, borders and social structures may appear real but, when they are scrutinized, one finds they are tools for social control and describe phenomena that are in flux. In short, the metaphor of LC is unfortunate considering that the artificiality of Africa's history and arbitrary borders act as edifices separating families. It is worth recalling that citizenship was selectively denied to certain groups on the basis of skin color. For example, in Rhodesia/Zimbabwe, citizenship was accorded in the 1940s to 'civilized people,' a shorthand referral to Whites, thus excluding Africans. In South Africa, the same policy was used until recently. The limitations of LC and LR in African sociolinguistics reflect the ahistorical nature of a historiography of LR and HR in Africa (Shi-xu 2012).

Language and human rights as political communication
In this section, we argue that discourses of LR and HR should be explicitly treated as forms of dialogical, political communication between different institutions or groups. The dialogic communication we are classifying as LR and HR varies substantially in terms of how different communities received it because it does not speak to the political experiences of these communities in identical ways. Furthermore, identical rights discourses may be received in different and, at times, conflicting ways by different generations of the same communities. Even though a mobilization of LR and HR may have been one of the consequences of political liberalization, or multipartyism, in the early phases of countries like Zimbabwe (Englund 2001), discourses of HR are construed more recently in the same countries from a governmental perspective as a form of Western-inspired elite political oppositional discourse. The rights discourses are also received differently. For example, the subaltern may respond to their violations differently than the elites. Rather than articulate their political opposition in terms of a violation of HR, subalterns articulate it as a challenge to their group dignity and individual selfhood. It is, therefore, critically important to be sensitive to establishing who is speaking and who are the hearers or to find the discourses irrelevant to their material conditions (Shi-xu 2012). Although liberal approaches typically emphasize individual rather than group rights, Kymlicka (2001) puts forward the thesis that the construct of an individual, which is central to liberal politics, is compatible with the idea of group rights.

Conclusions
This article has presented arguments that LR are an important part of HR. It has also been argued that HR and, indeed, LR discourses must be interpreted within a specific context, hence the importance of depending primarily on lay, emic

views about LR rather than on universalistic legal frameworks (Paulston 1997). Because interpretations of HR and LR are mediated by diverse cultural and linguistic factors, these interpretations are likely to vary among different individuals. The argument made in this article is that even though the interpretation of HR and LR is context determined, the local interpretation may paradoxically enhance the universalistic knowledge of HR and LR. Furthermore, claims made about LR appear to be 'pie in the sky,' yet accessing such state resources as water and sanitation may depend on language. If a relatively large number of minority speakers do not feel empowered by such promotion, then it is logical to inquire why such a research strand is continued when local communities do not necessarily subscribe to and are not much interested in it. Even if minority research approaches in Africa are designed in collaboration with the local communities themselves, the projects' success is not inevitable because of the heterogeneity and potential conflict within communities. However, collaborating with local communities may enhance their success in the long run. Reporting the results to the communities might contribute to the development of a healthy relationship between communities and researchers. However, even if the research is carried out jointly with local communities and linguists, the problem does not disappear. On the one hand, African linguists and African elites feel under a burden to respond to the pressures of Western scholarship, and on the other hand, the issues, concerns, and beliefs of local communities may run counter to their training.

Reporting their results to the communities themselves in order to resolve this double bind may not successfully address the unequal power relations between the researchers and local communities. In fact, interventionist minority research may accentuate power differences between the communities and researchers. Even if these power differences are reduced, the material benefits that accrue to the communities may not be distributed equally, hence the relevance of our closing question: who is winning?

This article has also highlighted the importance of the role of NGOs in the sociolinguistics of Africa. The role of NGOs compels us to rethink the centrality of a state-centric perspective of sociolinguistics that has dominated sociolinguistics of language planning in Africa while, at the same time, remain cognizant of the fact that an extremely thin line exists between advocating minority languages and appropriating them. We have built on arguments from an integrationist perspective by proposing a way of reframing notions about LR, individual/group rights, ethnicity, and identity, demonstrating sensitivity to the fluidity of African sociolinguistic contexts; something toward which linguistic citizenship gestures but does not capture.

The arguments made in this paper have significant implications for non-Western perspectives on scholarship that go beyond LR and HR and are relevant to other areas of sociolinguistics in Africa. Notably, one of the major critiques leveled against African scholarship and readily apparent in this paper is the tendency for African scholarship to act as a Western social laboratory: to serve as a space to test the validity and efficacy of theories formulated in Western contexts, which is more akin to what Hountondji (2002) calls 'theoretical extraversion.' Theoretical extraversion manifests itself as responses to Western scholarship. Although Hountondji's (2002) philosophical stance is pessimistic, optimism is present in that the subaltern and the elites, over the years, have always resisted, subverted, and reconfigured Western epistemologies.

Research into LR and HR has to be adapted and sufficiently contextualized to be relevant to complex, labile, and polyvalent African contexts. *Contextualization* refers to triple factors: the cultural contexts in which the analytical frameworks emerge, the contexts in which the knowledge is disseminated, and the multiple and pluralistic contexts in which the knowledge is interpreted. Non-Western academia in which LR and HR are construed is important because knowledge may be interpreted and read in local cultures and embedded in discourses radically differently than it is in Western academia. Therefore, it is important to understand the degree to which scholarship is readily portable, a point worth stressing in a global world characterized by intense movement of people, ideas, and technology.

Research into Rights has to be sensitive to the dynamics of African pastels but should not be overwhelmed by it.

Current formulations of LR and LC reviewed in this paper do not meet these criteria of sensitivity and capacity to reinvent the past. Because of the inseparability of knowledge and power, the call for an Africa 'able to stand up on its own' is not only economic and political but also epistemological. A powerful nexus also exists between economic dependence and theoretical extraversion. One way out of the impasse created by 'theoretical extraversion' is to develop and take full advantage of endogenous knowledge practices, vernacular discourses, and dialogues with scholarship from other regions of the world. Endogenous knowledge practices render it possible to exploit local forms of knowledge, while vernacular practices make it possible to analyze the various ways in which the knowledge is expressed. A combination of endogenous knowledge practices and vernacular discourses renders it conceivable to analyze the many and sometimes contradictory reactions of African communities' orientation to issues about LR and HR. It is instructive to bear in mind that vernacular discourses in terms of LR and HR (if there are any) are increasingly gliding away from academic and professional understandings and ways of talking about LR and HR. This disjuncture or discursive divorce (Appadurai 2001) is a challenge from which scholars in non-Western

African environments cannot escape. African scholarship on LR and HR discourses is, therefore, always intervening into a previous era, even when it is claimed to be contemporary.

The challenge is that academics and modes of collecting, analyzing, and reporting data may not merge or coalesce with what local communities may regard as ways of collecting information. Some of the intractable problems with which Africa is confronted cannot be fully addressed by an appeal to LR and HR, however desirable issues about LR and HR might be. Research into LR and HR may have some limited significance and relevance if it is not carried out either in conjunction with more powerful social projects and/or is submerged in them.

The involvement of research in LR and HR preempts possibilities of a parachute, 'guest-like' research (Edwards 2006) or 'academic tourist'. The argument is not that academic research should not be carried out in African communities but, rather, that it is likely to be more socially and academically valid if it enhances the ways in which communities understand their own needs and life demands. The emphasis in liberated sociolinguistics in Africa will, therefore, be on improving the needs of Africans and not industrial production, a tall order but one worth focusing on.

Since we are scholars and have been engaged in language promotional activities, it is appropriate to bring this paper to an end by citing a sobering observation of our role in such enterprises: "Without scholars [the revival] cannot succeed; with scholars as leaders it is bound to fail" (Moran 1900: 268, as cited in Edwards 2006: 8).

References
Appadurai, Arjun (2001). "The globalization of archaeology and heritage: A discussion with Arjun Appadurai" *Journal of Social Archaeology* 1, no. 1: 35-49.

Batibo, Herman (2005). *Language Decline and Death in Africa: Causes, Consequences and Challenges*. Clevedon: Multilingual Matters.

Bernstein, J. (1996). "Runyakitara: Uganda's 'new' language" *Journal of Multilingual and Multicultural Development* 19, no. 2: 93-107.

Bhebhe, Ngwabi, and Terence Ranger (2001a). "General introduction" In Ngwabi Bhebhe and Terence Ranger (eds.), *The Historical Dimensions of Democracy and Human Rights in Zimbabwe*, vii-xx. Harare: University of Zimbabwe Press.

Bhebhe, Ngwabi, and Terence Ranger (001b). *The Historical Dimensions of Democracy and Human Rights in Zimbabwe, Vol. 2: Pre-Colonial and Colonial Legacies*. Harare: University of Zimbabwe Publications.

Blackledge, A., Creese, A., Barac, T., Bhatt, A., Hamid, S., Wei, L., Lytra, V., Martin, P., Wu, C., and Yagcioglu, D. (2008). "Contesting 'language' as 'heritage': Negotiation of identities in late modernity" *Applied Linguistics* 29, no. 4: 533-554.

Cobbah, J. (1987). "African values and the human rights debate: An African perspective" *Human Rights Quarterly* 9, no. 3: 309-31.

Cook, S. (2009). "Street Setswana vs. school Setswana" In Jo Anne Kleifgen and George C. Bond (eds.), *Languages in Africa and the Diaspora:Educating for Language Awareness*, pp.96-119. Clevedon: Multilingual Matters.

Edwards, J. (2003). "Contextualizing language rights" *Journal of Human Rights* 2, no. 4: 551-571.

Edwards, J. (2006). "Players and power in minority-group settings" *Journal of Multilingual and Multicultural Development* 27, no. 1: 4-20.

Englund, H. (2000). "The dead hand of human rights: Contrasting Christianities in posttransition Malawi" *The Journal of Modern African Studies* 38, no. 4: 579-603.

Englund, H. (2001). "Chinyanja and the language of rights" *Nordic Journal of African Studies* 10, no. 3: 299-319.

Englund, H. (2004). "Rights talk in new democracies" *Discourse and Society* 15, no. 5: 527-551.

Fardon, Richard, and Graham Furniss (1984). *African Languages, Development And The State.* London: Routledge.

Hardt, Michael, and Antonio Negri (2000). *Empire.* Cambridge: Harvard University Press.

Harris, R. (2008). *Mindboggling: Preliminaries to a Science of Mind.* Luton: Pantaneto Press.

Harris, R. (2009). *After Epistemology.* Gamlingay: Bright Pen.

Haugen, Einar Ingvald (1966). *Language, Conflict and Language Planning.* Cambridge: Harvard University Press.

Heller, Monica (2007). *Bilingualism: A Social Approach.* London: Palgrave/MacMillan.

Hellsten, S.K. (2004). "Human rights in Africa: From communitarian values to utilitarian practice" *Human Rights Review* 5, no. 2: 61-85.

Hountondji, P. (2002). *African Philosophy: Myth and Reality.* Ohio: Ohio University Press.

Hutton, C. (2001). "Cultural and conceptual relativism, universalism and the politics of linguistics" In R. Dirven, B. Hawkins, and E. Sandikcioglu (eds.), *Language and ideology I: Cognitive theoretical approaches,* , 277-296. Amsterdam: John Benjamins.

Hutton, Chris (2002). "The language myth and the race

myth: Twin evils of modern identity politics?" In Roy Harris (ed.), *The Language Myth In Western Culture*, 118-138. London: Curzon.

Hutton, Christopher (2010). "Who owns language? Mother tongues as intellectual property and the conceptualization of human linguistic diversity" *Language Sciences* 32: 638-647.

Kayambazithu, Edrinnie (1989). "Patterns of language use in Malawi, a sociolinguistic investigation" *Journal of Contemporary African Studies* 8, no. 9: 109-131.

Khubchandani, Lachman (1997). *Revisualizing Boundaries: A Plurilingual Ethos.* Thousand Oaks: Sage.

Khubchandani, Lachman (2002). "Demographic imperatives in language planning" Plenary session of the Linguapax World Congress on Language Policies, April 16-20, in Barcelona, Spain. Accessed 5 July 2020 at: http://www.linguapax.org/wp-content/uploads/2015/07/CMPL2002_Plenari_LKhubchandani.pdf

Kymlicka, W. (2001). *Politics in the Vernacular: Nationalism, Multiculturalism, Citizenship.* Oxford: Oxford University Press.

Makoni, Sinfree (1998). "In the beginning was the missionary's word: The European invention of African languages: The case of Shona in Zimbabwe" In Kwesi Prah (ed.), *Between Extinction and Distinction: The Harmonization and Standardization of African Languages*, pp.157-165. Johannesburg: Witwatersrand University Press.

Makoni, Sinfree, and Alastair Pennycook (2007). *Disinventing and Reconstituting Languages.* Clevedon: Multilingual Matters.

Makoni, Sinfree, Janina Brutt-Griffler, and Pedzisai Mashiri (2007). The use of 'indigenous' and urban vernaculars in Zimbabwe. *Language in Society* 36: 25-49.

Makoni, Sinfree, and Barbara Trudell (2009). "African perspectives on linguistic diversity: Implications for language policy" In Jo Anne Kleifgen & George C. Bond (eds.), *Languages in Africa and the Diaspora: Educating for Language Awareness*, 32-47. Clevedon: Multilingual Matters.

Makoni, S., B. Makoni, and A. Rosenberg (2010). "Wordy worlds of music in southern Africa" *Journal of Language Education and Identity* 9: 1-16.

May, Stephen(1999). *Indigenous Community-based Education.* Clevedon: Multilingual Matters.

May, Stephen (2000). *Language and Minority Rights: Ethnicity, Nationalism, and The Politics of Language.* London: Longman.

Mazrui, A. (2004). *Power, Politics, and the African Condition. Collected Essays of Ali A. Mazrui.* Vol. 3. Trenton, NJ and Asmara, Eritrea: Africa World Press.

Mazrui, Alamin. 2007. "Globalization and some linguistic dimensions of human rights" In Paul Tiyambe Zeleza and Philip J. McConnaughay (eds.), *Human Rights, the Rule of Law, and Development in Africa*, 52-72. Philadelphia: University of Pennsylvania Press.

Meeuwis, Michael (1999). "Flemish nationalism the Belgian Congo vs. Zairian anti-imperialism: Continuity and discontinuity in language ideological debates" In Jan Blommaert (ed.), *Language ideological Debates: Language, Power and Social Process*, 381-424. Berlin: Mouton de Gruyter.

Moran, D. (1900). "The Gaelic revival" *New Ireland Review* 12: 257-272.

Mufwene, S. (2010). "The role of mother tongue schooling in eradicating poverty: A response to language and poverty" *Language* 86, no. 4: 910-932.

Nettle, Daniel, and Suzanne Romaine (2000). *Vanishing*

Voices: The Extinction of the World's Languages. Oxford: Oxford University Press.

Pattanayak, D.P. (2000). "Multilingual contexts and their ethos" In Adama Ouame (ed.), *Towards a Multilingual Culture of Education*, pp.31-47. Hamburg: UNESCO Institute of Education.

Paulston, C. (1997). "Language policies and language rights" *Annual Review of Anthropology* 26: 73-85.

Phillipson, R. (1992). *Linguistic Imperialism.* Oxford: University Press.

Shi-xu (2005). *A Cultural Approach to Discourse.* Basingstoke, England: Palgrave Macmillan.

Shi-xu (2012). "Understanding contemporary Chinese political communication: A historico-intercultural analysis and assessment of its discourse of human rights" *Journal of Language and Politics* 11(1), 93–114.

Skutnabb-Kangas, Tove (2000). *Linguistic Genocide in Education or World Wide Diversity and Human Rights.* Mahwah: Erlbaum.

Smolicz, J.J., and R. Radzik (2004). "Belarusian as an endangered language: Can the mother tongue of an independent state be made to die?" *International Journal of Educational Development* 24: 511-528.

Southall, A. (1976). "Nuer and Dinka are people: ecology, ethnicity and logical possibility" *Man* 11(4) 463-491.

Stroud, C. (2000). "African mother tongue programs and the politics of language: linguistic citizenship versus linguistic human rights" *Journal of Multilingual and Multicultural Development* 22, no. 4: 339-356.

Stroud, Christopher, and Kathleen Heugh (2004). "Language rights and linguistic citizenship" In Jane Freeland and Donna Patrick (eds.), *Language Rights and Language Survival: Sociolinguistic and Socio-*

cultural Perspectives, ed. pp.191-218. Manchester: St. Jerome Publishing.

Suleiman, Yasir (2004). *A War of Words: Language and Conflict in The Middle East*. Cambridge: Cambridge University Press.

Toolan, Michael (ed.) (2009). *Language Teaching: Integrational Linguistic Approaches*. London: Routledge.

Udogu, E. Ike (2004). "Human rights and minorities: A theoretical overview" In Paul Tiyambe Zeleza and Philip J. McConnaughay (eds.), *Human Rights, the Rule of Law, and Development in Africa*, pp.81-94. Philadelphia: University of Pennsylvania Press.

Wee, L. (2005). "Intra-linguistic discrimination and linguistic human rights: The case of Singlish" *Applied Linguistics* 26, no. 1: 48-69.

Zeleza, Paul Tiyambe (2004). "Introduction: The struggle for human rights in Africa" In Paul Tiyambe Zeleza and Philip J. McConnaughay (eds.), *Human Rights, the Rule of Law, and Development in Africa*, pp.1-21. Philadelphia: University of Pennsylvania Press.

V

Complementary and conflicting discourses of linguistic diversity: implications for language planning
(with Barbara Trudell)

Although the promotion of linguistic diversity is one of the main goals of language policy and planning in Africa, few attempts have been made to analyse how linguistic diversity has been construed in Africa within the different types of language planning discourses, and the implications of such discourses on language policy and planning. In this article we identify three main types of discourses of linguistic diversity: (i) linguistic diversity and the autonomy of language, (ii) linguistic diversity as problematic oddity, and (iii) linguistic diversity, identity and rights. In the article we demonstrate that these various discourses of linguistic diversity are both complementary and conflicting. We conclude the article by exploring the complexity of the relationships between these discourses as they affect language policy and planning.

Introduction
Beliefs about the nature of linguistic diversity are shaped by the discourses within which it is defined. Such beliefs are largely unexamined in popular use, and yet they are highly influential in a broad range of contexts, from national-level language planning to local decisions regarding education and language choice. It is thus important to understand the discursive sources of these beliefs, the perspectives to which each discourse is hospitable, and how the different discourses complement or contradict each other. These issues are the focus of this paper.

Three Perspectives
The discourses regarding linguistic diversity in Africa can be grouped into three broad categories: those which view language as an autonomous phenomenon; those which see linguistic diversity in a negative light, either as exotic or politically unwelcome; and those which see linguistic diversity in terms of the political and cultural rights of the local communities which speak those languages.

Linguistic diversity and the autonomy of language
The propensity to regard language as autonomous has a long history in linguistics. With roots in positivistic paradigms of scientific inquiry, linguistics developed as the science of language (Yngve & Wasik, 2004; Yngve, 1996). The focus of linguistic enquiry and description has tended to be on the nature of language itself; language data are seen as largely unrelated to humans except for being the necessary source of that data. The fundamental belief underpinning such linguistic description is the belief that languages are natural and not historically contingent, and that they are countable, discrete and bounded.

      Mühlhäusler (2004) describes this discourse as concerned with the enumerability of language. When languages are seen as discrete phenomena, they can be distinguished from each other and counted. Thus Adegbija lists over 450 languages in Nigeria (Adegbija, 2004). The *Ethnologue* (Gordon, 2005), arguably the most exhaustive catalogue of languages of the world, is also located in this discourse. In the arena of language policy, this discourse has influenced the emphasis on the number and proper selection of particular languages as a key feature of language policy (Makoni & Pennycook, 2005). South Africa has eleven official languages, for example. Across Africa, many descriptions have been written of the unique phonological and grammatical features of African languages (see for example the *Jounal of African Languages and Linguistics*, the *Journal of West African Languages* and the *South African Journal of African Languages*); since many African languages are still neither written nor otherwise developed, descriptive linguistics continues to be popular.

Related to the notion of enumerability is that of 'language as object.' This is manifested in an argument that language has existence and value apart from its actual use in a society. Languages can thus be objectified, studied and counted with at most only a passing reference to their location within particular human cultures (Wurm, 1996). The objectification of language also encourages a view of communication as consisting of the transference of private messages from one code to another, the so-called 'conduit' metaphor (Reddy, 1979).

The notion of language as an autonomous object has recently come under sustained criticism from a number of different theoretical positions including Harris (1980, 1998), Yngve (1996, 2004a, 2004b), Reagan (2004), Makoni and Pennycook (2005, 2006). Canagarajh (2002) argues that one way out of this conceptual impasse is to include locally grounded views of language. Terms such as *language shift* and *language loss* (Fasold, 1990) have characteristically been used to describe sociolinguistic processes linguistically, without reference to the societal or political causes or impact of such processes.[1] But not all locally grounded views of language can necessarily form the basis on which a viable applied linguistics project can be founded (Makoni & Meinhof, 2007).

These aspects of autonomy discourse have been contested by scholars such as Djite (1988), who argues that the creation of artificial linguistic boundaries in West Africa has exaggerated the linguistic complexity of the region, making language planning problems more complex than they would be if actual communicative characteristics formed the basis of description of the linguistic situation.

The ecology of language

An important development within the discourse of linguistic autonomy has been the ecological approach to linguistic diversity (Nettle & Romaine, 2000). In this paradigm languages are seen not as isolates, but as existing in a larger psychological and sociolinguistic environment. UNESCO describes this paradigm as treating language as an analogue to biodiversity, maintaining that 'just as there are hotspots of biodiversity, there are also hotspots of linguistic diversity'.[2] Thus language ecology is the study of the interactions between a language and this larger environment (Haugen, 1972). Hornberger (2003) more specifically describes language ecology as encompassing processes of language evolution, language environment and language endangerment.

---

[1] One notable exception to this rule is the linguistics text *African Voices* (Webb and Kembo-Sure 1999). Intended primarily as an introductory linguistics text, this treatment of linguistics is heavily seeded with sociopolitical commentary on linguistic processes as played out in African societies.

[2] http://portal.unesco.org/education/en/ev.php

The biodiversity analogy has engendered the use of metaphors such as *survival*, and *death* (Crystal, 2000) and even more emotively, *killer languages* and *linguistic genocide* (Skutnabb-Kangas, 2000). This terminology highlights an ethical judgement that language loss is morally wrong, regardless of the particular conditions of its social uses, and that linguistic diversity is inherently good. This is a radical departure from the positivist approach to language change which has for so long been a hallmark of linguistic theory (see Reagan 2004 for a critique of such a position). We are using the term positivist to describe one of the overarching frameworks which are evoked in the 'language-as-object' discourse. Although the ecolinguistics approach has moved significantly away from that perspective, it nevertheless remains within the paradigm of 'language as bounded phenomenon' because it is derives from the notion of language as species.

The notion of language endangerment in particular has caught the popular imagination in the West and has fuelled the arguments of language rights advocates. Keebe (2003: 47) describes this as a claim 'that the loss of a language is the permanent, irrevocable loss of a certain vision of the world, comparable to the loss of an animal or a plant'. Losing a language, irrespective of the number of speakers of that language, deprives humanity of a part of our universal human heritage insofar as the language embodies a unique worldview and knowledge of local ecosystems (Nettle & Romaine, 2000:166).

Hill (2002), however, argues that the tendency to treat endangered languages as treasures in this way is 'hyperbolic valorization'. The 'treasure' which such languages represent is perhaps more highly valued by the linguist than by the local communities which speak them. This does not mean that noting and recording rare linguistic structures does not enrich linguists' knowledge of language, but Dorian (2002:137) urges linguists to look at rarity 'from a community-centered perspective rather than only from the perspective of global frequency of occurrence'.

Clearly, the ecological approach to linguistic diversity takes into account the sociolinguistic and political milieu of language development and language change, in a way which earlier linguistic paradigms have not. However, it is important to note that in this discourse language is still described as an autonomous phenomenon, and at times is itself accorded agency. This perspective may be seen in UNESCO's argument for language preservation:

> The world's languages represent an extraordinary wealth of human creativity. They contain and express the total 'pool of ideas' nurtured over time through heritage, local traditions and customs communicated through local languages.[3]

The view of language as autonomous is the basis of most criticism of such approaches. Ecological paradigms, it is argued, fundamentally misrepresent the nature of language (and by implication linguistic diversity) because they treat language as if it were a natural, independently occurring phenomenon which is a vehicle of culture, rather than as a cultural artefact in itself. This inhibits opportunities to understand the role of human and political agency in language change and shifts in language ecology. Certainly, human existence is enriched through biological diversity, and the strongest ecosystems are characterised by diversity; but if languages are cultural artefacts rather than natural phenomena, then the ecological argument regarding the social good served by linguistic diversity is considerably weakened. It thus cannot be assumed that because biological diver-

---

[3] http://portal.unesco.org/education/en/ev.php

sity enriches human heritage, linguistic diversity necessarily has the same effect (Keebe, 2003; Pennycook, 2006).

Other, less contested assumptions about linguistic diversity which are made in the ecological approach include the individuality and equal value of all languages, including the weakened and endangered ones. This particular assumption derives from a belief in the value of all human cultures and individuals, no matter how vulnerable or disempowered. Elson (1987) articulates this view in his 'linguistic creed':

> [A]ny language is capable of being a vehicle for complicated human interaction and complex thought, and can be the basis for a complex culture and civilization. Therefore, all languages deserve respect and careful study. . . . Interest in and appreciation of a person's language is tantamount to interest in and appreciation of the person himself. All languages are worthy of preservation in written form by means of grammars, dictionaries, and written texts. This should be done as part of the heritage of the human race.[4]

The values expressed in this statement underlie much of the work currently carried out in the documentation and development of endangered languages. The value set on language in this context is directly related to its use by a unique people. The reference to language as a heritage of the human race also expresses the notion of the universal value of language. This notion informs the universalist approach to language rights which is discussed below.

The ecological discourse regarding linguistic diversity can have the effect of allowing 'language' to take the place of 'people', minimizing the essentially communicative

---

[4] http://www.sil.org/sil/linguistic_creed.htm. Accessed 10 January 2006.

and symbolic role of language within human society. Romaine (2004) acknowledges the problem:

> In discussion of language maintenance, revitalization, etc. there is a tendency to reify languages, when it is communities ... we should be talking about. When we lose sight of people and the communities that sustain language, it becomes easy to argue as a number of critics have that there is no reason to preserve languages for their own sake.

Describing minority languages in terms of endangered biodiversity carries a further risk: it tends to exoticise the people who speak those languages or treat the speakers 'as if they were plants' (England, 2002:141). Clearly, protection of vulnerable languages must not encourage the marginalization of the speakers of those languages; the rhetoric of endangerment must not do disservice to the very people it is seeking to protect. As an indigenous person of South America once told one of the authors, 'we are not interested in being in a human zoo'. The voices of the communities whose languages are being threatened have to be given substantial attention.

Linguistic diversity and language preservation
In the arguments recounted above, language preservation is assumed to be a key strategy for maintaining linguistic diversity. However, the notion of language preservation is not in itself unproblematic. It tends to ignore the diversity within languages in favour of one form. The fact that standardization and corpus planning are generally carried out under the aegis of non-native speakers of the languages adds further to the possibility that the written form of a language may not be perceived by its speakers as belonging to them in the way the oral forms of the language do.

This prompts another observation. Notions of linguistic autonomy and ecolinguistics have their roots in Western philosophical traditions and current Western values. Although that fact does not negate their utility, it does raise the question of whether African correlates to these discourses exist, and, given a concern with diversity, what their implications might be. The following African examples, suggest some of the issues.

One interesting case in which ecological concerns and cultural concerns have been combined is the celebrated environmental work of Dr Wangari Maathai, a Kenyan activist and Nobel Peace Prize winner. Dr Maathai has clearly linked preservation of the natural environment with the vitality of Kenyan cultures.[5] It is notable, however, that her articulation of this link does not extend specifically to the preservation of local languages, some of which are significantly under threat. The same attitude may be seen in a variety of disciplines in which environmental discourses are used[6] but rarely in connection with language preservation.

In other cases, however, the need for language development and cultural preservation are clear to threatened ethnic communities. Abundant anecdotal evidence from the ethnic communities of southern Sudan indicates that as these communities have been faced with what they perceived as ethnocide at the hands of the northern Sudanese government, their interest in committing the details of their culture and languages to writing has soared (Gilley, 1999). This vivid perception of language endangerment on the part of the speakers themselves led to active participation in local language planning and development activities. It appears that a people's perception of the importance of their linguistic (and

---

[5] http://www.gbmna.org
[6] See the *Special Issue of the Journal of Southern African Studies*, 26.4 (2000).

cultural) distinctives is enhanced when they find themselves in such a climate of extreme hostility to their ethnic and cultural identity.

Still, it appears that the notions of linguistic autonomy and ecolinguistics strike few familiar chords among African language communities. For African scholars, the concern with linguistic diversity tends to centre far more on issues of multilingualism and political inclusion (Roy-Campbell & Qorro, 1997; Muthwii & Kioko, 2004; Adejunmobi, 2004). An exception to this is the recent work by Batibo (2005), in which the author makes an impassioned case for the need to 'deal with the problem of language shift and death among the minority languages' (p.vii).

In another case, in South Africa the notions of language shift and language death have been used in a vigorous debate on Afrikaans at the University of Stellenbosch, even though there is no overwhelming evidence of large-scale language decline in the immediate community. The University reports that 70% of its students and 65 % of its teaching staff speak Afrikaans. Such use of notions of language death and language preservation should be interpreted not as pointing to language death or massive language shift, but as a strategy to pre-empt decline or create opportunities for an expanded use of Afrikaans as the 'language of tuition' (www.su.ac.za).

Language diversity as a problematic oddity

The discourse set which sees linguistic diversity as both exotic and problematic arguably has its genesis in the colonial domination of Africa. The supposedly 'exotic' nature of African languages, along with their associated cultures, was a theme of colonial European sociopolitical discourse. Linguistic features such as tone, length, and clicks, not found in European languages, contributed to the perception, as did the rich range of language varieties found in many parts of the continent (See, for example, Migeod, 1925). To the Europeans, this made them of curious academic interest. The post-colonial pendulum swing takes fundamentally the same view of language in asserting the opposite: linguistic diversity as a resource.

The evidence of abundant linguistic diversity led merchants, colonial officers and missions authorities in the British colonies to conclude that English was a preferable alternative to local languages for the administrative, communicative and educational tasks they had set themselves in Africa (Migeod, 1925:21). An English-based Pidgin developed in the British colonial holdings in West Africa (Vernon-Jackson, 1967), affirming the belief that any variety of English was preferable to attempting to communicate in the plethora of African languages in use by the colonised populations.

The swift takeover of European-style education – in European languages – in African communities over the first decades of the colonial era confirmed the marginalised place of African languages and cultures in the new world order. Further marginalization of African languages in 'modern' Africa came with the introduction of so-called *adapted education* in the British colonies (King, 1971). This attempt at education reform, originating in the United States and Britain, advocated a curriculum embedded in local knowledge and local languages (Wolf, 2001). The vigorous rejection of adapted education by African parents, who suspected it as an attempt to keep them from acquiring European knowledge and power (Ball, 1983), included rejection of both the local knowledge curriculum and the local language in which it was to be taught. This sense of the inappropriateness of African language as a medium of conveying knowledge in the formal classroom continues to be a widespread perception among African parents.

As independence swept across the African continent in the second half of the 20th century, the influence of the discourse of linguistic diversity as both exotic and anachronistic continued. The economic and political agenda of African states' new Western partners continued to favour the primacy of non-African languages and cultures in the continent's sociocultural development. At the Conference of African States on the Development of Education in Africa (1961), ministers of the newly independent African nations presented their hopes for a uniquely African education which would include serious attention to cultural and linguistic diversity. In response, their Western partners at the conference emphasised the need to refashion African education to match their own vision for economic development – a vision which revolved around global realities, not African ones. In the end, recognition of cultural and linguistic diversity failed to appear on the international agenda for the development of African education.

Antagonism to linguistic diversity has been further exacerbated by the advent of the nation-state in Africa. Formal recognition of multiple languages – and language communities – was, and is, seen as a significant barrier to national integration (Blommaert, 2006). Bamgbose (1991:14) describes the two facets of this argument: the notion that multilingualism inhibits national integration, and the notion that national integration necessarily involves the emergence of a nation state with only one national language. Bamgbose points out that in fact, the most serious challenges to national integration come from quite other sources than language; nevertheless, the notion that linguistic diversity is a threat to national unity has persisted.

So it has been that post-colonial governments have maintained and even extended the position of European languages in national education and political systems.

Adegbija (1994: 33-4) analyzes the post-colonial place of European languages in this way:

> Post-colonial policy makers in Africa have largely rubber-stamped or toed the line of language and educational policies bequeathed to them by the colonial masters. . . . Educational systems, which have widened and extended beyond what they were in colonial days, have been further used to entrench and perpetuate the feeling of the inviolable worth of colonial languages.

In this environment, linguistic diversity becomes a characteristic to ignore as far as possible. However, in recent decades challenges have emerged to the entrenched notion that linguistic diversity is troublesome and anachronistic. Spearheaded by international institutions such as UNESCO, there have been powerful moves to popularise the idea that linguistic diversity deserves to be addressed in political and educational spheres. As a result, African government language policies tend to be increasingly positive towards acknowledgement of the languages within their borders. In particular, the larger African languages are receiving some degree of official recognition: examples in eastern Africa include Setswana in Botswana (Nyati-Ramahobo, 2004), Chichewa in Malawi (Kayambazinthu, 2004), and most notably, KiSwahili in Tanzania (Roy-Campbell & Qorro, 1997). However, the support for linguistic diversity found in national language policy statements or in the emphasis on it as a resource is seldom played out in the actual provision of means for implementation of such policies.

Is the discourse of linguistic diversity as exotic and problematic any less foreign to Africa than the discourse of linguistic autonomy and ecology of language discussed above? Certainly, both originated with colonial Western views of African languages and cultures. Their embedding in post-colonial national policies can be traced to the nature of the political structures brought about by colonial domination of the continent. However, after so many decades of neglectful or negative policy regarding linguistic diversity by African governments, it is difficult to maintain that the discourse in which linguistic diversity is conceived as problematic is essentially foreign to Africa any more.

Linguistic diversity, identity and rights
A third discourse set regarding linguistic diversity focuses on the maintenance of language as an aspect of cultural identity, political enfranchisement and human rights.

The discourse of language and identity is grounded in the belief that language and culture are profoundly entwined. Whether language actually predisposes its speakers to see the world in a certain way (Sapir, 1929: 207), or whether language is itself a reflection of culture, the role of language in mediating and defining social relations is considered within this discourse to be crucial (Kramsch, 1998: 77). This is not to say that the nature of the language-culture connection is static; but May (2001) argues that language is nevertheless a significant feature of ethnic identity:

> To say that language is not an inevitable feature of identity is not the same as saying it is unimportant ... Language cannot be relegated, as some commentators would have it, to a mere secondary or surface characteristic of ethnicity (May 2001: 129)

In sub-Saharan Africa, certainly, language functions as one of the most obvious markers of culture. Webb and Kembo-Sure (2000: 122) note that in Africa, 'people are often identified culturally primarily (and even solely) on the basis of the language they speak'. Describing the role of language in traditional Zambian societies particularly, Serpell (1993: 97) notes that the Zambian languages are

> intimately bound up with many of the society's traditional practices, and enshrine in multiplex and subtle ways the epistemological foundations of indigenous moral values.

Hence in this discourse linguistic diversity becomes symbolic of cultural diversity, and the maintenance or revitalization of language signals ongoing or renewed validity of the culture associated with that language. For speakers of Africa's true minority languages – those which are unwritten and largely unacknowledged – this is a powerful argument for language development and the preservation of linguistic diversity.

A related discourse links language use and language choice to issues of power imbalance. It is undeniably true that communities of speakers of smaller languages tend also to be the less politically empowered communities. Indeed, May (2000) contends that

> Language loss is not only, perhaps not even primarily, a linguistic issue – it has much more to do with power, prejudice, (unequal) competition and, in many cases, overt discrimination and subordination. . . . Language death seldom occurs in communities of wealth and privilege, but rather to the dispossessed and disempowered. (p.368)

Romaine (2004) also describes the power imbalances underlying the material, political and economic domination of 'most of the world's small language communities'. And, in his study of the motivations underlying language planning and policy, Ager (2001: 158) notes that

> because of their majority or minority status, many communities within the state are vociferous in support of their own identity and desire to ensure that their language, customs and traditions are not lost. . . Language is an almost inevitable point of contention between communities.

This discourse of language-related power imbalances could be seen as contradicting Bamgbose's contention (cited above) that linguistic diversity is not an inherent threat to national unity. However, both of these arguments are linked by the crucial point that linguistic diversity per se is not a political problem: rather, *ignoring* linguistic diversity is the problem. Distinct language practices are often a feature of communities that are marginalised from access to resources and power, but national unity need not imply cultural or linguistic uniformity. Indeed, as national authorities recognise the right of individual communities to distinct language and cultural practices, and do not withhold resources or power from such communities, the resulting unity is likely to be stronger and more representative. Those most concerned with national unity must ask themselves whether their goal is not unity, but rather a particular configuration of national power structures.

Linguistic human rights
In a further move along the continuum of language and politics, the discourse which relates language issues to the political and cultural rights of communities gives rise to a more militant approach to linguistic diversity which focuses on the dominance and perceived imperialism of large, prestigious world languages – primarily English (Phillipson, 1992) – over the smaller languages of the world. The notion of linguistic human rights arises within this discourse. Freedom to

use one's own language is seen as a human right, and language diversity becomes symbolic of the defence of this universal human right. This discourse may at times use the terminology of language ecology to describe endangered and disempowered language communities (Skutnabb-Kangas, 2000), but its basis is not actually that of biodiversity or of language as a natural phenomenon needing protection from endangerment. Rather, a legal and political framework underlies the discourse of language rights (*Universal Declaration of Linguistic Rights,* 1998)

In the following section we describe the nature of the African political context within which rights regimes have become increasingly salient, and then analyse the nature of the rights discourses, focusing on what they reveal about the nature and conceptualizations of languages and language diversity within Africa.

The rights regimes became increasingly prominent in the 1990s, a period characterised by the appearance of democratic movements and multiparty elections in Africa. The main proponents of human rights in Africa have been non-governmental organizations and professional associations of teachers and lawyers. The African state has also contributed towards the consolidation of human rights regimes through a series of human rights protocols, even though there is increasing awareness of the potentially limited role which rights regimes have to effect social, political and economic equality. In addition, the interest and commitment to human rights regimes by African states can be seen at a pan-African level. A number of important pan-African structures have been set up to implement and protect human rights regimes, including (i) the Pan-African Parliament, (ii) the African Court of Justice (iii) the Economic, Social and Cultural Council, (iv) the Peace and Security Council, and (v) the African Commission on Human Rights and People's rights.

Yet in spite of the high profile of the rights discourses in Africa and the apparent commitment of African states to enforce and protect different types of rights, the situation is complicated by the African state's general proclivity to compromise rights ostensibly for the purposes of maintaining political and military security. The relationship between rights and security is further complicated by the abiding controversy in African scholarship on the nature of rights as a construct (Bhebhe & Ranger, 2001; Zeleza, 2004). Those who make a universalist argument insist that every individual has inalienable rights, and that these rights are not contingent upon a specific historical context. Those who maintain a relativist position, on the other hand, argue that a unique set of rights and discourses has developed in Africa as a product of its unique historical context. These rights are expressed and articulated in a paradigm which places a premium on human dignity more than rights. Language diversity is not a defining characteristic of this type of rights discourse.

However, the discourse of linguistic human rights does draw from this larger rights discourse. Ogechi (2003: 280) identifies the United Nations Universal Declaration of Human Rights, promulgated in 1948, as a primary pillar of language rights:

> Everyone is entitled to all the rights and freedoms set forth in this Declaration (of human rights) without distinction of any kind, such as race, colour, sex, language, religion, political or other opinion, national or social origin, property, birth or other status.[7]

Ogechi further notes that language rights are integral to numerous subsequent UN documents. Musau (2004:59) des-

---

[7] United Nations Universal Declaration of Human Rights, as quoted in Ogechi 2003.

cribes a broad range of linguistic human rights, 'aimed at the promotion of linguistic justice and the removal or prevention of linguistic inequalities or injustices that may occur because of language'. Musau and Ogechi do not entirely agree in their analyses of the status of linguistic rights in their country of focus – Kenya – but both are clearly situated in the rights discourse regarding linguistic diversity.

However, the notion of linguistic human rights has been subjected to considerable criticism (Stroud, 2000; Makoni & Pennycook, 2005, 2006). This criticism coalesces around a deep-seated scepticism regarding the definition of language that underpins this discourse, itself related to scepticism regarding western notions of language in non-western contexts. This perspective can be understood as part of a broader critique of linguistics and some of its notions of language (see Harris, 1981; Yngve 1996; Yngve & Wasik 2004; Makoni & Pennycook 2006).

For other scholars such as Ngugi wa Thiong'o and Mazisi Kunene, however, it is only through a renewed focus on the use of indigenous languages in language rights discourse that rights may be protected and enhanced. These scholars see contemporary discourses of rights as deeply entrenched in, and shaped by, European linguistic constructs. Rights discourses that are entrenched in European idiom will not have the desired effect when the people who are meant to be affected have limited knowledge of European languages (Mazrui 2004).

Not only so, but the profound connection evident between language and culture means that the protection of linguistic diversity among African populations is more difficult to maintain when languages are characterised as autonomous rather than as culturally constructed. The tendency to assign agency to language is still reflected in the Asmara Declaration of African Languages of January 17, 2000: article 1 states that 'African languages must take on the duty, the responsibility, and the challenges of speaking for the continent'. This approach carries all the limitations of the autonomous approach to language described above.

In the light of this complex situation, it is important to ask to what extent the discourse of identity, culture and rights resonates among African citizens and decision makers? The identification of specific languages with specific cultures varies across the continent, depending in part on the role that the various languages play in these largely multilingual cultures. Certainly for the 66% of African citizens who live in rural areas[8] (and so are unlikely to be fluent in international languages), the mother language is closely identified with their way of life. The desire to preserve and develop their languages is not uncommon among communities which speak small minority languages, as one author (Trudell) has experienced in African countries as diverse as Kenya, DR Congo, Ghana, Senegal, Cameroon, Benin and Sudan.

The rights discourse clearly has a strong recent history on the African continent. Whether language is widely considered to be a human right is debatable, however; scholarly attention to compliance with linguistic human rights by African nations does not seem to be matched by a more general sense of the place of language in human rights discourse.

Conclusion

In examining the array of discourses of linguistic diversity which influence beliefs and policy in sub-Saharan Africa, a few conclusions seem clear. One is that Africans tend to value multilingualism highly (Simire 2004; Roy-Campbell and Qorro 1997). This deep-seated and generalised value is

---

[8] Population Reference Bureau, <http://www.prb.org>. The definition of 'rural' used in this database of population statistics is a community environment of less than 2000 persons.

highly pragmatic, with few obvious theoretical roots in discourses of ecology or rights. However, the fact that it is so widespread lends support to positive discourses of linguistic diversity on the continent.

Another conclusion is that the pressure of a largely monolingual movement towards global culture is maintaining English – and to a lesser extent French – in a place of dominance in the minds of many Africans. Formal schooling, higher education, the Internet and modern telecommunications all increase the value of fluency in English. This fact, although not inherently inimical to multilingualism or the maintenance of African languages, does provide fuel to those discourses which denigrate African languages.

These colliding values account for the tension that exists between the various discourses of linguistic diversity as they are found in sub-Saharan African societies. Constructive resolution of this tension is only possible as the value of multilingualism, including fluency in European languages, is broadened to allow space for the continued development of minority languages for education and communication.

A related tension also characterises discussion of linguistic diversity in Africa: the tension between regarding language as simply a means of communication and regarding language as a profound marker of cultural identity. Discourse choices which downplay the self-identity role of language by denying its bounded nature entirely are not adequate models of linguistic diversity for Africa. Equally, those discourses which ignore the contingency of language on social and communicative choices are incomplete models. The discourse of 'language as communicative tool' must be balanced where needed by the discourse of 'language as cultural marker' if the benefits of both are to be attained by the millions of Africans who live the reality of linguistic diversity.

References

Adegbija, E. (2004) *Multilingualism: A Nigerian case study*. Lawrencevill, NJ: Africa World/Red Sea.

Adegbija, E. (1994) *Language attitudes in Sub-Saharan Africa: A sociolinguistic overview*. Clevedon: Multilingual Matters Ltd.

Adejunmobi, M. (2004). *Vernacular palaver*. Clevedon: Multilingual Matters Ltd.

Ager, D. (2001). *Motivation in language planning and language policy*. Clevedon: Multilingual Matters Ltd.

Badauf, R.B., Jr. and R.B. Kaplan (eds.) (2004). *Language planning and policy in Africa, Volume 1: Botswana, Malawi, Mozambique and South Africa*. Clevedon: Multilingual Matters Ltd.

Ball, Stephen J. (1983). "Imperialism, social control and the colonial curriculum in Africa" *Journal of Curriculum Studies*, 15(3): 237-263.

Bamgbose, Ayo (1991). *Language and the nation: The language question in Sub Saharan Africa*. Edinburgh: Edinburgh University Press.

Batibo, Herman (2005). *Language decline and death in Africa: Causes, consequences and challenges*. Clevedon: Multilingual Matters Ltd.

Bhebhe, N. & T. Ranger (2001). *The historical dimensions of democracy and human rights in Zimbabwe: Precolonial and colonial legacies*. Harare: University of Zimbabwe Press.

Blommaert, Jan (2006). "Language policy and national identity" In Ricento, T (ed.), *An introduction to language policy: Theory and method*. Oxford: Blackwell Publishing. x-xii.

Canagarajah, A.S. (2002). "Celebrating local knowledge on language education" *Journal of Language, Identity and Education*, 1 (4):243-261

Conference Of African States On The Development Of Education In Africa, Addis Ababa. 1961. *Final Report*. UNESCO.

Crystal, David (2000). *Language death*. Cambridge: Cambridge University Press.

Djite, Paulin (1988). "Correcting errors in language classification: monolingual nuclei and multilingual satellites" *Language problems and language planning*, 12(1):1-14.

Dorian, Nancy (2002). "Commentary: broadening the rhetorical and descriptive horizons in endangered-language linguistics" *Journal of Linguistic Anthropology*, 12(2): 134-140.

England, N. (2002). "Commentary: Further rhetorical concerns" *Journal of Linguistic Anthropology*, 12(2): 141-143.

Fasold, R. (1990). *The sociolinguistics of language*. Oxford: Blackwell.

Gilley, Leoma (1999). "Facilitating orthography development with mother-tongue speakers" *Notes on Linguistics*, 2(4): 185-192.

Gordon, Raymond (ed.) (2005). *Ethnologue*. 15th ed. Dallas: SIL International.

Harris, R. (1980). *The language-makers*. Ithaca, NY: Cornell University Press.

Harris, R. (1981). *The language myth*. London: Duckworth.

Harris, R. (1998). *Introduction to integrational linguistics*. London: Pergamon.

Haugen, E. (1972). *Linguistic Ecology*. Stanford: Stanford University Press.

Hill, J. (2002). "'Expert rhetorics' in advocacy for endangered languages: Who is listening, and what do they hear?" *Journal of Linguistic Anthropology*, 12(2):119-133.

Hornberger, N. (2003). "Multilingual language policies and

the continua of biliteracy: An ecological approach" In Hornberger, N (ed.), *Continua of biliteracy: An ecological framework for educational policy, research and practice in multilingual settings.* Clevedon: Multilingual Matters Ltd.

Hudson, R.A. (1995). *Invitation to Linguistics.* Oxford: Blackwell.

Kayambazinthu, E. (2004). "The language planning situation in Malawi" In Baldauf and RB Kaplan (eds), *Language planning and policy in Africa, Volume 1: Botswana, Malawi, Mozambique and South Africa.* Clevedon: Multilingual Matters Ltd. 53-118.

Keebe, D. (2003). "Language policy and linguistic theory" In J Marais and M Morris (eds), *Languages in a globalising world.* Cambridge: Cambridge University Press. 47-58.

King, K. (1971) *Pan-Africanism and education: A study of race, philanthropy and education in the Southern States of America and East Africa.* Oxford: Clarendon Press.

Kramsch, C. (1998). *Language and culture.* Oxford: Oxford University Press.

Makoni, S. & A. Pennycook (2005). "Disinventing and reconstituting language" *International Journal of Critical Language Studies,* 2(3):137-156.

Makoni, S. & A. Pennycook (eds). (2006). *Disinventing and reconstituting languages.* Clevedon: Multilingual Matters.

Mesthrie, R., J. Swann, A. Deumert & W. Leap (2000). *Introducing Sociolinguistics.* Philadelphia: John Benjamins.

May, S. (2000). "Uncommon languages: The challenges and possibilities of minority language rights" *Journal of Multilingual and Multicultural Development,* 21(5): 366-385.

May, S. (2001). *Language and minority rights: Ethnicity, nationalism and the politics of language*. Essex: Pearson Education Ltd.

Migeod, F. (1925). *Through British Cameroons*. London: Heath Cranton.

Musau, P. (2004). "Linguistic human rights in Africa: Challenges and prospects for indigenous languages in Kenya" In Muthwii, MJ & AN Kioko (eds), *New language bearings in Africa: A fresh quest*. Clevedon: Multilingual Matters Ltd. 155-165.

Muthwii, J.J. & A.N. Kioko (eds.) (2004). *New language bearings in Africa: A fresh quest*. Clevedon: Multilingual Matters Ltd.

Nettle, D. & S. ROmaine (2000). *Vanishing voices*. Oxford: Oxford University Press.

Nyati-Ramahobo, L. (2004). "The language situation in Botswana" In Baldauf, RB Jnr & RB Kaplan, *Language planning and policy in Africa, Volume 1: Botswana, Malawi, Mozambique and South Africa*. Clevedon: Multilingual Matters Ltd.

Ogechi, N.O. (2003). "On language rights in Kenya" *Nordic Journal of African Studies*, 12(3): 277-295.

Phillipson, R. (1992). *Linguistic imperialism*. Oxford: Oxford University Press.

Reagan, T. (2004). "Objectification, positivism and language studies: A reconsideration" *Critical Inquiry in Language Studies: An International Journal*, 1: 47-60.

Reddy, M.T. (1979). "The conduit metaphor: A case of frame conflict in our language about language" In Ortony, A (ed.), *Metaphor and thought*. Cambridge: Cambridge University Press. 164-201.

Romaine, S. (2004). "Linguistic diversity, sustainable

development, and the future of the past" Paper given at the Linguapax 2004 Conference on Linguistic Diversity, Sustainability and Peace, Barcelona, 2004.

Roy-Campbell, Z. & M.A.S. Qorro (1997). *Language crisis in Tanziania: The Myth of English vs. Education.* Dar es Salaam: Mkuki Na Nyota Publishers.

Sapir, E. (1929). "The status of linguistics as a science" *Language*, 5: 207-214.

Serpell, R. (1993). *The significance of schooling.* Cambridge: Cambridge University Press.

Simire, G.O. (2004). "Developing and promoting multi-lingualism in public life and society in Nigeria" In Muthwii, MJ & AN Kioko (eds), *New Language Bearings in Africa: A Fresh Quest*. Clevedon: Multilingual Matters Ltd.231-244.

Skutnabb-Kangas, T. (2000) *Linguistic genocide in education – or worldwide diversity and human rights?* Mahwah, NJ: Lawrence Erlbaum.

Stroud, C. (2000). "Language and democracy: The notion of linguistic citizenship and mother tongue" In Legère, K & S Fitchat (eds), *Talking Freedom: language and democratization in the SADC region*. Windhoek: Gamsberg: Macmillan.67-74.

Universal Declaration of Linguistic Rights. (1998). Barcelona: Universal Declaration of Linguistic Rights Follow-up Committee.

Vernon-Jackson, H.O.H. (1967). *Language, schools and government in Cameroon.* NY: Columbia University Teacher's College Press.

Webb, V. & Kembo-Sure (eds.) (2000). *African voices*. Oxford: Oxford University Press.

Wolf, H.G. (2001). *English in Cameroon*. Berlin: Mouton de Gruyter.

Wurm, S.A. (1996). *Atlas of the world's languages in danger of disappearing*. Paris: UNESCO.

Yngve, V. (1996). *From grammar to science: New foundations for General Linguistics*. Amsterdam & Philadelphia: John Benjamins.

Yngve, V. (2004a). "Issues in Hard Science Linguistics" In Yngve, V & Z Wasik (eds) *Hard-Science Linguistics*. New York: Continuum.14-27.

Yngve, V. (2004b). "An introduction to Hard-Science Linguistics" In Yngve, V & Z Wasik (eds) *Hard-Science Linguistics*. New York: Continuum. 27-35.

Yngve, V. and Z. Wasik (2004). *Hard-science Linguistics*. London & New York: Continuum.

Zeleza, P. (2004). "Human rights and development in Africa: New contexts, challenges and opportunities." Paper presented at the International Conference on the African Commission on Human and People's Rights, Uppsala, Sweden.

Language and Education

VI

The consequences of a Chomskyan perspective on rules in second language acquisition

Abstract
The aim of this article is to outline the role and status of rules in second language acquisition in order to demonstrate the consequences of such a conceptualization for second language acquisition. The Chomskyan framework was initially designed as an account of first language acquisition. However, it has been extended to second language acquisition. In this article I argue that the extension of a Chomskyan framework outside its original area of conceptualization simplifies second language acquisition. A number of key concepts in Generative Linguistics such as creativity and stable state grammars are identified and I argue that their scope needs to be restricted, if they are to have much explanatory power in second language learning, because second language users are relatively less 'creative' in the generative sense of the word and their grammars more unstable. In a bid to explain the instability, descriptions of second language grammars need to incorporate variation as part of their description.

Introduction
The aim of this article is to explore the insights second language acquisition and teaching could gain from a Chomskyan version of linguistics by focussing on the concept of rules. In order to do this, I intend to outline the following factors, which arguably have a bearing on the way rules are conceptualized and the format the rules assume in a linguistic description:

1. The role and status of rules in generative grammar and the consequences of such views for a conceptualization of second language learning.
2. The developmental stage of second language acquisition and the variable nature of learners' production.
3. The mechanisms which bring about the rammaticalization of second language acquisition rules.

Rules In second language acquisition
Sharwood Smith (1993) points out that there is no general consensus among linguists about either the conceptual desirability of rules in linguistic descriptions or their theoretical significance. In this section, I intend to focus on a theoretical approach which, at least, accords some significance to rules in its description of languages with the aim of demonstrating: the consequences of a Chomskyan conceptualization of rules and parameters on second language acquisition.[1]

---

[1] In this article I seek to examine the consequences of a Chomskyan, and not Chomsky's perspective, on second language acquisition (SLA). Following Botha I would say the perspective is Chomskyan and not Chomsky's because with the exception of one or two flippant remarks Chomsky has never demonsmted much public interest on SLA. This has however not discouraged scholars like Sharwood Smith, Cook, etc. from extending his theoretical framework into SLA. Their work, in the light of Botha's distinction, would be categorized as Chomskyan.

One of the main aims of a generativist enterprise is to describe the Internalized knowledge (I-language) of a mature adult native speaker. I-language as a matter of convention, is contrasted with Externalized language (E-language). Cook (1988) gives a lucid and accessible account of some of the properties which are characteristic of I- and E-language approaches. The I- and E-language distinction echoes and mutually reinforces the contrasts found in other binary terms in the generative literature: grammaticality and acceptability; competence and performance.

Unfortunately, the I- and E-language distinctions do not have a comparable epistemological valency, because with I-language, Chomsky seems to have had in mind an abstract cognitive configuration, a stable mental state below the level of language, but with E-language the thrust is more towards the ability to actualize language behaviour—something comparable to Hymes' (1972) communicative competence.

Instructional methods seeking to foster the development of E-language require a radically different set of design features from those seeking to develop I-language. With E-language the analyst is concerned with analyzing real time rules deployed by language users every millisecond during production and indeed during reception. (It is however, relatively easier to construct real time rules for production than for comprehension.)

Language production in real time is rendered possible by human creativity. Creativity, on which I- language is based, has a special meaning different from its artistic meaning. Cook defines creativity thus

> In all Chomskyan models a characteristic of competence is its creative aspect; the speaker's knowledge of language must be able to cope with sentences that it has never heard or produced before (1988: 15)

I will argue later on in this article that concepts of steady state grammars and creativity are problematic and have limited applicability in second language acquisition. Earlier generativist models uied to capture the character of steady state grammars mainly through transformations. For example, it was said that interrogatives and passives were formed by moving elements around (Chomsky, 1965; 1980). In more recent formulations of generative grammar such as Government and Binding (GB), transformations have by and large been replaced by principles and parameters. The only transformation which Chomsky has retained in his current thinking is (move α). The few rules which remain not only play a modest role but a different one as well.

> The rules in the current generative models are to be explained as the interaction of principles and lexical properties rather than as existing in their own right and account for idiosyncratic and specific aspects of language. (Cook, 1988: 23)

The dispensing with rules has general consequences on the conceptualization of the acquisition of grammatical systems. A language learner is seen within the principles and parameter setting models

> not as a creator of rules, but rather, as someone, who uses input to fill out, tune or reset an already existing set of parameters. The truth of the matter is that learners do not take in the rule they take in examples of the rule (Sharwood Smith, 1993: 170)

Format of principles and parameters
Typically, parameters are described in terms of clusters presented in the format of 'where there is A there is always B' (Sharwood Smith, 1993). For example, languages which

optionally omit grammatical subjects (pro-drop) typically permit free subject-verb inversion. Italian and Spanish are frequently cited as examples. Free subject-verb inversion is one of the deductive consequences of the omission of grammatical subjects. Unfortunately, the empirical evidence to support whether the configurationality found in first languages is analogous to that in non-mother tongue speech, is not overwhelming particularly with regard to principles such as pro-drop (Bley-Vroman, 1989: 64). The principles and the parameters are also couched in a very abstract way that their relevance and applicability to second language learning and teaching is not self-evident and more importantly 'no-one actually speaks a universal grammar' (Davies, 1991: 41), although all the languages spoken could be said to be manifestations of universal grammar in one form or other. The crux of the matter is that applied linguists are much more concerned about the acquisition and teaching of a specific language by language learners who are flesh and blood while linguists are concerned with as Davies (1991: 39) puts it 'uncovering, revealing, describing, explaining the knowledge of the idealized native speaker', hence the interest of the linguists in universal grammar for which there can never be any mother-tongue speakers.

The point I am making should not be construed to mean that there should not be any idealization in second language acquisition and language teaching. It is not unusual for disciplines to aim at different degrees of abstraction. Linguists working within a universal grammar framework may idealize at a higher degree of abstraction than second language acquisition and language teaching: that degree of abstraction could be appropriate to Universal Grammar-inspired linguistics, but is not necessarily appropriate to second language acquisition and teaching. Conversely, the low degree of abstraction in second language acquisition and language teaching could be appropriate to these activities and not Universal Grammar linguistics. The moral of the story is that although the abstraction required in second language acquisition and language teaching is low, it is impossible to escape from some abstraction; the very act of data collection, whether as part of an experiment or ordinary classroom work involves some partial analysis, some degree of idealization (Davies, 1984). In other words, although the data used in universal grammar work is highly artificial, there is nothing like naturally occurring data because 'collection and transcription already imposes partial analysis' (Davies, 1984).

Steady State grammars in second language acquisition
There are two very central assumptions underlying discussions about Steady State grammars. It is, as a matter of course, assumed that the competence underlying Steady State grammars is 'singular and monolithic' to use Hurford's (1990: 94) phrase and that, on the one hand, adult mother-tongue speakers have fully acquired their 'native' language i.e they have the end product available, but on the other hand they are still in a real sense in the process of acquiring their mother tongue, and I suspect the process is a never ending one. It is a life long exercise. The acquisition of new vocabulary items or new senses to 'old' words and registers is an ongoing activity throughout one's life. So if implicit in the notion of Steady State grammar is the idea that language learning is completeable, if it can be demonstrated that language acquisition is an ongoing activity, then adult native speaker grammars may not be in an extremely steady state after all; at least not in the sense implied in generative literature. The point I am making that language acquisition is a continuous process, is valid with the caveat that, strictly speaking the lexicon is regarded as outside the structural properties of language, at least in the generative literature.

The issue about the relative stability of grammars may be of minor significance in adult native-speaker grammars; it however assumes a special significance in second language learning where it is more productive to think, not in terms of what Hurford (1990: 94) calls a 'singular monolithic competence', but of 'pluralistic competencies in which language learner language' at each stage is made up of rules from different developmental stages rendering the grammars unstable: indeterminate. It is in an attempt to capture this indeterminacy that Ellis (1987;1992) in a series of articles has proposed the 'multiple competence hypothesis'.

The multiple competence hypothesis seeks to capture the variable nature of second language acquisition in which the same linguistic rule may have a number of different variants.

Format of variable rules
P includes Q 90% of the time in context.

Some data demonstrating variability of the third person singular in second language acquisition Third person singular forms used in parallel coordinate constructions in unplanned discourse in first and second clauses, e.g.

Clause	-s	o	-ing
First clause	18	19	0
	(49%)	(51%)	0%
Second clause	11	26	0
	(30%)	(70%)	0%

Example: Everyday he *climbs* a bus and he get off at the bus stop near the tavern. (Makoni, 1992: 81).

From a second language learning perspective, it means the third person singular is a variable rule in second language production, and that there is a higher frequency of suppliance of the (-s) form in the fist clause than in the second clause, and that the rule has three variants, the (-s), (o), (-ing). (The presence of the [-ing] form is not evident in the data reported here.) One merit of variable rules is that they capture the tendencies in second language production and the factors which bring about the variation. For example, in the light of the data supplied above. the third person singular varies depending on the linguistic context i.e. first clause or second clause. There are a number of structures including tense marking, plural formation and the copula which research in second language acquisition has demonstrated to be variable. For example, Ellis (1987) has produced empirical evidence demonstrating variability in the use of tense among second language learners. Young (1991) describes variability in 'the use of plural forms during interlanguage production.

If language teaching is to achieve its desired impact it needs to take into account the variable nature of second language rules and the factors which contribute to that variability such as discourse plannedness (Makoni, 1992; Ellis, 1987). Unfortunately, the probabilistic nature of second language rules is frequently overlooked because it is conceptually much easier to think of language learner language as categorical; a linguistic form is either categorically present or absent. The signals being sent out loud and clear from second language acquisition variability studies, and more recently in the renewed interests in grammaticalization, Creole studies and language teaching is, that although it is inconceivable to imagine a language without the traditional subcomponents of language i.e. morphology, syntax, semantics and pragmatics, language should be thought of as a system of systems in which there is no formal separation of the additionally recognized subcomponents in language (Le Page & Tabouret-Keller, 1982; Davies, 1990). The idea of language as a system of interacting systems is one of the insights from second language acquisition *to* linguistics.

Creativity in second language acquisition

There are two senses to the idea of creativity as an ability to understand and produce an infinite number of sentences as cited earlier on. The two senses of creativity have direct implications on the issue of rules.

At a mundane level, Miller (1993) argues that creativity in one sense, simply means 'taking syntactic patterns and using them with new vocabulary'; at a more abstract level, creativity involves using syntactic resources of language to construct new complex constructions. Because the source of evidence for most of the generative literature is drawn from carefully constructed sentences by highly literate users; creativity is as a result associated with written discourse. Perhaps, the creativity which generativists have in mind is more a property of the written language than a 'primitive' characteristic of language. This is an anomalous situation of considerable interest to me because it is language, or more accurately issues beyond language, for which language simply provides the necessary evidence which are the main concerns of generativists.

In this section I intend to do two things. Firstly, to demonstrate how problematic it can be to establish whether language learner language is a manifestation of creativity or a lack of knowledge. Secondly, to demonstrate the extent to which second language learners may not be as endlessly creative as is implied in the literature.

Creativity, innovation and error

Davies raises an important issue relating to the problematic nature of the distinction between creativity and error when he says,

> it seems to be the case that often non-native speakers will invent terms, whether words, expressions or sentences which native speakers choose to categorise as errors; and yet by the same token, similar inventions or creations by the native speaker are not regarded as being errors. Instead they are creative additions to the language. (Davies, 1992: 87)

In other, words, whether the same type of language is classified as erroneous or genuinely creative leading to a deliberate violation of rules depends to a large extent on the sociolinguistic status of the language speaker. Celebrated second language users like Joseph Conrad do not commit grammatical errors because their language production is regarded as creative, but if the same type of creativity was produced by a less celebrated writer than Conrad, her production would have been categorized as erroneous.

The generative and indeed artistic senses of the word creative overlook the extent to which as Miller (1993) puts it

> much of language is formulaic and that imitation combined with the learning and manipulation of formulas plays an important part in first and indeed even more so in second language learning.

There is a good deal of everyday use of language which is quite properly described in 'behaviouristic terms' and can be attributed to our acting out of particular roles in the maintenance of socially prescribed ritualistic patterns of behaviour. The intellectual reluctance to accept the extent to which much of language consists of an adjustment of preassembled and memorized patterns is an indirect consequence of Chomsky's (1959) victory in a polemic with Skinner.

Pawley & Syder (1983) argue that the knowledge of a mature speaker is made up of thousands of lexicalized sentence frames which are in varying degrees of 'frozenness'. The most frozen ones are idiomatic expressions—in idiomatic expressions such as by hook or by crook; look before you leap; a stitch in time saves nine.

The relationship between the lexical items is fixed to such an extent that the items are best thought of as composite units or as Widdowson (1989) in a witty and elegant way puts it, 'the rules are in suspended animation'. At the other end of the continuum of frozen constructions are a series of 'institutionalized clauses' which unlike idiomatic expressions permit some amount of variation, albeit restricted in scope. Because of the scope of the variation, the senses cannot be said to have been freely generated by the syntax. The following are examples of institutionalized sentences with some restricted variation. The examples are taken from Miller (1993):

- who do you think you are?
- what does she think she is?
- what kind of report does she think this is?

are variations of the basic theme: wh + pronoum/NP-do-pronoun/NP think with changes in tense and an alternation of NP's and pronouns.

The moral of the story for the applied linguist is that second language users are not as endlessly creative as is frequently implied in the generative literature and that second language users need to develop a feel of constructions which should not be decomposed (an awareness of the limits of analyzability). They also need to develop a feel of the limits of the scope of variation permitted within some constructions as the examples from Miller demonstrate. 'An ignorance of the limits of analysability, of the variable application of rules constitutes incompetence' (Widdowson, 1989 132). If the unanalyzed schematic units are so widespread in language it might be more appropriate to describe language acquisition as a process of adapting an increasing number of idioms 'supplemented by generative rules' rather than viewing language as a system of generative rules with a restricted number of idiosyncratic expressions (Widdowson, 1985: 327). In other words, to use terms borrowed from the generative literature what we are witnessing when language learners are manipulating preassembled chunks, is an instance of 'performance without competence' (Widdowson, 1985).

A phenomenon not unknown in first language acquisition.

Relocating rules within the mind of the learner
Within the Chomskyan enterprise descriptions of grammatical knowledge, as pointed out earlier, are highly abstract and decontextualized. The decontextualization and abstraction are a necessary methodological consequence of seeking to provide a description of an idealized native speaker hearer, who because she operates at such a high degree of abstraction, is not flesh and blood. The feelings or the perception of the users of the rules are neither significant nor relevant to the construction of the grammar. What is important is the grammaticality and not the acceptability of the constructions. The feelings of the users are insignificant because users are dispensed with in a vigorous way in the process of *decontextualintion and idealization.* In second language acquisition the opposite is the case. What generativists *take such meticulous care* to exclude we *vigorously reinstate because the users' feelings and perceptions are of central importance* in understanding the nature of these rules. Klein (1985) is an excellent example of an attempt to reinstate the second language learner's feelings into the grammatical descriptions in what he calls Test grammars. Test grammars are a good example of what I was calling the need for low level idealization in second language acquisition.

Psychological status of Test Grammars: 'Detection of anomaly with no development[2]

At every stage of second language development a learner entertains, according to Klein, subjective perceptions concerning the acceptability of her language. Each interlanguage rule according to Klein is associated with a confirmation index ranging from 0 to 1 with 0 meaning that the learner feels that the rule is in need of revision. (The fact that the learner feels that the rule is false does not mean that it is not used.) A rule with an index of 1 is correct and stable. A value of 0.5 means maximum insecurity.

Maximum insecurity does not in itself result in rule revision. The learner, however, revises rules which she feels are not only insecure but are critical as well. In other words, a learner may be able to detect a mismatch between her language rules and the feedback she is receiving but still insists on operating with her old rules because the old rules are not yet sufficiently critical to merit a radical revision in spite of their being deviant. Rules are judged as critical for a number of reasons. For example, rules which result in the learner being socially stigmatized may be regarded as critical by the learner and hence in urgent need of repair. These rules may not necessarily be the ones which are the target of corrective feedback by the language teacher. The point I am making is that the impact of second language teaching is mediated by the value of the revision and criticalness indices put on them by the learner. Thus although language teachers may manipulate the input during teaching, caution is necessary when

---

[2] The term detection of anomaly with no development comes from Sharwood Smith's (1993) paper 'Input enhancement in instructed SLA' in which he makes the point that changes in input do not necessarily result in developmental changes in language learner production.

making claims about the consequences of such manipulation on interlanguage development.

Grammaticalization
So far the main thrust of my argument has been based on an assumption that the rules of the language learner have been grammaticalized already. It is this assumption of grammaticalization which I now intend to address. Hurford describes grammaticalization thus:

> The historical mechanism by which facts of discourse become facts of grammar, is often labelled grammaticalization. To prevent confusion, it should be stressed that the result of this process does not necessarily involve a class of previously ungrammatical strings becoming grammatical. What gets *grammaticalised* is a pattern or *configuration of facts,* not some class of strings which happen to participate in such a pattern. (emphasis is added) (1990: 119)

Since second language learning is, by and large, a developmental process, it is arguably an excellent example of grammaticalization. Rutherford (1988: 43; 50) cites excellent examples of grammaticalization.
   Some examples of grammaticalization
1. a. Elephant nose is long
      Topic comment
   b. Grammaticalized into
      The elephant's nose is long.
2. a. The problem is the destroy of nature
   b. The problem is the destruction of nature.

   In (1) a topic-comment configuration is syntacticized through the possessive marker. In (2) grammaticalization involves the formation of verbal nouns.

In order to understand the role and status of rules in second language learning, it is also crucial to understand the mechanisms underlying the conversion of a loose configuration into a syntactic pattern. Second language teaching therefore needs to 'manufacture' strategies which can facilitate such types of grammaticalization.

Conclusion

With this article I have provided an overview of quotations regarding the role and status of rules within a Chomskyan perspective. I have argued that the degree of abstraction of the rules renders their relevance to language teaching doubtful. I have also argued that if the rules are to be useful for the purposes of language teaching, then some degree of 'deabstraction' is called for but at the same time some form of abstraction and idealization is inevitable in any language analysis. The de-abstraction enables the analyst to reintroduce the learner's perceptions of the acceptability of her language. I have also argued that the issue of creativity overlooks the extent to which language use is formulaic and the conceptual problems of distinguishing between errors and creative innovations in language production was touched on. My conclusion is that Universal Grammar, as a way of doing linguistics, might have revealed a lot of interesting facts, but is of limited relevance for second language acquisition and teaching.

References

Bley-Vroman, Robert (1989). "What is the logical problem of foreign language learning?" In Gass, S. & Schachter, J. (Eds.). *Linguistic perspectives on second language acquisition.* Cambridge: Cambridge University Press, pp.41-69.

Botha. Rudolph P. 1992. *Challenging Chomsky: the Generative Garden Game.* Oxford: Basil Blackwell.

Brumfit, Christopher (1991). "Applied linguistics in higher education: riding the storm", *BAN. Newsletter,* Spring. pp.45-50.
Cameron, Deborah (1994). "Putting our practice into theory", *British Studies in Applied Linguistics,* pp.15-24.
Chomsky, Noam (1965). *Aspects of the theory of syntax.* Cambridge, Mass: MlT Press.
Chomsky, Noam (1980). *Rules and representations.* New York: Columbia University Press.
Cook. Vivian (1988). *Chomsky's universal grammar:* an *introduction.* Oxford: Basil Blackwell.
Cook, Vivian (1990). "Observational data and the U.G. theory of language acquisition" In Roca, I.M.(Ed.) *Logical issues in language acquisition.* Dordrecht: Foris Publications, pp.33-45.
Cooreman, A. & Kilbom, K. (1991). "Functionalist Linguistics: discourse structure and language processing in second language acquisition'. In Ferguson, C. & Huebner, T. (Eds.). *Cross currents in second language acquisition and linguistic theory.* Amsterdam: Benjamin Press, pp.195-224.
Crystal, David (1985). *A dictionary of linguistics and phonetics.* New York: Basil Blackwell.
Davies. Alan. 1991. The *native speaker in applied linguistics.* Edinburgh: Edinburgh University Press.
Eckman, Fred R. (Ed.). (1993). "Introduction: one approach to the interaction of linguistics, second language acquisition and speech-language pathology" In *Confluence linguistics, L2 acquisition and speech pathology.* Amsterdam/Philadelphia: Benjamins, pp.vii-xv.
Ellis. Roderick (1987). "Interlanguage variability in

narrative discourse: style shifting in the use of the past tense', *Studies in Second Language Acquisition,* 9(1): 2-20.

Ellis, Roderick (1992). *Second language acquisition and language pedagogy, multilingual matters.* Clevedon.

Hilles, S. (1986). "Interlanguage and the pro-drop parameter", *Second Language Research,* 2: 33-52.

Hudson, Richard A. (1981). "Some issues on which linguists can agree", *Journal* of *Linguistics,* 17(2): 333-343.

Hurford, James (1990). "Nativist and functional explanations in language acquisition" In Roca, I.M. (Ed.). *Logical issues in language acquisition.* Dordrecht: Foris Publications. pp.85-132.

Hymes. Dell (1992). "On communicative competence" In Pride, J.B. & Holmes, J. *Sociolinguistics.* Harmondsworth: Penguin.

Klein. Wolfgang (1986). *Second language acquisition.* Cambridge: Cambridge University Press.

Le Page, Robert & Tabouret-Keller. A. (1982). "Models and stereotypes of ethnicity of language", *Journal of Multilingual and Multicultural Development,* 3(3): 161-205.

McCawley, James (1984). "Review of White 1982" *Language* 60: 431-436.

Makoni, Sinfree B. (1992). "The effects of linguistic context on unplanned discourse: a study in interlanguage variability'. *Issues in Applied Linguistics,* 3(1): 69-91.

Miller, James (1993). *Speaking, writing and language acquisition.* Unpublished manuscript.

Pawley, A.K. & Syder, F.H. (1983). 'Two puzzles for linguistic theory: native like selection and native like fluency'. In Richards, J.C. & Schmidt, R.W. (Eds.). *Language and commumication.* London: Longman.

Peters, Ann (1983). *The units* of *language acquisition.*

Cambridge: Cambridge University Press.

Roca, Iggy M. (Ed.). (1990). *Logical issues in language acquisition.* Dordrecht: Foris Publications.

Rutherford, William (1988). *Second language grammar: learning and teaching.* London: Longman.

Rutherford, William (1993). "Linguistics and SLA: The two-way street phenomenon'. In Eckman. Fred R. (Ed.). *Confluence linguistics, L2 acquisition, and speech pathology.* Amsterdam/Philadelphia: Benjamins, pp. 1-1 4

Sharwood Smith, M. (1990). 'Second language learnability'. In Roca, LM. (Ed.). *Logical issues in language acquisition.* Dordrecht: Foris Publications, pp.259-273.

Sharwood Smith, M. (1993). 'Input enhancement in instructed SLA', *Studies* in *Second Language,* 115; 165-179.

Tarone, Elaine (1988). *Variation in interlanguage.* London: Edward Arnold.

Widdowson. Henry C. (1989). "Knowledge of language and ability for use" *Applied Linguistics,* 10(2): 128-138.

Young, Richard (1991). *Variation in interlanguage morphology.* New York: Peter Long.

VII

English and education in anglophone Africa
Historical and current realities
(with Busi Makoni)

In this chapter, we focus on the historical and contemporary role of English in "anglophone" Africa.[1] We use this term circumspectly because it emphasizes the connection between language and place—what Canut (2002) refers to as *territorialization*. The connections between language and place implicit in terms such as *anglophone, lusophone, francophone* are rendered difficult to maintain because of people's constant movement across different geographical regions. The complexity of using local categories arises not only because of the inconsistencies in the ways the terms are used within the same local communities. In addition, even when the

---

[1] We are using the term *anglophone Africa* advisedly because "anglophone," "lusophone," and "francophone" African nations have a great deal in common in terms of language, social practices, and ethnocultural histories. These commonalities are easily overlooked when Africa is viewed through colonial categories. We are, therefore, using the term *anglophone Africa* for stylistic convenience, not because we necessarily subscribe to the ideology that it represents (Makoni, Smitherman, Ball & Spears, 2003).

same community uses the term consistently, it may be interpreted radically differently by educated and non-educated speakers.

The place of English in Africa, particularly in what is known as anglophone Africa, has been shaped over centuries by historical, social, and political forces. Unlike other parts of the world in which English usage and English-language teaching are relatively recent linguistic phenomena, Africa has a long history of contact with and usage of the English language. Unquestionably, Christian institutions played a significant role in establishing English as a language of prestige in British colonial Africa. Today, however, attitudes and uses of English are mediated by far more influential institutional forces of state, society, and economics.

In this chapter, we analyze the role that institutions such as Christianity and colonial governments have played in shaping and determining the prestige of English in anglophone Africa. The role of these institutions was also in part shaped by African demands for education in English, which continues to partially determine the status of English in popular imagination in Africa. We also comment on the ethical and moral dilemmas of language planning research, which advocates an expanded use of African languages in contexts in which there is a strong pro-English educational orientation both from parents and students (Ferguson, 2003).

English in Colonial Africa: Mission Perspectives
The historical role of Christianity in establishing English as the language of prestige and formal employment in anglophone Africa is undeniable. As the founders of formal education systems in the British colonies, Christian missionaries were integral to the formation of early colonial policy on language in education. However, debates on language choice were vehement and frequent among mission educators and among mission-educated Africans as well. These debates

centered on questions of cultural integrity, the communicability of the Christian gospel, the new meanings that African words and speech acts assumed under the impact of Christianity, and "appropriate" knowledge for the Africans being educated, especially according to the Africans themselves. Africans literate in Western formal education did not regard their cultural identities as compromised through learning English. Even if Africans may have associated Western formal education with English, it is not self-evident that they readily accepted nonnative teachers of English because in African popular imagination English was construed as White.

The debates among African intellectuals did not focus on whether it was appropriate to use English as a medium of instruction; that was taken for granted. Instead, the debate focused on the standardization of African languages because missionaries could only incorporate a relatively restricted range of Africans' stylistic repertoire, thus excluding associative discourses characteristic of oral cultures (Makoni & Meinhof, 2003). African languages that were a product of this standardization were received with mixed feelings by educated Africans. It is, therefore, instructive to note that, at least in Zimbabwean social linguistic history, the term *colonial language* was first used by African intellectuals to refer *not* to English but to standardized African languages because of the limited input and serious involvement by Africans in the standardization process and the perceptible shifts in the meaning and forms of African languages due to standardization.

In fact, the English language did not arrive on the African continent through the mission's medium. Adegbija (1994) argues that it was first mercantile contact and then the conquering colonizing powers that brought English and other European languages into the linguistic picture for Africans. At the moment of African encounters with Europe, it is unlikely that Africans maintained any firm distinctions between the various European languages. However, the early association of these languages with military and economic gain might set the stage for their subsequent high regard in the minds of the conquered. Adegbija notes that:

> The basis for the European languages as languages of the masters, of power, of high position of prestige and of status were solidly created in these early days. Many Africans began to look up to the European languages as the master's language and yearned to learn them. (p. 31)

Although Adegbija's argument is well made that Africans might have expressed strong interest in European languages, this was not necessarily accompanied by a desire to acquire European cultural habits. This strong interest in learning European languages has to be situated within a context in which Europeans, in order to facilitate their control of colonized Africans, learnt African languages, albeit their own written versions, as part of an unfolding European colonial project.

Although Christian missionaries in the early colonial period tended to be highly sympathetic to the use of local African languages for education and communication, and inimical to the use and promotion of European languages in terms of policy, some missions clearly favored the use of local languages. The crucial issue, however, is not so much that the missionaries promoted the use of local languages but rather what they understood by the concept of "local language" and the impact of their linguistic perspective on local African linguistic ecologies. These perspectives facilitated the emergence of new relationships between languages and dialects and, in some cases, even led to a breakdown of pre-colonial social structures. An example of the latter can be found in the development of a missionary-based *lingua franca* (Tsonga) in colonial southern Africa, which facilitated the breakdown of some traditional systems of chieftainship and kinship (Spolsky, 2003).

The activities of missionaries in some contexts led to the emergence of new language varieties, as well as a new social and political hierarchy between particular local languages. The work of Protestant and Catholic missionaries in Zimbabwe led to the emergence of five different dialects, namely Karanga, chiManyika, Zezuru, Korekore, and Ndau, which were associated with different religious denominations (Errington, 2001). Karanga was subsequently associated with the Dutch Reformed Church, chiManyika with the Anglican Church, and Zezuru with the Roman Catholic Church (Chimhundu, 1992). Furthermore, in Botswana, Nyati-Ramahobo (2004) links the development of the Setswana language to the influence of eighteenth century missionaries with the London Missionary Society.

Furthermore, there was considerable latitude in how the missionaries understood African multilingualism and the use of African languages. For example, in southern Africa, the American Mission Board continued to use isiZulu for their everyday work (e.g., medical advice and farming) in a region in which the Africans actually spoke chiNdau (Jeater, 2007). Similarly, the Basel missionaries operating in what was then the British Cameroons used the Mungaka language (spoken by the Bali people) extensively, even in regions where the dominance of the Bali was strongly resented by the local non-Bali populations (Trudell, 2005b, p. 74).[2]

---

[2] Debates about what constitutes a local language are still pertinent even in contemporary Africa. For example, the general scholarly tendency has been to construe English as alien and "indigenous" languages as local, overlooking Africanized varieties of English.

In this environment, mission-educated Africans entered into the language debate as well, not just regarding whether to use English but also regarding which of the local languages should be used in schools. In colonial Rhodesia of the 1930s, fierce debate raged between mission-educated Africans who supported the continued use of Zulu in Ndebele schools as part of a pan-African nationalist project and Ndebele nationalists who supported the introduction of Ndebele as part of a cultural nationalist project. The London Missionary Society, which had played a key role in systematizing Ndebele, was also in favor of the introduction of Ndebele (Ranger, 1995; Samkange, 1936). However, the pan-African nationalists argued for the continued use of Zulu because they felt that introducing Ndebele would divide the Ndebele in Rhodesia from those in South Africa. They used English as a model to support their argument, contending that just as in England where there are still counties that have the main language as the King's English but speak their own dialects, so maintaining Zulu as the language of education would be preferable to the introduction of Ndebele in schools. Pan-African nationalists also disparaged Ndebele, describing it as a mixture of Zulu words and Kalanga (a dialect of chiShona).

Thus, questions of language in education fueled extended and fervent debate. The missionaries' enthusiasm for developing and teaching local languages was rooted largely in their belief that, in order that their evangelistic endeavors be effective, Christian texts such as the Bible needed to be available in "the language of the soul." For the missionaries, competence in local languages included but was not restricted to an ability to translate from English into local languages in order to facilitate the translation of Christian texts. By using local languages instead of European languages, the missionaries created opportunities for Christianity to be understood through African languages, since the religious concepts that they used were embedded in African languages. Notions of God, sin, and prayer were not introduced as new concepts but were derived from existing concepts for new evangelistic purposes. In southern Africa the term *God* was translated in a number of different ways, one of them being *wedenga*, derived from *kudenga* (meaning "in the sky"), a word that, although already existing, excluded the possibility of a god of the caves (Pennycook & Makoni, 2005).

In addition to the Bible, the texts most frequently produced by missionaries were lists of words or vocabularies. The preponderance of vocabularies over grammars reflects an orientation toward "using words" rather than speaking (Fabian, 1986; Jeater, 2007). The missionaries' production of local-language texts established a connection between Christianity and literacy and situated Christianity within a specific literate tradition. Since the church provided opportunities for becoming literate, those who became literate in the colonial days were also perforce exposed to Christianity. This is not to say that there were no literacy practices that predated Christianity or were developed independently of Christianity in Africa; Swahili was previously written in an Arabic script, and the Vai language in Liberia had an orthographic system that predated Christianity and colonialism in that region. Nevertheless, the connection between Christianity and local-language literacy practices in Africa was strong.

Christian missions thus involved two types of conversion (Errington, 2001): the conversion of local people to Christianity and the conversion of African languages from unwritten into written forms. The development of orthographies for indigenous languages, carried out in many cases with a great degree of linguistic naïveté, affected the way indigenous languages were codified and distinguished. In some cases, distinctions were made between varieties of the same language, as the case of Runyakitara in Uganda and

Nguni languages in South Africa illustrates (Bernstein, 1996). In addition, phonological characteristics not commonly found in European languages (such as tone or vowel quality) were often either ignored or underrepresented in early orthographies of African languages, rendering reading in these languages extremely difficult. The constant changes made to African orthographies and the limited literature available also made reading in these languages extremely difficult.

Stylistically, the missionaries tended to use a very restricted range of the African language stylistic continuum. They were also frequently not well disposed to the associative rhetorical styles typical of African cultures, favoring instead linear reasoning styles. The reduction of African languages to writing, therefore, contributed to the emergence of new rhetorical styles, some of which were distant from traditional African rhetorical patterns. The impact of the conversion of African languages into written forms was also evident at a lexical level. For example, Willan (1984) describes the efforts of early African novelist Sol Plaatje to extend the range of Tswana words to include words that were not included in early dictionaries (Makoni & Meinhof, 2003).

The determination to use local African languages in mission contexts caused Christian missionaries to campaign energetically in favor of language policies that favored African language development and use in education. Adejunmobi (2004) observes that: "European advocates of vernacular literature in Africa during the colonial period made their views known in books, journal articles, and at international conferences linked to specific interest groups, namely missionaries, education officials, linguists and anthropologists" (p. 5). Missionaries' energies on this question were directed toward the persuasion of expatriate authorities, and their arguments often contributed to debates about the status of Africans that were taking place in Europe. For example, the argument that African languages were as complex as European languages was used to demonstrate that Africans were not racially inferior to Europeans (Irvine, 1989).

Missionary protest against the use of English in education was linked to larger beliefs about the integrity of African cultures, as well as a significant degree of distrust of the European-educated African, the so-called "trousered African" (Mamdani, 1996). Many missionaries and educationists involved in this debate expressed both respect for African cultures and regret for the negative impact of European colonialism on those cultures.

At the 1926 Le Zoute Conference, a gathering of the leaders of Christian missions to Africa, the value of "the African as a man [sic]" was affirmed, and doubt was expressed as to "the desirability of imposing European institutions on Africans instead of developing their own" (Smith, 1926, pp. 13-14). However, neither opposition to English instruction nor support for English instruction was unanimous. For example, de Vries (2004) reports on an acute division in the Kom community's reaction to mission schools. While Catholic education was warmly received by the religiously converted, the non-Catholic were deeply wary of surrendering their children to the white men, seeing education as deeply ideological. Arguing on behalf of the demonstrated desire of African parents for education in the language spoken by the colonial powers, Smith (1926) describes the pro-English sentiment of many educators at the time:

> The African wants to learn English—indeed this is clearly why he clamours for education ... any attempt to adopt the vernacular as the medium of instruction would meet with the strong opposition of certain classes of literate Africans who would feel that the door of opportunity was slammed in the face of their children. (p. 68)

Indeed, this was a highly accurate reading of the reality for African parents. Keen to advance in the colonial African context, parents looked to European language education as a primary means to this end. According to Adejunmobi (2004), "[P]arents wanted an education that would enable their children to compete for the best paying jobs in the colonial administration or set up business independently of European control" (pp. 9-10). Missionary education was, therefore, not always imposed on unwilling locals. Certain segments of the local community were even empowered by English education. However, African parents were also aware of the potentially socially adverse effects of English education, such as the production of an African elite that was ill suited to its local communities and alienated from it. Roy-Campbell (2001) describes a similar situation in colonial Tanganyika, in which English was valued over Kiswahili: "By the end of the colonial period, Kiswahili remained in the minds of many Africans a second class language, while English was the prestigious language of modernization, the conveyor of knowledge" (p. 57). The source of this attitude lay in the political, economic, and social realities of the colonial state, regardless of the opinions of the English speaking missionaries.

Along with the desire for an education that would provide real opportunities for their children, African parents had more political motivations for demanding education as well. Inviting missionaries to set up schools in their areas was a way to protect their land from possible takeover by the colonial government, since it now fell under the jurisdiction of the missionaries. The Africans thus used schooling as a strategy for protecting and advancing their interests within the constraints of colonial rule (Summers, 2002).

However, in analyzing the development of African education, Summers (2002) observes that even though African parents might have been unanimous in their demands for education in English, their sons and daughters were not always in agreement with them. That the sons and daughters were not as enthusiastic about schooling as parents is understandable, given the significant expectations on them for carrying out physical work at schools and the threat of corporal punishment.

Still, formal education in English was in Africa to stay. In this environment of parental demand for English-language education, Christian missions in Africa eventually came to recognize that communities would tolerate Christian presence and influence only if the missionaries offered a Western-type education that featured English as well as other concepts such as "time discipline, literacy, arithmetic, and other essentials of European culture, ranging from the new forms of cleanliness to the complex codes of manners, and dignity inherent in furniture and clothes" (Summers, 2002, p. 87). Mission schools thus had little choice but to oblige African parents and communities, as well as government, in this regard. The missionaries lost their campaign for local languages at this point, a fact that is often missed in historical analysis of language policy. Adejunmobi (2004) remarks that:

> In hindsight, one cannot but be struck by the irony of the fact that subsequent generations of Africans have tended to attribute sole responsibility for the prominence of English in the school system to the missionaries, in much the same way as they have held missionaries responsible for privileging the humanities over instruction in vocational skills in colonial schools. (p. 11)

This loss of local-language instruction may not have been recognized at the time, but it was nevertheless significant to the quality of learning that took place in schools. Most of the reading material used in the teaching and reading of English was foreign to Africans' cultural traditions and ways of thinking, and reading in English came to be treated as a technical exercise rather than an intentional effort to produce meaning. Nor was the shift to English purely linguistic in nature; it was also characterized by replacing African construal of learning and teaching with Western norms. Western education also introduced an emphasis on individualism, undermining the communal practices of African societies. The individualizing practices of this form of education are evident today:

> Teachers call on students to perform both privately and publicly without assistance from their peers: they are required to write exams, do assignments, and speak out in front of others. Teachers may take steps to prevent collective or collaborative efforts to ensure that any information supplied within such interactions can be attributed exclusively to the demonstrator. School personnel diligently supervise tests and exams. They penalize students during testing situations for such things as talking or soliciting information. (Ryan, 1992, p. 105)

Parental demands for English-language education during the colonial period can be situated within a broader context of the general orientation of Africans toward Western education. Africans were laying claim not only to a particular type of education but also to being treated in a manner that they thought was commensurate with their social status as educated Africans, reinforced by education in English (Summers, 2002).

The subsequent development of formal education in anglophone Africa was characterized by the establishment of

English as the standard. English fluency became the key characteristic behind the formation of a small, educated elite who could successfully negotiate the language and content of formal education and whose resulting economic and social successes stood (and still stand) in stark contrast to those of the majority of the population (Trudell, 2005b, p. 121). English was frequently used to stratify educational provision; in colonial Zimbabwe and Tanganyika, for example, highly discriminatory parallel education systems for Africans and for Whites were put in place, with language of instruction acting as a key differentiating marker (Roy-Campbell, 2001).

With independence, this trend continued. Postcolonial governments maintained and nominally extended the position of English in national education systems in terms of policy, not necessarily in terms of practice. Adegbija (1994) analyzes the postcolonial place of European languages in this way:

> Post-colonial policy makers in Africa have largely rubber-stamped or toed the line of language and educational policies bequeathed to them by the colonial masters. ... Educational systems, which have widened and extended beyond what they were in colonial days, have been further used to entrench and perpetuate the feeling of the inviolable worth of colonial languages. (pp. 33-34)

The language policies instituted in newly independent Ghana and Malawi exemplified this trend. In 1957, the independent Ghanaian government established an English-medium policy for primary education across the country. Despite subsequent recommendations from a committee of educators who were concerned that there were not enough competent primary school teachers of English to carry out the policy, the Ghanaian minister of education decided in 1963 to confirm the 1957 pro-English policy (Bamgbose, 1991, p. 114). In Malawi, the postcolonial language policy established in 1969 upheld earlier government decisions to prioritize Chichewa and English as the languages of education over the Christian missions' choices of Tumbuka and Chinyanja (Kayambazinthu, 2004, p. 110).

Professional educators and linguists have had a very limited impact on the way African governments formulate their policies and implement them, and the situation is unlikely to change. It is, therefore, more reasonable for professional educators and language educators to expend their energies on seeking to alter changes at the micro-level rather than at a macro-level (Ferguson, 2003), thus establishing a mode of operating maximally even under policies that they might not fully endorse and that may raise ethical problems for some applied linguists.

Current Policies on English and Education in Anglophone Africa

The fact that debates regarding the appropriateness of English in education are virtually nonexistent in anglophone Africa is ironic. Even more ironic is the fact that some present-day Christian teachers insist on English-only teaching. Contemporary missionaries can learn from the early sponsorship of the vernacular by early missionaries, while at the same time becoming aware that the teaching of the vernacular among early missionaries consisted largely of a transference of modes of teaching and assessment from English.

English remains embedded in the community understanding of proper education. The policy to use English in schools is reinforced by the interests of foreign donors in spreading the teaching of English, which they support through the donation of teaching materials, training of teachers, and supply of expatriate teachers and consultants (Bamgbose, 1991, p. 77). While local languages have gained entry into schools, it is with the clear understanding that English fluency is still the ultimate goal. In such situations, African languages are seen as the building blocks of transition toward English. In other words, even when African languages are used as media of instruction, a hierarchy between the languages is introduced in which English has a higher status than local languages. Psycholinguistic models of language learning, such as additive bilingualism are based on the idea that learning a second language is facilitated after consolidating the learning of one's mother tongue. Pushing aside the inherent sociolinguistic complexities of determining what constitutes one's mother tongue in heteroglossic situations in Africa and sociologically inferring from the additive bilingual model, there seems to be a subtle assertion that learning African languages is useful only as a basis for learning English.

This assumption is evident not only among government decision makers but within the research community as well. Questions being addressed have more to do with the best means of increasing access and improving English ability than with whether English is the appropriate language to use in schools. For example, Kyeyune (2004) decries the low level of English ability among Ugandan students who have studied it and used it as medium of instruction for years and recommends more intentional English instructional strategies in school (pp. 78-79). Ferguson (2003) argues that since it is unlikely that African governments will radically shift away from English, applied linguists might use their time and resources more productively by exploring ways of mitigating the effects of shifting from local languages toward English, rather than trying to convince African governments to change their pro-English policies. This perspective on English is highly pragmatic, based on awareness of the realities of globalization and the dominant position of European academic education in anglophone Africa.

Where local language use in education is promoted, it is generally based on beliefs regarding the greater effectiveness of mother tongue-medium instruction in attaining educational outcomes, such as school-leaving examinations (Benson, 2002; Trudell, 2005a). Sympathy exists in certain quarters for the use of local languages, as Kembo-Sure (2004) demonstrates in his argument for making room for bilingual education in developing an English syllabus for Kenyan schools (p. 114). Such sympathy is rooted in the ongoing vitality and dynamism of African languages, especially in popular culture and the media. Despite the relatively long history of English use in Africa, relatively few Africans (outside South Africa) speak English as their first language. The "dystopic vision of linguistic catastrophe" within which studies of the spread of English have been framed thus might be misplaced (Jacquemet, 2005).

However, what seems clear is that in anglophone Africa today the debate regarding English is by no means the purview of Christian missions or the Christian church. Powerful forces of state, community, and international agencies keep English in its dominant position in African education systems. This situation underlines the fact that language policy analysts in Africa lack an in-depth understanding of how the state makes its decisions in Africa. Researchers may complain that policy makers do not take into account their recommendations about the effects on children of learning in a language they do not fully understand, e.g., English or French. But the reality is that policy makers inhabit a world in which popular opinion is key and research evidence is of secondary importance. Levin (2005) explains:

> From a political perspective, however, evidence is only one factor that shapes decisions, and it will

often be one of the less important factors. I have had politicians tell me on various occasions that while evidence I was presenting for a particular policy might be correct, the policy was not what people believed, wanted or would accept. As Bernard Shapiro, whose experience includes a stint as Ontario Deputy Minister of Education, put it, "All policy decisions are made by leaping over the data. For politicians, what people believe to be true is much more important than what may actually be true." (p. 619)

Current Christian Institutional Perspectives on Language

In the current pro-English environment, the stances of Christian institutions regarding language vary. The Christian church, which in the vast majority of cases has become truly African owned, tends to accept use of local languages, particularly in rural areas. Regarding South Africa, for example, Kamwangamalu (2004) notes, "In general, every church [denomination] has (on a national level) a sizable representation of 10 or more languages. At the local level, especially in the rural areas, there are however many monolingual congregations" (p. 221). Urban or multilingual congregations, however, require use of a language of wider communication, whether African (such as kiSwahili in Kenya or Pidgin in anglophone Cameroon) or European. Nyati-Ramahobo (2004) notes that in Botswana, the Christian church has helped to increase the use of Setswana and English over local languages (pp. 33-35). The two are used alternately in church services and events, although Setswana is dominant in rural churches. The orientation of the African Christian church seems largely pragmatic: one uses the language(s) that can communicate best to a given congregation in a given place. It is also true that, like government leaders, denominational leaders in anglophone Africa tend to be members of the educated elite who would naturally choose English as the language of prestige.

Denominational providers of formal education in Africa today are controlled by government language policy regarding education and, therefore, take their cues from that policy. For example, Kayambazinthu (2004) notes that mission schools in Malawi are controlled by government language policy, which stipulates vernacular language use in early grades, transitioning to the use of the English and Chichewa languages (p. 99).

Non-African Christian institutions are involved to a certain extent in English-language teaching in anglophone Africa today. This activity is primarily found in denominational seminaries and Bible schools, which may still utilize non-African staff and use English as the medium of instruction. One of the major international, faith-based institutions involved in language development and language teaching in Africa is SIL International, formerly known as the Summer Institute of Linguistics. SIL's focus in Africa is almost entirely on the development of African languages, particularly the smaller and less developed languages of the continent. Given the lasting damage done to the vitality and use of African languages through the dominance of English in educational and national life, it is not surprising that SIL's language development focus does not include English at all. It seems that by its exclusion of English, SIL is trying to avoid some of the mistakes of the colonial past.

On the other hand, the enthusiasm that African populations, even those in rural areas, show for English-language fluency and literacy is not lost on SIL or its national partner organizations in anglophone Africa. In response, local-language literacy programs may include instruction in English as a foreign or second language. One such adult literacy program, offered by a Ghanaian NGO called the Ghana Institute of Linguistics, Literacy, and Bible Translation (GILLBT), consists of two terms of local-language literacy learning and two further terms of ESL and English literacy instruction (Aggor & Kofi, 2003). In other anglophone nations such as Kenya (Schroeder, 2004) and anglophone Cameroon (Gfeller, 2000), SIL supports multilingual primary education initiatives in specific rural areas. This focus on local languages draws criticism from two very different sources: those who see English as the future and consider local-language development initiatives to be detrimental to national progress and those who object to the involvement of non-Africans in language and culture change among minority African populations.

The impact of Christian institutions on English-language use and teaching in anglophone Africa today is thus neither consistent nor extensive. Compared to the impact of government language policy, community opinion, and the globalizing influences of media and education, the contribution of specifically Christian institutions adds little to the prestigious position of the English language.

Conclusion
In this chapter, we examined the historical and contemporary roles of Christian institutions in shaping the nature of English-language policy and practices in Africa. While African parents demanded education in English, missionaries were more likely to emphasize local languages. The tension between these groups regarding the use of English in educational contexts continues to be played out in contemporary anglophone Africa, where Africans engaged in language planning research are likely to continue to argue for the beneficial role of using local languages in school, while policy makers are reluctant to implement such language policies. An historical view of education and language policy in anglophone Africa is thus very helpful to understanding the place of English in African societies today.

As for the desires of African communities and parents in particular, Pennycook (2001) may well be correct in his concerns about the deleterious effects of English on local-language speaking societies. Nevertheless, it is difficult to dismiss Africans' experience and understanding of their own socioeconomic and linguistic realities and to ignore the primacy they give to English-language fluency. In addition, the continued use of local languages, combined with the continued interest in English, should lead us to question whether the "dystopic vision" of English swamping out local African languages does not require reconsideration (Jacquemet, 2005). The future of effective education in anglophone may depend on the ability of researchers, communities, and policy makers to find common ground in which linguistically contextualized learning and mastery of English are part of every child's schooling experience.

References

Adegbija, E. (1994). *Language Attitudes in Sub-Saharan Africa: A Sociolinguistic Overview*. Clevedon, UK: Multilingual Matters.

Adejunmobi, M. (2004). *Vernacular Palaver: Imaginations of the Local and Non-Native Languages in West Africa*. Clevedon, UK: Multilingual Matters.

Aggor, R. A., & Kofi, S. (2003). *Literacy: A Key to Development — the GILLBT Literacy Programme in Ghana*. Accra: Ghana Universities Press.

Bamgbose, A. (1991). *Language and the Nation*. Edinburgh, UK: Edinburgh University Press.

Benson, C. (2002). "Real and potential benefits of bilingual programmes in developing countries" *International Journal of Bilingual Education and Bilingualism,* 5(6), 303-317.

Bernstein, J. (1996). "Runyakitara: Uganda's "New"

Language" *Journal of Multilingual and Multicultural Development,* 19(2): 93-108.

Canut, C. (2002). "Perceptions of languages in the Mandingo region of Mali" In D. Long, & D. Preston (Eds.), *Handbook of Perceptual Dialectology* (pp. 33-39). Amsterdam: John Benjamins.

Chimhundu, H. (1992). "Early missionaries, and the ethnolinguistic factor during the invention of tribalism in Zimbabwe" *Journal of African History,* 33(1), 87-101.

De Vries, W. H. (2004). "The interface between prophecy as narrative and prophecy as proclamation: A study of three prophetic legends" In J. H. Ellens, D. L. Ellens, R. P. Knierim, & I. Kalimi (Eds.), *God's Word for Our World: Volume I, Biblical Studies in Honor of Simon John De Vries* (pp. 211-246). London, New York: Clark/Continuum.

Errington, J. (2001). "Colonial linguistics" *Annual Review of Anthropology, 30,* 19-39.

Fabian, J. (1986). *Language and Colonial Power.* New York: Cambridge University Press.

Ferguson, G. (2003). "Classroom code-switching in post-colonial contexts: Functions, attitudes and policies" *AILA Review,* 16(1), 38-51.

Gfeller, E. (2000). *La Société et l'Ecole face au Multilinguisme.* Paris: KARTHALA.

Jacquemet, M. (2005). "Transidiomatic practices: Language and power in the age of globalization" *Language and Communication,* 25(3), 257-277.

Jeater, D. (2007). *Law, Language, and Science: The Invention of the "Native Mind" in Southern Rhodesia, 1890-1930.* Portsmouth, NH: Heinemann.

Irvine, J. (1989). "When talk isn't cheap: language and political economy" *American Ethnologist,* 16(2), 248-267.

Kamwangamalu, N. (2004). "The language planning situation in South Africa" In R. B. Baldauf, Jr., & R. B. Kaplan (Eds.), *Language Planning and Policy in Africa, Volume 1: Botswana, Malawi, Mozambique and South Africa* (pp. 197-281). Clevedon, UK: Multilingual Matters.

Kayambazinthu, E. (2004). "The language planning situation in Malawi" In R. B. Baldauf, Jr., & R. B. Kaplan (Eds.), *Language Planning and Policy in Africa, Volume 1: Botswana, Malawi, Mozambique and South Africa* (pp. 79-149). Clevedon, UK: Multilingual Matters.

Kembo-Sure (2004). "Establishing a national standard and English language curriculum change in Kenya" In M. J. Muthwii, & A. N. Kioko (Eds.), *New Language Bearings in Africa: A Fresh Quest* (pp. 101-115). Clevedon, UK: Multilingual Matters.

Kyeyune, R. (2004). "Challenges of using English as a medium of instruction in the multilingual contexts: A view from Ugandan classrooms. In M. J. Muthwii, & A. N. Kioko (Eds.), *New Language Bearings in Africa: A Fresh Quest* (pp. 77-88). Clevedon, UK: Multilingual Matters.

Levin, B. (2005). "Improving research policy relationships: The case of literacy" In N. Bascia, A. Cummig, A. Datnow, K. Leithjwood, & D. Livingstone (Eds.), *International handbook of educational policy* (pp. 31-62). New York: Springer.

Makoni, S., & Meinhof, U. H. (2003). "Introducing applied linguistics in Africa" In S. Makoni & U. H. Meinhof (Eds.), *Africa and Applied Linguistics* (pp. 1-12). Amsterdam: John Benjamins Publishing.

Makoni, S., Smitherman, G., Ball, A. F., & Spears, A. K. (Eds.) (2003). *Black Linguistics: Language, Society,* and *Politics in Africa and the Americas*. London: Routledge.

Mamdani, M. (1996). *Citizen and Subject: Contemporary Africa and the Legacy of Late Colonialism*. Princeton, NJ: Princeton University Press.

Nyati-Ramahobo, L. (2004). "The language situation in Botswana" In R. B. Baldauf, Jr., & R. B. Kaplan (Eds.), *Language planning and policy in Africa, Volume 1: Botswana, Malawi, Mozambique and South Africa* (pp. 21-78). Clevedon, UK: Multilingual Matters.

Pennycook, A. (2001). *Critical Applied Linguistics: A Critical Introduction.* Mahwah, NJ: Erlbaum.

Pennycook, A., & Makoni, S. (2005). "The modern mission: The language effects of Christianity" *Journal of Language, Identity and Education, 4*(2), 137-157.

Ranger, T. (1995). *Are We Not Also Men? The Samkange Family and African Politics in Zimbabwe*. Cumbria, UK: James Currey.

Roy-Campbell, Z. M. (2001). *Empowerment Through Language: The African experience: Tanzania and Beyond.* Trenton, NJ/Asmara, Eritrea: Africa World Press.

Ryan, J. (1992). "Eroding Innu cultural tradition: individualization and communality" *Journal of Canadian Studies*, 26(4), 94-111.

Samkange, Reverend T. D. (1936). "Sindebele or Zulu as a standard language" *Bantu Mirror*, April 18, 1936, p. 23.

Schroeder, L. (2004). "Mother-tongue education in schools in Kenya: Some hidden beneficiaries" *Language Matters,* 35(2), 376-389.

Smith, E. W. (1926). *The Christian Mission in Africa: a*

Study Based on the Proceedings of the International Conference at Le Zoute, Belgium, September 14-21, 1926. London: International Missionary Council.

Spolsky, B. (2003). "Religion as a site of language contact" *Annual Review of Applied Linguistics,* 23, 81-95.

Summers, C. (2002). *Colonial Lessons: Africans' Education in Southern Rhodesia 1918-1940.* Oxford, UK: James Currey.

Trudell, B. (2005a). "Language choice, education and community identity" *International Journal for Academic Development,* 25(3), 237-251.

Trudell, B. (2005b). *The Power of the Local: Education Choices and Language Maintenance Among the Bafut, Kom and Nso' Communities of Northwest Cameroon.* Unpublished doctoral dissertation, University of Edinburgh, UK.

Willan, B. (1984). *Sol Plaatje: South African Nationalist, 1876-1932.* Berkeley: University of California Press.

VIII

"I am starving with no hope to survive" Southern African perspectives on pedagogies of globalization
(with Busi Makoni)

In this article we briefly describe key issues central to what Spring (2007/this issue) refers to as the "industrial-consumer paradigm" and the role of English as the global language characterized by what Harvey (1990) called "time and space compression." We also comment and provide a critique of some of its primary principles examining its relevance to Southern Africa. In view of the commentary provided, we then propose, in the latter part of the article, an alternative model of education that draws on principles of popular culture in Africa, which is a thriving area of social and artistic creativity that provides a sharp contrast to images of the total collapse of Africa and endemic violence (Barber, 1997; Brusilla, 2003; Chitando, 2002; Zeleza, 2003). The principles of popular culture will also draw its parallels from leisure studies and the role these can play in educational settings.

The article is divided into five sections. The first section is a schematic description of Spring's (2007) model and commentary, whereas the second section provides an overview of a Southern African perspective on consumerism and pedagogies of globalization. In exploring Southern African perspectives on the consumer model, we address the question of the extent to which Spring's consumer model reflects experiences from Southern Africa and the role English plays, and how pedagogies are discursively described. The third section focuses on the role of English in consumerism. In that section, we emphasize that discourses about English have tended to focus on its role in the state, and rarely in the everyday lives of those struggling to survive on the margins of society. Drawing from data on the study of cityscapes in the townships in South Africa, it is suggested that English is used for survival; sometimes playfully but artfully so.

The fourth section deals with the integration of security and education, and the last section is an outline and rationale of a proposed African educational model based on African popular culture and leisure studies. That section suggests that, paradoxically, although the main tenets of the proposed model are founded on African popular culture and leisure studies some of them resonate with the key principles identified in "traditional" African education (Boateng, 1990; Fafunwa, 1974) and may echo descriptions of education and learning that have been identified in other non-Anglo contexts (Ramanathan, 2005).

SPRING'S CONSUMER MODEL AND PEDAGOGIES OF GLOBALIZATION

Spring's (2007) industrial-consumer model is founded on the centrality of consumption in the contemporary world. The model is based on the assumption that for consumption to be successfully sustained, ideally ad infinitum, it is necessary to reinforce old consumption habits, wherever possible, while at the same time creating new needs for both young and old consumers. Consumption (and its converse wastage) is a key principle in an industrial–consumer model. It is not only personal but is also political, and it is at times used to engender a sense of nationalism. It is important to stress that in the 18th and 19th centuries consumption was the "hallmark illness" (Sontag, 1978) of the first coming of capitalism; and, by the end of 20th century, in a sense it had become the defining characteristic of modernity. The emergence of consumption as a site for crafting society and identity is intimately related to the changing conditions of work under contemporary conditions (Comaroff & Comaroff, 2002).

Within the industrial–consumer model, English plays an important role as it is one of the key commodities for servicing the global economy (Spring, 2007). Unlike in previous centuries, communities are now opting to learn English, and it is not imposed on them. Spring, citing evidence drawn mainly from Asia, suggests that families and communities are volunteering to learn and be taught in English, in which case, English cannot therefore be said to be imposed on them.

SOUTHERN AFRICAN PERSPECTIVES ON CONSUMERISM AND PEDAGOGIES OF GLOBALIZATION

Discursively, consumption in South Africa is best encapsulated in slogans such as *"local is lekker."* Lekker is an Afrikaans word for *good*. It seems that the slogan has its roots in a government-sponsored campaign called Proudly South African. This campaign encourages consumption of locally produced products. However, one of the unintended but not officially discouraged effects of this campaign and its accompanying consumption slogan is the tendency to define in a pejorative manner non-South African goods. Such goods are referred to as *amaFongKong* (Fong Kong is a blend of *false*, and Hong Kong; ama- is a plural prefix in Nguni languages) as opposed to the *real makoya* (authentic locally produced products and not false imitations of brand names). Makoya is drawn from Tsotsitaal, a variety of language associated with South African youth, thus rendering the message authentic in the views of the local population because Tsotsitaal is a widely used "anti-language" (Finlayson, Calteaux, & Myers-Scotton, 1998; Halliday, 1978). In this regard, foreign produced products are often construed in the public imaginaire as non-authentic, and the only real thing is one rooted in the South African geographical and political production space. Yet, although we are living in an authenticity "discursive regime," the notion of authenticity is complex and contradictory (Coupland, 2003; Heller, 2003; Taylor, 1991).

The consumption slogans underwritten by authenticity inadvertently contribute to the creation of a xenophobic discursive regime when they migrate to human beings and are used to distinguish between those who are South African and those who are not and are derogatorily referred to as *amakwerekwere* (those who chirp like birds). This word is claimed, etymologically, to have originated from Sesotho implying limited competence reflecting a compromised capacity to engage in intercourse with authochotonmous society (Comaroff & Comaroff, 2002). The term amakwerekwere is, however, rarely if at all used to refer to Whites who are non-South Africans, although it is used by White South Africans to refer to Blacks who are non-South Africans. Thus, it seems likely that the discourses of consumption parallel and feed into xenophobic discourses in South Africa despite the fact that the foreigners from neighboring countries and further afield have worked in South African industries and farms for over one century. Xenophobia is, however, not a peculiarly South Africa problem, as the social histories of a number of African countries—notably Ghana, Nigeria, and Ivory Coast, and so forth—amply demonstrate.

The second part of Spring's (2007) consumer model deals with the centrality of English in pedagogical issues in Singapore and how English is used as an entrée into the global market. Although Spring may be correct in arguing that English plays a crucial role in servicing the industrial–consumer model, in South Africa a wide range of linguistic resources are used to promote and legitimate consumerism. Some of these resources are from official languages, whereas others include nonofficial languages such as Tsotsitaal as shown in the real makoya slogan.

What is notable in the South African experience of consumerism is that English does not play as significant a role as it does in the Asian experience described by Spring (2007). Instead, South Africa's quest for national identity is apparent in how it prides itself in its multiple languages as shown by its eleven official languages policy. The pride in the diversity of South Africa is captured through the discourses of the "rainbow nation." However, what is accomplished through the use of such discourses? The metaphor of a rainbow suggests that South Africa is a multicultural society and thus draws attention to multicultural issues. However, race and indeed social class are avoided in the image of the rainbow nation because the colors do not represent distinct cultural and racial groups (Baines, 1998). Thus, within the discourses of the rainbow nation in South Africa, race and class are remarkably occluded from its official imagination (Anderson, 1991).

The discourses about the industrial–consumer model in Spring (2007) are also compatible with some of the current discourses on language as a commodified entity that are a product of and in turn shape discourses of globalization (Duchêne & Heller, 2007). The discourses of the commodification of language may prove to be a powerful corrective measure to discourses of language rights in that such discourses facilitate a shift in language discourses from the discursive regime of rights to those of economic development, and the role of language therein (Blommaert, 2001; May, 2001).

The manifesto, "shop til you drop," which Spring (2007) highlights, may be applicable to Asian contexts and yet may carry completely different meanings when extended to southern Africa, as its significance is dependent on the viability of the economy at hand. In the Asian case that Spring describes, the notion of shopping until you drop dead is founded on the assumption that the economies are sufficiently robust and the citizens have adequate disposable income to shop. In contexts of runaway inflation, the idea of shopping til you drop means something else. In countries such as Zimbabwe in which inflation is running beyond 1,000%, the possibility of dropping dead before you shop is more likely than shopping until you drop dead. This is not to suggest that the demon of shopping has been exorcised by high inflation as Zimbabweans cross over to neighboring countries so they could shop until they drop. As shown in Figure 1, consumerism as an ideology might still be retained even when there is little to consume.

Figure 1 shows Zimbabweans packing their commodities into a bus in Johannesburg after a shopping trip. The picture was taken in December, 2006 shortly after Christmas; clearly, the shopping was not part of the usual Christmas rush experienced in many cities. In essence, the shop til you drop manifesto becomes applicable when Zimbabweans cross over to South Africa where all the goods that are not readily available in Zimbabwe are available in abundance. If the frenzy with which Zimbabweans purchase goods in South Africa is anything to go by, it appears that run away inflation in Southern Africa enhances rather than attenuates excessive consumption habits. This seems to suggest that postcolonial Africa has successfully created contexts in which excessive consumption and ostentatious display of wealth have become key features of social and individual identity rendering, ironically, the industrial–consumer model applicable in African contexts as well.

FIGURE 1 Zimbabweans packing commodities onto a trailer in Johannesburg

FIGURE 2 A Kiosk in Alexandra Township, Johannesburg

THE ROLE OF ENGLISH: FROM CONSUMERISM TO SURVIVAL

Figure 2 was taken from Alexandra Township in Johannesburg, South Africa as part of a project on the cityscapes of Southern Africa in December, 2006. Figure 2 shows an interesting use of English in that, although the kiosk is based in an urban slum where the majority of the residents hardly understand English, English is used for advertisement purposes.

"From six to sixx" refers to the times when the kiosk opens and it is founded on the South African 7-Eleven, which is a chain of stores that opens at 7 a.m. and closes at 11 p.m. An analysis of the inscriptions on the kiosk shows that *six* is spelled in two different ways in the same line. Barely visible under *six* is *sex*, written in red, which shows the radical changes in meaning when one vowel is changed and perhaps, reflecting the range of commodities on sale (i.e., *paraffin, biscuits, to sex*), all cited as commodities that are sold from *six to six*!

FIGURE 3 An old man begging with a sign: "I am starving with no hope to survive."

FIGURE 4 An old man begging with a sign in English in Johannesburg.

If Figure 2 tries to capture the visual representations of English in the underbelly of the global economy, Figures 3 and 4 show a serious effort to use English not as an international language, but as the language of begging. The quotation, "I am starving with no hope to survive," used in the title of this article was taken from the inscriptions on a placard a beggar was holding in Johannesburg in January, 2007. The placard and the use of English raise issues about resources and survival, which are central to the industrial-consumer model. English is one of the social resources that the gentleman has at his disposal to make ends meet in Johannesburg, South Africa. The picture belongs to the same genre as the one used in the title of the article, except that in Figure 2 the use of English might not reflect the same level of literacy or literary sophistication as the one from whose placard the title in the article was taken. Of course it might be worth recalling that Nelson Mandela, looking forward to his retirement, once remarked, "In a few months I will be standing by the road with a sign; 'Please help, unemployed with a new wife and a big family'" (Salopek, 1999, p. 3).

In addition to the aforementioned examples where English is used for begging, the youth are interpreting and utilizing popular culture in innovative ways. The creative ways in which they are using English and mixtures of English and African languages is evident when one analyzes the use of language written inside taxis in African cities. The following examples are drawn from Harare, the capital city of Zimbabwe (March 4, 2007):

1. The driver is instructed to run away from the police.
2. The driver is instructed not to stop at railway crossing.
3. How is your wife and my kids?
4. Front seat is for beautiful ladies only.

These inscriptions on taxis reflect the degree to which English is embedded—at least in its written form—in popular culture and is used to capture an anti-establishment position as reflected in lines 1 and 2, or capture the real or imagined social experiences of drivers as shown in sentences 3 and 4. In African taxis seating in the front seat is a special privilege, which for the driver of the taxi in line 4 is reserved for "beautiful ladies only." However, lines 3 and 4 also reflect a gendered perspective about taxis and taxi drivers in Southern Africa. Most taxi drivers are male, who, in line 4, would appreciate beautiful ladies sitting next to them in the front seat.

If English, its varieties, and mixtures of English and African languages are widely available as resources, albeit unequally in Southern Africa, this has implications for the ways in which its role is conceptualized and framed. Whether English or any language for that matter is acquired voluntarily or not is central only as a direct result of envisaging the relation of hegemony to exist between languages rather than between social agents who are empowered or disempowered under specific conditions of language. "Language is objectified in the politics of discourse, but it may be the imposition on others of discourses about language rather than language itself and practices to do with language that constitute the hegemonic relation" (Fardon & Furniss, 1994, p. 16). The way in which the imposition of English is discursively framed can be challenged in that both what Pennycook (2007) called the *homogeny* and *heterogeny* positions are inadvertently drawing attention to the role of imperial powers in shaping and influencing the politics of language and the linguistic practices of countries in the socalled periphery of the global economy.

    The objectification in the conceptualization of language evident in the separation of language from culture and society is one of the central tropes of African sociolinguistics that unfortunately does not serve the objectives of an African sociolinguistics which seeks to effect change. By proposing a perspective which defines language as social practice, as a form of social action, as a resource that (albeit) circulates in unequal and multiple ways in communities leads to the conclusion that the hierarchies are not inherently linguistic, but rather social and political. Construing language as social practice enables one to re-envision how one can change things, what sites of action may act to intervene in (Duchêne & Heller, 2007). If language is separated from society, the point of intervention is language, and this inadvertently leads to a logical but socially ineffective strategy (i.e., an intervention into language with the belief that this will change society). If language is taken to be part of society and not a stand-alone element outside society, possible alternative strategies suggest themselves. In this regard, the intervention has to be at the level of society, and so forth, and not begin and end at the level of language.

Although there is a considerable amount of attention drawn to the role of imperial ex-colonial powers such as Britain, France, and the current superpower, the United States, the threatening presence of China in African Affairs and (that of India on the horizon) is gradually dawning on African scholarship and popular press as reflected in the headline of the McCarthy-Tribune *News Service*, which posted an article entitled "African Nations Wary of China's Aid" on Tuesday, February 20, 2007 commenting thus:

> Africans are increasingly wary of Chinese involvement within African affairs in part because of the manner in which China's massive exportation of "cheap" commodities are adversely affecting local African industries, and the long term contracts which African regimes have signed with China guaranteeing China secure access to oil and other natural resources (p. 13)

The credibility of China is undermined by its overt support of African governments with dubious human rights records such as Sudan. The Chinese government's self-serving interests are apparent in their silence up until now on Darfur, which has experienced the worst ongoing humanitarian crisis. Darfur in Southern Sudan has been a focus of international aid and yet China has been conspicuous in its silence on issues related to Darfur. Perhaps this has been influenced by the fact that Sudan is a key supplier of Chinese crude oil. Sudan exports half its crude oil to China. China has also purchased 45 per cent shares in an oilfield offshore in Nigeria. It declared 2006 the African year. Forty African heads of state were invited to Beijing and 2,500 "partnerships" agreements were signed ranging from aid and training to investment in commerce, and so forth.

Although African scholarship has tended to be fixated with the abiding legacy of European colonialism, it has consequently not paid adequate attention to emerging colonial threats. It is important for African scholars to learn something from a chameleon (i.e., its capacity to have one eye looking backward while the other is "resolutely looking ahead at the same time"; Chitando, 2002, p. 96). Thus, Africa needs to keep a watchful eye on China as a possible future imperial power. In fact, the impact of the Chinese involvement in African affairs as a potential imperial power (a status the Chinese government vehemently rejects) and the possible role and status of Chinese within the African linguistic scene still needs to be analyzed. Currently, there are plans to set up Confucian language learning centers in which Africans are taught to read and speak Chinese. It is not clear at the moment whether this will result in a widespread acquisition of Chinese because research has shown that some imperial powers have not sought to impose their own languages on Africa, whereas others have.

The model that China, if it turns out to be an African imperial power, opts for will only become clear in the long term. It is, however, possible to speculate that the Chinese may not be anxious to promote the use of Chinese in African countries because it may be more beneficial for them to have Africans purchase some of their commodities, such as cheap electrical appliances, and to have Chinese clothes flooding the market than to teach Chinese because electrical appliances and clothes are more lucrative to the Chinese as commodities than promoting Chinese as a lingua commodity. However, because the labels on clothes and the manuals for the electrical appliances are written in Chinese, it might very well be beneficial to the Chinese to commodify the Chinese language as well. Similarly, if these items are to be massively produced locally by big Chinese business, African workers might need some working knowledge of Chinese which again may mean China has to commodify not just the goods but Chinese as well. Because the Chinese goods are likely to be marketed globally, this may lead to the emergence of Chinese as an international language with possibly an African variety.

INTEGRATING EDUCATION AND ECONOMIC NEEDS IN SOUTHERN AFRICA

Spring (2007) reports on how Singapore has attempted to integrate education and economic needs in the industrial-consumer model. Similarly, South Africa has attempted to integrate education and economic needs through the National Qualifications Framework, which is a national resource representing a national effort at integrating education and training into a unified structure of recognized qualifications to encourage lifelong learning. Working hand in hand with the South African Qualifications Authority, the Department of Labor has promulgated two pieces of legislation that aim at skills development in order to cope with technological development, innovation, and globalization. First, the Skills Development Act (1999/2000) aims to develop and improve the skills of the South African workforce. Because the global economy requires a different set of skills, existing skills need to be realigned through several reskilling initiatives as mandated by the Skills Development Act. Second, the Skills Development Levies Act prescribes how employees should contribute to the national skills fund for purposes of skills development especially in areas that have been identified as scarce skills. In South Africa the thrust has not only been on reskilling but on the development of what are defined specifically as scarce skills, particularly among the previously disadvantaged populations.

To what extent, then, is Spring's (2007) consumer model different or similar to the southern African experience? Clearly, the above discussion on consumerism in parts of southern Africa, the role of English in pedagogies of globalization and the integration of education and economic needs resonate, to some extent, with southern African experiences, although there are differences largely influenced by contextual factors. Thus, we now propose an alternative model of education which draws on principles of African popular culture — a thriving area that serves as an antidote to images of total collapse of Africa and endemic violence (Barber, 1997; Brusilla, 2003; Chitando, 2002; Zeleza, 2003). The following section enumerates key principles of the proposed model of African education.

EDUCATIONAL MODEL BASED ON POPULAR CULTURE:
"TEACHER DON'T TEACH ME NONSENSE"

Most of the educational models in language teaching currently in circulation in Africa have been informed by research in sociolinguistics, psycholinguistics, and rarely by studies in African popular culture and leisure. However, there have been serious efforts to design models of African education drawing on indigenous knowledge (Reagan, 2006). The educational model we are proposing is based on popular culture as an attempt to capture contemporary African experiences as a possible template for framing educational models in Africa.

Despite the burgeoning nature of research in African popular culture and leisure as an area of study, there has not been a substantial number of systematic efforts to explore its relevance in the crafting of educational models as reflected in research into hip hop in other parts of the globe (Alim, 2007; Morgan, 2005; Norton & Vanderheyden, 2004; Pennycook, 2007). Because African popular culture and leisure is a thriving area of development and creativity, perhaps drawing insights and parallels from it might invigorate African education. The central tenets of an educational model based on African popular culture and leisure studies might neutralize distinctions in the following pairs of terms:

1. Work and play.
2. Imitation and creativity.
3. Novice and expert.
4. Membership and affiliation to multiple as opposed to a single community.

To revitalize the youth's interest in education, curriculum development should be based on areas that are of interest to them and thus neutralizing the distinction between play, learning, and work. If formal education draws from African popular culture and leisure, it will be construed more as play and not as a chore hence increasing the motivation of African youth and perhaps reducing the drop-out rate. Perhaps it is by drawing on activities such as popular culture that the youths are actively taking part in that distinctions between work and play are neutralized and thus can avoid the scathing attacks by one of Nigeria's musicians and icons of social and political rebellion, Fela Kuti, encapsulated in his song, "Teacher Don't Teach Me Nonsense."

The new forms of education that are produced through strategies of playfulness, constructive imitation produce what du Bois (1903) called "double voice," I which might enable Africans to face the challenges of contemporary Africa. The playfulness or artfulness enables African youth to live between spaces engendering a sense of liminality and thus live simultaneously between spaces, one of the consequences of globalization.

Unexpectedly, popular culture is also relevant to the industrial–consumer model but in unanticipated ways. According to Dolby (2006), the youths are "voracious consumers and producers of popular culture initially through imitation" (p. 32), but subsequently through creative adaptation. This means that the youths are actively producing popular culture and not only passively consuming it, and in some cases seek to accomplish individuality through consumption (Brusilla, 2003, p. 227). The youths are interpreting and utilizing popular culture in innovative ways. The capacity to utilize in novel ways the material that the youths are exposed to is characteristic of Africa's extraversion (i.e., "the ability to draw in and creatively absorb materials from outside in order to fuel local contexts and projects"; Barber, 1997, p. 6). It is this extraversion and creative imitation that should form one of the key principles of African education. In fact, the processes involved in extraversion are captured well by Samper (2004):

> Culture brokers acquire local cultural capital from their ability to decontextualise and deterritorialise local forms and meanings, blend them with global texts, and then re-embed them into local discourse in ways which are artful, playful, ironic, mimetic and reflexive. (p. 38)

From such a perspective, if the capacity of youth to utilize information in new and novel ways is exploited, then educationally we may be able to minimize the frequent complaints about the tendency of African students to simply repeat information verbatim or choral responses (Ramanathan, 2005). Because the youths are likely to be intimately familiar with various aspects of popular culture, perhaps more so than their elderly teachers, it radically changes the notion of expertise, and consequently alters education from being teacher fronted and gives the notion of life long learning an additional meaning particularly for teachers.

CONCLUSION

In this article we have sought to propose an educational model in Africa founded on African popular culture and leisure. We focused on African popular culture and leisure because of its dynamic and continuously evolving character, and how it has been able to work within traditions while at the same time radically changing some aspects of the traditions. Our argument is that we need to integrate other disciplines to revitalize youths' interests in education.

REFERENCES

Alim, H. S. (2007). "Critical hip hop language pedagogies: Combat, consciousness, and cultural politics of communication. *Journal of Language, Identity and Education*, 6(2): 161-176.

Anderson, B. (1991). *Imagined communities: Reflections on the origin and spread of nationalism*. London: Verso.

Baines, G. (1998). "The rainbow nation? Identity and nation building in post-apartheid South-Africa" *Mots Pluriels, 7*. Retrieved March 10, 2007, from http://www.arts.uwa.edu.au/MotsPluriels/MP798gb.html

Barber, K. (1997). *Readings in African popular culture*. London: The International African Institute School of Oriental and African Studies.

Blommaert, J. (2001). "Asmara Declaration as a sociolinguistic problem: Notes in scholarship and linguistic rights. *Journal of Sociolinguistics*, 5, 131–142.

Boateng, F. (1990). "African traditional education: A tool for intergenerational communication" In M. Asante & K. Asante (Eds.), *African culture rhythms of unity* (pp. 109–123). Trenton, NJ: Africa World Press.

Brusilla, J. (2003). *"Local music, not from here" The discourse of World Music examined through three Zimbabwean case studies: The Bhundu Boys, Virginia Mukwesha and Sunduza*. Helsinki, Finland: Society for Ethnomusicology Publications.

Chitando, E. (2002). *Singing culture: A study of gospel music in Zimbabwe*. Uppsala, Sweden: Nordiskia Afrikainsteinstuitet.

Comaroff, J., & Comaroff, J. (2002). "Alien nation,zombies, immigrants and a millennium capital" *South Atlantic Quarterly, 101,* 780–803.

Coupland, N. (2003). "Sociolinguistic authenticities: Contextualizing the authentic speaker. *Journal of Sociolinguistics, 7,* 417–431.

Dolby, N. (2006). "Popular culture and public space: The possibilities of cultural citizenship" *African Studies Review, 49*(3), 31–49.

du Bois, W. (1903). *The souls of Black folk.* New York: Dover.

Duchêne, A., & Heller, M. (2007). "Discourses of endangerment: Sociolinguistics, globalization and social order. In M. Heller & A. Duchêne (Eds.), *Discourses of endangerment: Interest and ideology in the defense of languages* (pp. 1–13). London: Continuum.

Fafunwa, B. (1974). *A history of education in Nigeria.* London: Allen & Unwin.

Fardon, R., & Furniss, G. (eds.) (1994). "Introduction: Frontiers and boundaries, African languages as political environment" In R. Fardon & G. Furniss (Eds.), *African languages, development and the state* (pp.1–29). London: Routledge.

Finlayson, R., Calteaux, K., & Myers-Scotton, C. (1998). "Orderly mixing and accommodation in South Africa" *International Journal of Sociolinguistics, 3,* 395–420.

Halliday, M. (1978). *Language as social semiotic.* London: Edward Arnold.

Harvey, D. (1990). *The condition of postmodernity.* Cambridge, England: Blackwell.

Heller, M. (2003) "Globalization, the new economy, and the commodification of language and identity" *Journal of Sociolinguistics, 7,* 473–492.

May, S. (2001). *Language and minority rights*. Harlow, UK: Longman.

Morgan, M. (2005). "After ... word! The philosophy of the hip hop battle" In D. Darby & T. Shelby (Eds.), *Hip hop and philosophy: Rhyme 2 reason* (pp. 205–211). Chicago, IL: Open Court.

Norton, B., & Vanderheyden, K. (2004). "Comic book culture and second language learners. In B. Norton & K. Toohey (Eds.), *Critical pedagogies and language learning* (pp. 201–221). Cambridge, England: Cambridge University Press.

Pennycook, A. (2007). *Global Englishes and transcultural flows*. London: Routledge.

Ramanathan, V. (2005). "Rethinking language planning and policy from the ground up: Refashioning institutional realities and human lives" *Current Issues in Language Planning,* 6(2), 89–101.

Reagan, T. (2006). *Non-western educational traditions*. Mahwah, NJ: Lawrence Erlbaum Associates.

Salopek, P. (1999). "Mandela stresses success, struggle" *Chicago Tribune*, February 6, 1999, p. 3.

Samper, D. (2004). "Africa is still our mama. African identities: Kenyan rappers, youth identity and the revitalization of traditional values. *African Identities,* 2, 37–51.

Sontag, S. (1978) *Illness as metaphor*. New York: Farrar, Straus & Giroux.

Taylor, C. (1991). *The ethics of authenticity*. Cambridge, MA: Harvard University Press.

Zeleza, P. T. (2003). "The creation and consumption of leisure: Theoretical and methodological considerations" In P. T. Zeleza & C. R. Veney (Eds.), *Leisure in urban Africa* (pp. vii–xli). Trenton, NJ: Africa World Press.

Gerontolinguistics

IX

"They talk to us like children"
Language and intergenerational discourse in first-time encounters in an African township

Abstract
This paper analyses language discourse in first-time encounters between young and old women in an African township. Forms of address, stories and complaints are analysed in terms of generational differences and similarities in identity ascription. Young women identify themselves on the basis of their ethnic membership and class, while old women do so on the basis of family relations and implied ethnic membership, which can be gleaned from their name and place of birth or origin. The discourse is marked by frequent complaints by old women to young women about the youth. Some complaints may be interpreted as masked forms of bragging. Old women complain that "they [the youth] talk to us like children," but their words were initially used by the youth to describe old people. Within their use of language old women try to reinforce traditional power to withstand youth power and to retain some influence, even within non-familial intergenerational encounters.

Introduction
This paper analyses the use of language by old and young women in first-time encounters in an African township in post-apartheid South Africa. As far as the author is aware, no studies have been conducted on this topic in South Africa. The literature on the topic is predominantly from Western countries. Further, the majority of analyses of the discourse of older persons has been quantitative and from a psycholinguistic approach (see e.g. Coupland, Coupland & Giles, 1992).

Much of the psycholinguistic research has been fraught with methodological problems, and the results have been inconsistent and difficult to interpret. The research has been influenced by a deficit model which seeks to investigate the extent to which the comprehension and speech production abilities of older persons, particularly in the areas of syntax and vocabulary, decline with advancing age. Hamilton (1994) argues that psycholinguistic studies have overlooked how the expectations and communicative reactions of a healthy speaker shape the language of an older person who is being assessed. Coupland *et al.* (1992) point out that isolating the effects of age among subjects separated by at least two decades is extremely demanding as it involves controlling for a host of factors, including education, life history, motivation and the subject's intelligence. A lesson from the psycholinguistic studies is that it may be prudent to investigate the discourse of older persons by analysing typical discursive practices which include forms of address, self-identification and complaints.

Forms of address
According to Wood and Kroger (1993: 264) forms of address superficially appear mundane but the forms in fact have special pragmatic functions: they open the communicative act and set the tone of the conversations which are to follow.

The forms of address used in conversations between people who meet for the first time are particularly important in signalling either the distance or the degree of solidarity developing between the conversationalists. A comparison of the forms of address used in the interaction demonstrates the dynamics involved. For example, a predominant usage of group over personal names reflects the importance attached to conforming to group norms. (Groups may be gender or ethnic based.) Hence an old woman is expected to behave like an old woman and a young woman to behave like a young woman in the interaction (Raum, 1973; De Kadt, 1994).

Kinship and generational identities
Identity is a transitive phenomenon. To realise one's identity a person needs to identify with someone, some group or something else. Individuals have a range of identities. For example, older persons may gravitate towards or distance themselves from what they perceive to be elderly group norms. The identities may be organized along a number of dimensions, including gender, age, religion, ethnicity and kinship. All identities are not necessarily activated at the same time or, to use Giddens' (1991) words, identities which are "brought along" are not necessarily always "brought about." Coupland *et al.* (1992) investigated how old people activate different identities depending on whether they are interacting with peer older persons or relatively young conversationalists.

    Changes in identity can also occur within a single interaction. The variability is permissible within the constraints that are negotiable within an interactional event. In urban settings individuals may appropriate different types of discourse (cf. Rampton, 1995a); for example, older persons may appropriate ways of talking associated with younger persons, or with persons having a particular profession or belonging to a particular religion.

However, there are two major problems inherent in this approach to self-identification. First, the approach implies that the identity which an individual ascribes to himself/ herself, or has ascribed in an interaction, remains constant. This paper therefore seeks to examine some of the changes which occur within an interactional event, which suggest that an individual's identity is continually changing. Second, the approach claims that the central organizing principle is the notion of the self as the basis on which identity is constructed. An emphasis on individual identity downplays the extent to which "relations are structured by group identities" (De Kadt, 1994). Group identities are particularly important in intergenerational encounters since one "relates as a young man to an older man, as a child to a parent, etc." (De Kadt, 1994: 105).

Intergenerational discourse
The literature on intergenerational discourse has been strongly influenced by American constructs of communication. Central to these studies has been a simplistic notion of the self as speaker and hearer. A number of critiques have pointed out this weakness, notably Hsu (1985). Scollon and Scollon (1992) have more recently argued against what they call "American ontological individualism," whereby "... the individual has a primary reality whereas society is a second order, ... furthermore... even in the anthropological and sociological sciences, culture and society are seen as being built up out of the association of individuals, not as primary realities in themselves" (1992: 334).

Studies on intergenerational discourse, particularly those conducted in Europe and America, may not be directly appropriate to a cultural context in which the notion of a collective is extremely powerful. The research conducted by

Coupland and his associates into the role of "painful self-disclosure" in intergenerational discourse, because of the impact of ontological individualism on their thinking, fails to realise that in some cases "the person giving voice to the words may not be the author of the words. In such a case the source is composite of [at least] two persons" (Coupland *et al.,* 1992: 47). What is required is a more complex model of interaction which goes beyond the "straightjacket of first and second person" (Levinson, quoted in Scollon & Scollon, 1992: 233). To avoid some of the pitfalls of the American and European studies of communication, it is necessary to draw a distinction between individualistic and collectivistic conceptualisation of the self (Tracy, 1990). For example, there is a subtle but important distinction between giving voice to somebody's words and quoting; in the latter instance the person giving voice to the words is aware that the words are not his/hers and publicly acknowledges this, but in the former case the individual is giving voice to a collective experience which he/she feels part of, and to which he/she has a legitimate claim.

Complaints
The discourse of old people tends to be characterized by complaints, particularly when it is about young people, or directed at them. Cattell (1996) defines complaints as "... multivocal or multidimensional, simultaneously holding several meanings, fulfilling several needs, and/or having one or more intended results.... Complaints can be expressions of person-environment dissonance, or the sense of unease that follows from being in an environment in which one feels more or less like a stranger ..." The person-environment dissonance creates an environment conducive to complaints. In South Africa this dissonance may arise from the social and political changes that are taking place, whereby the black African youth have become empowered through the signifi-

cant role which they played in the politics of the country since the 1960s, particularly their political agitation towards the end of the apartheid era; however, older Africans were not empowered to a comparable degree. Since the April 1994 first democratic elections the youth have become yet further empowered; again, this has not been the case with older Africans.

An analysis of forms of address, self-identification and complaints in first-time encounters between old and young African women is made within the context of these rapid social and political changes in the country.

The study
Aims
The aims of the study were to investigate the nature and type of language used in first-time encounters between old and young African women. An effect of modernization has been changes in the traditional roles played by old women; for example, old women are no longer as responsible for the socialization of young women as they were in the past—a role which previously accorded them considerable influence. Some old women may indeed feel that they are unable to exercise as much influence as they were able to in the past. If this is true, Cattell's argument is valid that complaints arise in situations of "person-environment dissonance"; in such cases it would be natural to expect complaints to arise in intergenerational discourse because of a discrepancy between the power which old women would expect to wield and that which they will wield. Hence the study aimed to analyse what older people complain about, as well as a relationship between complaints and other types of speech acts such as bragging. In some cases the acts of complaining and bragging may fulfil multiple functions, e.g. they may function as a complaint and be an exercise in "complaint administration."

The study was conducted in late 1994 and early 1995 —a time of radical change in South Africa, when a division between the young and the old was becoming more marked.

Method

Ten women participated in five meetings (n = 50), which are referred to in this paper as "first-time encounters." Five women were "old" and five were "young". The old women were in their mid to late seventies and all were social pensioners. They were all recruited at a senior citizens' centre in Guguletu, a predominantly African residential area of Cape Town, The .women attend the centre five days a week where they are provided a meal, recreation and health support. The old subjects were all unimpaired and relatively healthy.

The young women were all in their twenties, and were relatively well-educated and studying part-time towards obtaining a postgraduate degree. Two of the young women were employed as junior teaching staff members at the University of the Western Cape (UWC) and three worked in the publishing field.

The meetings were held at the seniors' centre in Guguletu. At each meeting five old and five young women were paired. They were advised that the purpose of the meeting, or pairing was for them to get to know one other (Coupland, Coupland, Giles & Wiemann, 1988). Each woman was told that she would meet a woman of a different generation for the first time. It was explained that the purpose of the study was to observe the interaction between each pair of women.

Following on an earlier study by Coupland *et al.* (1988), the study was designed as an open-ended and exploratory investigation of talk between generations in a controlled and relatively formal setting. It was expected that the study would yield data suitable for a discourse analysis of complaints, stories and forms of address.

Recording
The conversations between the pairs of subjects were tape recorded and the recordings subsequently transcribed. The subjects agreed to have the conversations tape recorded on condition that they could afterwards listen to the recordings. The visible presence of a tape recorder had an unexpected effect on the old subjects. It was initially anticipated that these subjects might be reluctant to talk because of the presence of the tape recorder and that it would stifle vernacular elderly talk. However, it was found that the recorder actually stimulated rather than stifled talk, particularly among the old subjects who in their life times had never listened to their voices (cf. Milroy & Milroy, 1980).

The conversations each lasted between 30 and 40 minutes. The subjects spoke in Xhosa, the African language mainly spoken in the Western Cape province. Following on the conversations, retrospective commentary was obtained from the old subjects and recorded. The retrospective commentary was of about 15-minutes duration. Retrospective commentary was introduced to triangulate the analysis, and involved playing back the recorded conversations to the subjects and asking them for their reactions and comments. In the majority of cases, the retrospective commentaries were played back to the subjects about two weeks after they were recorded (cf. Erickson & Schultz, 1982; Rampton, 1995a). Triangulation is a research technique used to gather data from several sources to enable an investigator to arrive at a more reliable interpretation of a situation. The use of a triangulation strategy meant that the analysis did not only rely on the recorded conversations but could also use information from other sources to substantiate the findings.

The transcripts of the recordings and the retrospective commentary were subsequently translated from Xhosa into English for the purpose of analysis. The transcriptions were treated as documents which would provide insight into the use of language in the first-time encounters between the young and the old women (cf. Taylor, 1992).

Analysis
The analysis focussed on forms of address, the construction of identities and the nature of the complaints in the discourse. As such, the analysis went further than the analyses of Coupland *et al.* (1992) which focussed on discourse processes in painful self-disclosure.

Findings
Forms of address and the construction of identities
The extract below describes a conversational opening between a young woman (YW) and an old woman (OW). The young subject, referred to as YW1, is a staff member at the University of the Western Cape. The old woman (OW1) was involved in setting up the senior citizens' centre in Guguletu.

YW1: *Makhulu mandithi ndingu P ndisuka kuTsolo e Transkei. Ndisebenza eUWC. (Grandma, let me say I am P. I'm coming from Tsoio in Transkei. I'm working at UWC.)*
OW2: *Igama Iam nguS. Ndiyintombika V Maseko. (My name is S. I'm the daughter of V. Maseko.)*
YW1: *Maseko*
OW1: *Maseko*
YW1: *Ei*
OW1: *Ndanditshate no Mr Mgola. (I was married to Mr Mgola.)*

YW1: Identifies herself in Xhosa by name and the region which she comes from.

Greetings and self-identification are an obligatory preliminary phase of first-time encounters among Xhosa speakers.

The greetings and self-identification may be expected to be initiated by a young person and will occur in most intergenerational encounters. By identifying herself as coming from Tsoio in the Transkei, the young woman implicitly described herself (ethnically) as being a Xhosa speaker. To define and hence to identify herself, in addition to her ethnicity, she described her professional affiliation, i.e. she works at UWC. By referring to her profession as a university teacher, the young woman described her social class. A tendency to construct one's identity in terms of implied ethnicity and social class is typical of most young Xhosa women.

The old subjects on the other hand described themselves first in terms of their ethnicity, which may be inferred from their places of birth, before describing themselves in terms of their social relations. No mention was made of their social class, unlike in the case of the young women.

The following extract is from a conversation between an old woman (OW2) and a young woman (YW2).

OW2: *I was born at Peddi and moved to Qoboqobo where I got married. I'm Mrs Ratshi.*

The extract illustrates how the old woman (OW1) and the young woman (YW2) in the first extract differently constructed their identity. Subtle differences were also apparent between widowed and non-widowed women. The old women whose husbands were still living, or who had died and the women had remarried, defined themselves by using their husband's name: e.g. *I'm Mrs Rhatshi* (OW2). They only disclosed their father's name when explicitly asked to do so in a conversation, unlike the widowed woman (OW1) who began by introducing herself by using her father's name: *I'm the daughter of V. Maseko.* In the retrospective commentary it transpired that the husband of OW1 had died in 1940 and she had not remarried.

One older woman had a dramatic way of introducing herself: she simply presented her identity card. (It is compulsory in South Africa for all citizens to carry an identity card. The card bears the name of the holder, his/her date of birth, and the district in which the holder lives.) Cattell (personal communication) points out that when strangers meet in Kenya, they are quick to ask "Where are you from?" When one meets someone, one gives one's name. The other person will ask: "From where?" One then says "Machakos," meaning "I'm Mukamba," or "I'm Muluyia." (Cf. Coplan, 1994, for a similar description of how strangers greet one another in Lesotho.)

Scollon and Scollon (1992) demonstrate how relations between generations can differ along several dimensions. The authors identify seven dimensions, among which are the pluralistic-holistic, kin-peer, and egalitarian-hierarchical dimensions. It is the hierarchical-egalitarian relationship which is most relevant in the present analysis.

When old women counsel young women about matters relating to their social life, there is a tendency for them to use terms such as "my child," which gives authority to their advice and at the same time strengthens the relationship through the use of the quasi-kinship terms. The following extract is from a conversation between an old woman and a young subject.

YW3: *You will correct me if I make a mistake. To me there is a difference between* **umendo** *and* **umthshato**.

OW3: **Umendo** *is when a girl of so and so is married to a particular family name and she has to tell herself that. When we say that someone is married she is only married to her husband.*

Intergenerational discourse is characterized by a format in which young women typically ask questions about traditional social life. For example, in the above extract the young woman wants to know something about different types of marriage. The intergenerational relationship which emerges is radically different from the one described by Coupland *et al.* (1992), where the interrogatory rights of the young over the elderly are referred to. In the retrospective commentaries the old women emphasized how the encounters had given them an opportunity to socially educate the young women. The old women relished this opportunity, in view of the circumstances in the country whereby families have become dislocated and people of different generations spend relatively little time together. Further, the youth tend to spend a great deal of time either at school or away from home, working or seeking employment, which makes it difficult for old women to socialize young women and to exercise control over them. In addition, older persons would probably view educating or advising the young as positive functions, since even though young women tend to have higher formal education, the old still retain valuable knowledge.

By using the term "my child" an old woman underscores an hierarchical relationship. The use of the term *sisi* towards the end of a conversation reflected attempts by old women to move towards a more egalitarian relationship with a young woman. (The term *sisi* is also used among older women.) However, the move is not reciprocated by young women who maintain a sense of respect and distance. Even within families relations tend to be formalized (De Kadt, 1994).

Old persons seem to be fairly prescriptive in terms of the social discourse which they will engage in and the form which they maintain the discourse should take. They are willing to depart from the norms themselves but will not allow others to do so. For example, one old woman "complained" that *llkuba abantwana abakuhloniphi bathetha nawe njengomhlobo wabo. Kuthi elo lihlazo.* (If children do not respect you they talk to you as if you are their friend ... to us [older women] it is an insult.) Perhaps what this old woman objected to was informal discourse which she may have felt undermined her power. Paradoxically, in some of the retrospective commentary the older women commented on how they had appropriated terms which were initially used by the young to describe them, such as "radio gogo" and "local police." *Gogo* is an abbreviated term for grandmother. Some older persons are called "gogos" because they are perceived by youths to talk too much.)

An interesting clash of perceptions emerged. When the old women complained that "They [the youth] talk to us like children," they were objecting to the manner in which youths engage in intergenerational talk. When the young women described the elderly as "radio gogos," they were objecting to what they perceived to be a lack of taciturnity on the part of older people. What is apparent here is that there are different perceptions about the manner and quantity of talk between people of different generations.

The elderly were also described as "local police" - a term used by some youths to describe old people whom they perceive become overly involved in other's affairs. (During the apartheid era the local police were viewed negatively since they were seen to be part of the apparatus of the apartheid regime.) The term "local police" is clearly used in an abusive way and is arguably a metaphoric description of conflict between the generations. The youth, because of their involvement in politics, were likely to be in conflict with the local police who were supporting the apartheid regime.

However, the old women frequently used the terms "radio gogo" and "local police" humorously. In the retrospective commentary, when asked about their status as local police, they laughed in response. The laughter may be interpreted as a sign that the term had been partially rehabilitated, or its pejorative connotations removed. Despite rehabilitation, the term still conjures up images of the youth's description of the elderly. Bakhtin (1981:293) comments: "There are no neutral words and forms ... all words have the 'taste' of a profession, a genre, a tendency, a party, a particular work, a particular person, a generation, an age group, a day and hour. Each word tastes of the context and contexts in which it has lived its socially charged life."

However words do not have a single life, as they can be appropriated by new groups and assume a new life. The appropriation of youthful terms in elderly discourse is an instance of "crossing." Rampton (1995a: 280) defines crossing as focussing on code alternation by people who are not accepted members of the group associated with the second language (or the variety) which they employ. In this instance terms which were previously used by the youth to describe older persons in a negative way, are used in a positive manner by the old women.

In the retrospective commentary one of the issues which frequently emerged was how the youth no longer "listens" to the elderly. To listen in Xhosa, and indeed in most African languages, carries a meaning which goes beyond simply paying attention to what the other person is saying. If a parent complains that a child does not listen, he/she is alleging that the child is disobedient.

As part of their social resistance to what they perceive as increasing youth power, the elderly may have taken the sting out of the abuse of some terms. The process of social rehabilitation of words which previously had negative connotations is usually initiated by people or groups which were the targets of the abuse. The process of "semantic inversion," as Smitherman (1995: 19) terms it, is fairly widespread—particularly in situations where there is an asymmetrical power relationship between groups with the dominant groups assuming the right to name the less powerful group. Makoni (1995) shows how the term "kaffir" now carries with it a mark of solidarity when used by and among black South Africans. (The term was used as a racist marker under the apartheid regime.)

The process of rehabilitation of words is never a complete process; for example, some terms used by the young to describe the old may be regarded as abusive by older individuals. In the study an old woman (OW3) described how young people refer to elderly people as witches, particularly if they have outlived their peers.

OW3: *Do you know that old as we are, they say we are witches? They [young people] will tell you that you are the only old woman in the street, what are you still doing, you killed your friends. That is why they burn old people's houses.*

Individual and collective identity
A characteristic feature of intergenerational discourse is how it frequently slides into narration, not about an individual's experiences but about revelations of a common history, or group experience in which "the key aspect is no longer me vs you but us and me as the repository of the past articulated through me" (Rampton, personal communication, 1995b). In his description of stories told by Basotho migrant workers working on South African mines, Coplan (1994) stresses the importance of maintaining such a distinction.

The following extract is from a conversation between OW2 and YW2. Like most black South African women of her generation, OW2 spent a considerable part of her working life as a domestic servant to white employers. Because of this employment experience, a particular genre of stories has emerged reflecting, more often than not, how white women became dependent on black maids. In the extract,

OW2 tells the young woman how she was responsible for looking after an old white woman who had been deserted by her family and friends.

OW2: *Ndakhetha eyona-yena engcomo.* *(I chose the best one* [a dress].)
YW2: *For her.*
OW2: *Ndayeka ukumnxibisa.* (*And the woman stepped* [stood up] *and I dressed her.)*
OW2: *Ndamjonga.* *(I look at her ... don't think that the strength is coming from you. We get strength from God.)*

Stories about how frail elderly white women abandoned by their families became dependent on their domestic servants do many rounds in African township discourse. In the light of these collective stories it may be argued that old women are giving voice to collective experiences. The speakers would thus be seen as a "composite individual" revealing a common history. The intergenerational discourse becomes a type of reflection on collective experience. None of these complications nor a host of other complications can be easily encompassed within an ontological individualism assumed by a simple speaker-hearer model of communication.

Such collective stories differ from personal narratives. The following extract is a typical example of personal narrative.

OW2: *I don't know whether to explain now because I was living with many children. Those were children of my late father, four of them. There were also three of my granddaughters. I raised my daughter's children whose husband died, but I'm alone now with my son who is 34-years old. He must do away with this new life-style. I want him to follow the example of Daniel.*

The first part of the story is a fairly common experience. A woman looks after children on her own after the death of her husband. The second part of the account describes a set of details specific and perhaps only true to her—the age of her son and her wishes that the son does not succumb to new influences.

However, old women do try to find ways to resist change. Attempts are manifested in women's repeated efforts and appeals to Christianity. As OW3 put it: "The first thing we do as old people is to keep quiet. These children do not choose a correct way of talking. There is a verse in the Bible which says respect your father and your mother and you will live long. Do you know it?"

Complaints
The old women constantly compared the present with what they frequently regarded as a golden age in terms of moral behaviour. For example, an interaction frequently began: *Kwimihla yakudala, msithi umzekelo, xa ithe intombi yanzima abazali bayo babexelelana.* (In our days, let us say for example when a girl became pregnant, parents used to tell each other about it...) The older women were aware that the golden moral past which they constructed was fiction, albeit useful fiction. It was useful because it enabled them to compare the moral behaviour of the present young generation with their own behaviour when they were young. The complaints do not necessarily reflect the degeneracy of the present behaviour of the youth but are characteristic of the manner in which the elderly have been socialized into mastering the art of complaint. As one old subject put it: "Every mother of my age complains."

Complaints serve a number of different purposes. On the one hand complaints reveal that older persons think that some changes which they regard as undesirable have occurred. At the same time, paradoxically, some complaints, particularly about the so-called low morality of the youth, are meant to demonstrate the extent to which the elderly are still in control. For example, one of the most vociferous critics of the young generation's lack of discipline was quick to describe how she handled her household with an iron hand: *Andiwavumeli amantombazana alale enlwini yamngaphandle ngokulandela inkqubo efanelekileyo Andifuni kumbona. Andifuni mntu uzaa kuza izinto ezzimbi endliwiniyam.* (I don't allow girls to come and sleep in my house without following the right procedure ... I don't want to see her. I don't want a person who will come and do bad things in my house.) This type of complaint may also be construed as bragging. By complaining about how the youth no longer obey the instructions of older persons, the old woman is able to boast how she is an exception in this case as she is in firm control of her household.

Complaint discourse is not restricted to elderly talk; the young in turn complain that the elderly talk too much—hence the term "radio gogo". The two generations are also in some cases united in their complaints, e.g, against what they perceive as incompetent and corrupt government officials. President Mandela is however immune from complaints as he is "above Jesus and on the same side with God."

Conclusions
This paper has analysed some typical discursive practices in first-time encounters between old and young Xhosa-speaking women. The structure of the intergenerational dialogue was briefly described, and different forms of address and the manner in which the women constructed their identities were highlighted. Complaints seem to be common in this type of

discourse but are difficult to distinguish from other types of discourse practices such as bragging. The study was conducted in a quasi-experimental setting and further research is needed to analyse intergenerational language use and discourse within naturalistic environments.

References

Bakhtin, M. (1981). *The dialogic imagination.* Austin, Texas: University of Texas Press.

Cattell, M. (1996). "Old people and the language of complaint: examples from Kenya and Philadelphia" In: Hamilton. H. (Ed.) *Old age and language: multidisciplinary perspectives.* Philadelphia, PA: Garland Press.

Coplan, D. (1994). *In the time of the cannibals: the word music of South Africa's Basotho migrants.* Johannesburg: University of the Witwater- srand Press.

Coupland, N,, Coupland, J. & Giles. H. (1992). *Language, society and the elderly: discourse, identity and ageing.* Oxford: Basil Blackwell.

Coupland, N., Coupland, L., Giles. H. & Wiemann, J. (1988) "My life in your hands: processes of self-disclosure in intergenerational talk" In: Coupland, N. (Ed.) *Styles of discourse.* London: Croom Helm, pp. 210-254.

De Kadt, E. (1994). Towards a model for the study of politeness in Zulu. *South African Journal of African Languages.* 14(3): 103-112,

Erickson, F. & Schultz, J. (1982). *The counselor as gatekeeper: social interaction in interviews.* New York: Academic Press.

Giddens, A. (1991). *Modernity and self-identity: self and society in the late modern age.* Cambridge: Polity Press. In conjunction with Basil Blackwell.

Hsu, F. (1985). "The self in cross-cultural perspective" In: Marsetla, A.J., DeVos, G. & Francis, L.K. (Eds) *Culture and self: Asian and western perspectives.* New York: Tavistock, pp. 201-230.

Makoni, S.B. (1995). Language and identities in Southern Africa. Paper Tead at a conference on "Ethnicity, Meaning and Implications." Edinburgh, May.

Milroy, L. & Milroy, J. (1980). *Language and social networks.* Oxford: Basil Blackwell.

Rampton, B. (1995a). *Language crossing.* Oxford: Oxford University Press.

Rampton, B. 1995b. Personal communication. London, October.

Raum, O.F. (1973). *The social factors of avoidance and taboos among the Zulus.* Berlin: De Gruyter.

Scollon, R. & Scollon S.W. (1992). *Individualism and binarism, A critique of American intercultural communication analysis.* (Working Paper Research Report 22) Hong Kong: City Polytechnic of Hong Kong, Department of English.

Smitherman, G. (1995). "The chain remains the same. Communicative practices in the hip-hop nation" Paper read at a conference on "English in Africa." Grahamstown, June.

Taylor, B. (1992). "Elderly identity in conversation" *Communication Research,* 19(4): 493-510.

Tracy, K. (1990). "The many faces of facework" In: Giles, H. & Robinson, W.P. (Eds) *Handbook of language and social psychology.* Chichester, UK, Wiley, pp. 323-338.

Wood, L. & Kroger, R.O. (1993). "Forms of address, discourse and ageing" *Journal of Ageing Studies,* 7(3): 262-277.

X

Aging in Africa: a critical review

Abstract
My goal in this article is to analyze gerontological discourses in Africa using articles in this collection as a spring board. The broad intention is to explore the possible areas of intersection between research in African aging and other social science disciplines such as history, politics and linguistics as a way of demonstrating how gerontology may contribute to scholarship in other disciplines.

Aging in Africa: Towards a Critical Linguistic Framework
The collection of articles in this special issue is a fascinating snapshot of gerontological studies in Africa during the early twenty-first century. However, like any snapshot, it will inevitably miss other aspects of gerontology in Africa. As a linguist, in this essay, I set for myself a very simple goal. My goal is to analyze the rhetorical structures of discourses in gerontology research in Africa using articles in this collection as a spring board. My second objective will be to explore the possible areas of intersection between research in

African aging and other cognate disciplines such as history, politics, counseling, linguistics and public health as one possible way of demonstrating how gerontology may contribute to scholarship in other disciplines.

Discourses of Aging in Africa
One of the reasons frequently adduced in justifying research into aging in Africa is the increase in the number of elderly persons. The claim is that we are living longer, that is, once premature deaths resulting from HIV/AIDS related illnesses are factored out. There are indications that the number of people aged 60 and over will double to 10% by 2050. The increase in the number of the aged will present a challenge to an "unprapared continent" (GHachuhi and Kiemo 2005: 36). According to this particular view, an increase in the number of elderly is occurring rapidly in a continent currently beset by many other intractable problems. The increase in the number of problems should therefore be a cause for major concern to African governments and policy makers who have largely tended to ignore aging in Africa.

These demographic trends are, however, not unique to Africa. The demographic trends emerging in Africa are comparable to those found in other parts of the globe and indeed in Europe in mid-twentieth century. The difference, though, is that Africa is 'graying' faster than in developed countries. The unique aspect of aging in Africa is that the graying is taking place in a rapidly urbanizing society. Historically, although urbanization is occurring rapidly it is instructive to note that cities predate colonialism in Africa, although urbanization has been accelerated by post-colonialism. Rapid urbanization and the increase in numbers of aging persons are apparently weakening what were previously imagined to be robust 'traditionally extended family structures' which used to cater to the elderly and the sick.

The increase in the number of the elderly is a cause for concern because of the absence of systematic plans to cater for their interests and welfare. The low priority for gerontology in Africa, it is argued, is apparent at a policy level and in the halls of the academe. In the academe there are very few courses on gerontology in Africa which, inevitably, has led to few gerontologists being trained in Africa within African universities. Scholarly literature on aging in Africa is gradually increasing, and this special issue of JCCG attests to its increasing dynamism. The academic scenario is also beginning to change with the number of scholars and Non-Governmental Organizations (NGO's) directly dealing with issues about aging in Africa. In a foreword to an edited volume, one of Africa's most celebrated gerontologists, Apt (1994) states unequivocally in a positive mood:

> 'Twenty years ago it would have been impossible to put together a group of researchers in ageing'

When gerontologists in Africa talk about aging, they have a very different meaning of Africa, which oftentimes excludes the Arab North. As such, the differences in aging of Arab Africa and the rest of Africa remain under-researched, and yet there is anecdotal evidence that there may be a significant and fundamental difference in terms of aging between the two parts of Africa. In as much as there are very specific challenges which aging poses, such as slowing down of physical movement, loss of eye sight, and being hard of hearing, increasing in all communities, there are also differences as well. For instance, while in Western countries independence in old age is a sign of successful aging, dependence upon others is interpreted as unsuccessful aging. Yet in Africa (South of the Sahara and possibly in Arab Africa as well) depending upon others may be interpreted as interdependence and a sign of successful aging, in which case it is not regarded as a problem unlike in Western countries.

However, because of the "impending" aging population, African governments have been pressured by NGO's to formulate policies on aging. In response to the NGOs, the African Union (AU) formulated a policy that dealt directly with issues related to aging. Not withstanding the fact that the promulgation of a policy on its own will not bring about change, the response by the AU has been lauded as an important step in the recognition of aging in Africa. An increasing awareness of the importance of aging is also corroborated by the declaration of 1999 as the Year of the Elderly. Nonetheless, discourses on the impeding social problem resulting from the rapid increase in the number of aging persons has gradually been replaced by and at times co-exist with another type of narrative about aging in Africa. In this narrative, the elderly are neither an object of pity nor a social problem but rather an important resource because of the role which they play in mitigating potentially devastating effects of HIV/AIDS. In this trope, the elderly are actively involved as caregivers, to both the children of HIV/AIDS and adults succumbing to disease prematurely. I will return to this issue later in this article.

The types of discourses which, for purposes of clarity and ease of exposition, I will simply call lament discourses are an important aspect of aging in Africa. However, these discourses have to be critically examined and must not be taken at face value because they are not simply linguistic expressions, but also ways of thinking which have a bidirectional relationship with our experiences of aging (Foucault 1971). On the one hand, they shape our experiences of aging and yet, on the other hand, aging shapes our discourses, but not all experiences of aging, though, are translated into discourse. We have more experiences of aging than our discourses allow us to articulate. Our initial experiences of aging are through seeing the people that we are related to go through the process of aging, and not ourselves, hence, the need for an intergenerational perspective on aging. Nonetheless, since we are adopting a very specific view of discourses, it is useful to carefully scrutinize the rhetorical structures of these discourses.

Firstly, in the lament trope (the increase in the number of elderly persons in anunprepared continent), a statement that is often repeated but not critically examined is that aging is an individual and not a social problem. There is a sharp disconnect between the discourses of aging as a problem, and how aging individuals themselves experience their own lives (Cohen 1994).

Whether the elderly regard their lives as problematic is beside the point. Even if aging is problematic (there are no reasons to assume that it is not in one way or other) rarely are we presented with substantial empirical evidence by the elderly themselves in which they described in their own words how they are experiencing aging, and what it is they understand as problematic experiences. Furthermore, rarely is it made clear whether these problems are peculiar to them irrespective of class, gender, and ethnic differences amongst them. It is important that we get a sense of how aging Africans themselves describe their own conditions in their own terms. There is scant data from the elderly which draws attention to their situation. As a result, we cannot assume that becasuse something constitutes a problem to scholars, it inevitably does so to the subjects of enquiry, as in our case, the eldery themselves. Even though what the elderly say about themselves may obviously be constrained by larger facts such as the socio-political context they are in and the relationship they share with the generation before and after them, the elderly, like other people, make history with varied outcomes. If they make history even wthin limited constraints, then how they view themselves is a part of how they make ther own history.

Nevertheless, if the elderly are given space to articulate their own views about aging an "emic" view of who is old is invaluable. As researchers, we often use chronological age. Using chronological aging as a marker may not be sufficient because chronological aging is typically used for bureaucratic purposes. It is part of the "governmentality" (Foucault 1971). Governments rely heavily on classifying and counting people and things. In order to manage countries, chronology may be a proxy for aging, and yet in Africa people who qualify as old may depend not only on chronological age, but rather on a whole host of other factors such as marital status, wealth and traditional position/function. Thus, an individual may be regarded as old even when in terms of chronological age they may beclassified as young. Conversely, an individual may be considered young because they are unable to look after themselves or have not satisfied such criteria as marriage irrespective of their chronological age.

Even if chronology is used as a proxy for aging, there are intergenerational differences in the way in which chronological age is construed by different generations. For example, Giles *et al.* (2006) demonstrate that college students may regard as old people in their 50s. There are also interregional differences in the way in which chronological aging is viewed. In the Giles *et al.* study just mentioned, there were differences in the ways in which college students in Ghana and South Africa defined adulthood, middle age, and old age.

Ironically, gerontologists in Africa, and perhaps in other regions, frequently draw attention to an increasing number of aging individuals; the same gerontologists rarely write reflectively about their own aging, and how their own aging potentially shapes their own views on what constitutes aging. It is almost as if it is other people who age and geron-

aging are through seeing the people that we are related to go through the process of aging, and not ourselves, hence, the need for an intergenerational perspective on aging. Nonetheless, since we are adopting a very specific view of discourses, it is useful to carefully scrutinize the rhetorical structures of these discourses.

Firstly, in the lament trope (the increase in the number of elderly persons in anunprepared continent), a statement that is often repeated but not critically examined is that aging is an individual and not a social problem. There is a sharp disconnect between the discourses of aging as a problem, and how aging individuals themselves experience their own lives (Cohen 1994).

Whether the elderly regard their lives as problematic is beside the point. Even if aging is problematic (there are no reasons to assume that it is not in one way or other) rarely are we presented with substantial empirical evidence by the elderly themselves in which they described in their own words how they are experiencing aging, and what it is they understand as problematic experiences. Furthermore, rarely is it made clear whether these problems are peculiar to them irrespective of class, gender, and ethnic differences amongst them. It is important that we get a sense of how aging Africans themselves describe their own conditions in their own terms. There is scant data from the elderly which draws attantion to their situation. As a result, we cannot assume that becasuse something constitutes a problem to scholars, it inevitably does so to the subjects of enquiry, as in our case, the eldery themselves. Even though what the elderly say about themselves may obviously be constrained by larger facts such as the socio-political context they are in and the relationship they share with the generation before and after them, the elderly, like other people, make history with varied outcomes. If they make history even wthin limited constraints, then how they view themselves is a part of how they make ther own history.

Nevertheless, if the elderly are given space to articulate their own views about aging an "emic" view of who is old is invaluable. As researchers, we often use chronological age. Using chronological aging as a marker may not be sufficient because chronological aging is typically used for bureaucratic purposes. It is part of the "governmentality" (Foucault 1971). Governments rely heavily on classifying and counting people and things. In order to manage countries, chronology may be a proxy for aging, and yet in Africa people who qualify as old may depend not only on chronological age, but rather on a whole host of other factors such as marital status, wealth and traditional position/function. Thus, an individual may be regarded as old even when in terms of chronological age they may beclassified as young. Conversely, an individual may be considered young because they are unable to look after themselves or have not satisfied such criteria as marriage irrespective of their chronological age.

Even if chronology is used as a proxy for aging, there are intergenerational differences in the way in which chronological age is construed by different generations. For example, Giles *et al.* (2006) demonstrate that college students may regard as old people in their 50s. There are also interregional differences in the way in which chronological aging is viewed. In the Giles *et al.* study just mentioned, there were differences in the ways in which college students in Ghana and South Africa defined adulthood, middle age, and old age.

Ironically, gerontologists in Africa, and perhaps in other regions, frequently draw attention to an increasing number of aging individuals; the same gerontologists rarely write reflectively about their own aging, and how their own aging potentially shapes their own views on what constitutes aging. It is almost as if it is other people who age and gerontologists are above aging or are ageless researchers (Cohen 1994) and indeed do not belong to an ethnic or racial group, even though aging is culturally and racially variable!

The issue of having the elderly give their own 'emic' perspectives on aging and their experiences of aging also raises the question of what 'idiom' the elderly ought to use in such research studies. Undoubtedly, if, as gerontologists we take our research enterprise seriously enough to get insights into how and what the elderly tell us about their own lives, this has to be done in their own idiom, i.e., in African languages.

Using African languages as modes for studying aging in Africa is feasible if notions about African languages are radically re-conceptualized by taking into account contemporary ways of framing them. Prah (2000), a sociologist and the majestic doyen of scholarship in African languages, has put up a compelling argument that of the 600-700 million Africans, 80-85% speak 15 to 17 core languages either as first, second or third languages; indeed, because of the flux and fluidity of linguistic situations, it might be hard, if not conceptually impossible, to determine what constitutes a first, a second, or third language. In spite of the fluidity, a large majority of the core languages are spoken across borders, thus, rendering it possible for scholars working in different countries to collaborate and work on the same language.

Thus, carrying out gerontological research in African languages is indeed feasible. For instance, the Gbe/Ewe-speaking peoples can be found in communities all along the West African Coast from Ghana, Togo, Benin, and the Nigerian border. This cluster includes Aja in Badagra/Nigeria, Aja in Benin, Gun in Benin, Mina, Fon in Benin, Mina and Ewe inTogo, and Ewe in Ghana (Prah 2000: 4). The Ndebele are found in South Africa, Botswana and Zimbabwe. In addition, some languages have fewer than 1,000 speakers which, therefore, render the project of understanding how elderly Africans themselves describe their own cultural and linguistic idioms a relatively easier task to conduct than might be assumed. In other words, a perception of Africa as a Tower of Babel and the belief in its undue linguistic complexity has constrained our efforts to carry out gerontological research in African languages. The limited amount of research in African languages in Africa is unfortunate because whatever ways in which we define aging, a majority of the aging speak African languages and relatively few speak English, Portuguese, or French. Most of African gerontological research finds its way into the academe which is as it should be.

Unfortunately, a majority of the elderly who serve as our informants are rarely provided with opportunities to comment on the research findings of the research carried out ON them; ideally, we should carry out research not only ON them but WITH them and FOR them as well. Such an approach, I concede, would be scientifically messy initially, but it will increase the positive impact of gerontological research and the benefits might outweigh the costs as it enhances the research's ecological validity.

Even when we write and think about aging in Africa, our thinking is inevitably culturally specific and heavily influenced by Western academe even when writing about Africa. Our thinking is always going to be Euro-centric. I am using the term Euro-centric not in a negative way but as an inevitable way in which our scholarship is part of a scholarly tradition which accepts as "true statements about empirical reality ... as true. Scholars may, however, deny that they are Eurocentric" (Blaut 1993:9). A telling example of our Euro-centric mode of analysis is how little we know about how aging is framed in Islamic Africa or in scripts other than the Roman alphabet. For instance, very few gerontologists, if any, can read the old Semitic script from antiquity used to write Geez, Amharic and Tigrinya, and Vai, a syllabic alphabet which has been used in Liberia for many centuries. Our lack of literacy in Ajami, the Arabic script which has been used to write a number of African languages for many centuries such as Swahili, Hausa, Wolof, Fulfulde, Kanuri and Bambara among many others is a direct result of our Euro-centric analytic tools. If we are to carry out a cross-cultural analysis of aging in Africa, we therefore need to analyze how those using other writing systems have written about aging in their scripts. If our analysis is to have ecological, defensible historical and time depth, then learning how to read some of these ancient scripts will be invaluable, or working collaboratively with those who are literate in those scripts will enrich our knowledge of aging in Africa.

Aging has always been an important theme in anthropological research. Thus, although gerontology in Africa may be a relatively recent enterprise, this does not mean that aging research in its entirety is a new research enterprise (Apt 2002). Unlike in other parts of the world, gerontology in Africa creates its object by focusing on aging in a very specific way. It construes aging as an autonomous, independent, scholarly object resonating with strong positivist trends. While on the other hand, anthropological research views aging as strongly embedded and interconnected with other social institutions such as marriage, funeral rites, and kith and kin illuminating how such systems are organized. The interesting aspect about gerontology in Africa is that while there are very few elderly people who live in isolation and are not embedded in complex social relations, research in gerontology in Africa has had, for analytical purposes, to create an asocial elderly as part of its idealization, in order for it to make advances in its analysis.

Furthermore, aging research, as articulated by Apt (2002), has tended to be extremely nationalistic in its quest to find unique solutions to African aging. It has also tended to be state-centric in that most of the studies are country or state-specific, hence, one encounters studies such as aging in South Africa, Ghana, and Tanzania. Although it is indisputable that there may be peculiar aspects of aging that are directly related to specific circumstances of each individual nation state, excessive reliance on the nation/state as an analytical template tends to overlook similarities between countries and the inherent diversity within each country. More significantly, aging in Africa that draws heavily on the notion of a nation/state at a historical juncture when Africanists are increasingly questioning the value of such a template seems rather misplaced.

In view of the above, the overall argument is that aging, like other categories such as ethnicity is not pre-given but rather, socially constructed, fluid, performed from one moment and situation to another. Being elderly involves much more than chronological aging; it may involve ways of speaking, dress, and styles of gestures, stories told, etc., hence the relevance of the notion of performativity by Butler (1990) as a possible heuristic in the analysis of how aging is conceptualized.

After briefly describing the different types of discourses in gerontology in Africa, and the problematic nature of how to conceptualize aging, I now comment on the various articles in this collection. I am going to deliberately seek to examine the nature of the overlap and intersection between gerontology in Africa and other disciplines such as history, politics, and public health.

Gerontology and History: Opportunities and Potential Pitfalls

Mackinnon's paper challenges the notion of retirement particularly the view widely held by white officials in the 1950s in South Africa. He investigates how Africans, after spending years working in mines, return to the "traditional" homes to spend the rest of their lives in dire poverty. He describes the difficult conditions in which they find themselves upon returning "home." The archival analysis challenges the dominant ideology advocated by white South African governments in pre-apartheid South Africa that after working in mines, Africans retired to relative comfort and affluence. Methodologically, the article demonstrates how archival research into a very specific aspect of aging makes important contributions to history. Sagner (2002) follows a similar trend when through a careful analysis of archival research, he challenges the dominant ideology that Africans invariably looked after their elderly. There is a growing body of literature that uses archival data as a resource in order to gain insight into a wide range of issues from historical, social, linguistic and more recently aging. Although the trend of using archival data is welcome, the exercise is much more complicated than one might initially anticipate. The main challenge of using archival data is that the texts were produced for a purpose often different from the research question that a researcher is attempting to answer, thus the texts have to be "read against" their objectives. As such, the data from any archival resource has to be interpreted and treated with caution.

It is, however, encouraging that gerontology in Africa is making its contribution to a developing body of literature by using a research methodology that is now relatively common in diverse disciplines in the social sciences and humanities. However, as already stated, the texts have to be read with caution because they were not produced with aging explicitly in mind. Therefore, references to aging may be made variably and in connection with other issues. Thus, the analyst has to bring together the disparate references to aging and make them into a coherent whole.

In spite of the problems related to reading into a text issues which were not central to it, gerontology can still make an important ideological contribution to history. It questions some of the underlying beliefs about aging and this is an issue which is critically important in cross-cultural research. Gerontology research brings together history and linguistic analysis because history cannot be conceptualized outside language, so an analysis of how gerontology is articulated is a linguistic theory (Joseph 2006). Although there is a great potential for collaborative research between history and gerontology because of the intersecting nature of the research between historical concerns and aging this area of research still has to be widely taken advantage of. This may be a missed opportunity because historians rely at times quite extensively on data collected from the elderly (particularly when making use of oral sources), but they show very little awareness of how aging might indeed affect and shape the various ways the elderly may respond to their pasts. Historians, and to some extent dialectologists, assume that the elderly can serve as direct windows into the past; yet, this is a situation which needs to be studied more deeply if it is accepted as a principle that through intergenerational interconnectedness, the elderly may partially overlap with that of the youth.

If gerontology in Africa is to make a substantial contribution to historiography, a number of issues have to be taken into account. Oakley (2002), in a remarkable study, shows how an analysis of the life times of a single colored woman in South Africa can provide important insights into how her life was shaped by events: a noble effort because of the seriousness with which it views history through the experiences of an individual. However, there are a number of issues which those wishing to expand and build on the excellent work by Oakley and those like Mackinnon in this article need to identify and possibly clarify, especially when dealing with individuals from African communities:

1. Most of the narratives will inevitably or largely be elicited rather than spontaneous, and, thus, may not have the linguistic and conventions typically associated with such genres questioning their validity as sources.
2. Even though Oakley arranged the narratives in a chronological manner, most African societies "foster a non-formal and loosely institutionalized view of the past which is extremely difficult to capture, unwittingly burdened as we are in the academy by a more contemporary, highly text-bound linear and chronological understanding of history" (Hofmeyr 1993).
3. Gerontological narratives are gendered (Hofmeyr 1993) so the narratives which Mackinnon, and indeed Oakley, have need to be read against that background.

Another critical question which is clearly important as gerontology in Africa seeks to contribute to the writing either of history or contemporary issues, is to analyze how the elderly experience time. For instance, van Dongen (2002) shows the complexity of how the elderly experience time by drawing into her study the lives of people with mental illness in a long term psychiatric ward. She argues that in such situations "all days of the week seem alike with some fixed important time points everyday: breakfast, the coffee break at 10:30 in the morning, the meal at noon, tea in the afternoon, the meal at 6:00 P.M." (van Dongen 2002:91). Even though van Dongen does not have aging in Africa in mind, her point is that it cannot be readily assumed that those who are institutionalized treat and understand time as those who are not in an institution. Indeed, those who are HIV/AIDS-infected may experience time differently from those with whom they live and yet are not affected with complicated ideas about time and care.

Anthropology of Aging as Object of Historical Analysis

Like the studies cited above, Cattell, in this volume and some of her earlier work, explicitly explores possible intersections between history and anthropology. Based on her 20-year study among the Abaluyia in Kenya, she documents some of the changes which have taken place in Kenya as the Abaluyia were integrated into the modern economy. Her evidence is drawn from a wide range of sources such as auto-biography and family sources. The historywhich Cattell writes about is also based on her own experiences of researching amongst the Abaluyia over a quarter century. Her research in one site enables her to deeply appreciate the dynamics of the society. In most cases we encounter individuals when they are already aged (whatever that means), but we do not know exactly how they behaved prior to their aging status. By carrying out research in one site over a prolonged period, this problem is partially addressed as each individual becomes their own base line. The research methodology which Cattell uses has also been used by other gerontologists/anthropologists/historians such as van der Guest (2002) who has extensively studied aging in Northern Ghana over a number of decades. Other scholars who might not readily regard themselves as gerontologists have found repeated visits to the same site for a prolonged period more informative in their research into aging. One such example is Colson who has studied the Tonga in the Congo for over 60 years (Colson 2007; Dervish et al. 2002).

One of the issues which recurs throughout this commentary is how the past is handled. Cattell meticulously shows how she collected and wrote her research, but there are two key issues which are missing which we cannot infer from her studies. These relate to the limitations of relying heavily on social memory and the use of anthropological approaches to historical accounts. For instance, Colson (2007), drawing upon extensive research into diverse societies, argues that history is difficult to remember in the absence of a centralized state. Perhaps conquerors take great pleasure in remembering the past more so than the conquered and victims themselves do. Victims therefore tend to have a relatively short historical memory or what Colson felicitously calls a 'telescopic' account of history or events. In Cattell's studies, it is extremely difficult to determine where the Abaluyia may fit into this scheme between victors and the conquered. From a linguistic perspective it is worth stressing that the richness and depth of narrating the past is greatly weakened when it is not acknowledged that the audience played a significant role in the narrativization of the past, and that the 'teller together with gestural and dramatic skill' rendered the event into a multi-dimensional event. It is this multidimensionality, the utilization of multiple semiotic systems which is lost in a mono-modal presentation and analysis of the recounting of the past (Kress and van Leeuwen 1996; Iedema 2003).

Even though anthropology has made substantial contributions towards research into aging in Africa, it appears that according to some Africanists it has not escaped from its colonial and racist past. Clark and Pierre (2003) in Zeleza (2006) argues that anthropologists' concern with cultural difference is a metamorphosis of racist differences. Anthropology, according to some senior Africanists, has thus not escaped its own past. If this argument is valid, then anthropology has to be used circumspectly in its contribution to gerontology in Africa lest it be read as a retrospective justification of an unfortunate past through the use of academic terms which echo that past. For example, notions about cross-cultural differences in aging might be easily read as a new formulation of cultural hierarchy, which was at the core of colonial encounters.

The HIV/Aids Pandemic
We are all aware that HIV/AIDS is one of the most devastating pandemics which continue to face Africa more so in southern Africa than in other parts of the world. We do not need to reiterate its devastating effects which include: loss of income by able-bodied individuals at their prime and pressures to reconfigure families to care for children whose parents are adversely affected by the pandemic. There are two articles in this special issue which address different dimensions of these complex social and medical problems. Ice (in this collection) using multiple methods such as clinical history, physical examination results and a version of SF-36 presents detailed and sophisticated findings about the relationship between caregiving status, age and gender. Bock, in a related study, again in this collection, argues that although the elderly are increasingly replacing the middle-aged generation as they assume roles which the latter used to play, the elderly do not execute these duties as 'efficiently' as the middle-aged group would have otherwise done. Bock therefore suggests that there is indeed a significant difference between caregiving by the elderly and that by the middle-aged. Both studies are most welcome as they demonstrate the increasingly important role which the elderly have come to play in this pandemic, thus mitigating someof its potentially adverse effects.

The HIV/AIDS models may be approached from a wide range of perspectives; in this article, I want to argue for two key constructs which flow from two ideas:

1. The interconnectedness of generations
2. The linkage between public health and communication

The studies by Bock and Ice both show the potential stress of caregiving by the elderly. Linguistically, it is not clear how the African elderly would define what they are doing; that is whether they would define it as caregiving or something else. However, it seems that they would use a much more intimate term: *kuchengeta* (in Shona, language used in southern Africa mainly in Zimbabwe) which means looking after one's own child. *Kuchengeta*, as a concept, conjures the image of responsibility and obligation. *Kuchengeta* therefore, does not readily translate into caregiving. The term carries with it connotations of a much more intimate experience than caregiving. It is also not as distant as caregiving and cannot be readily translated into a burden. Looking after your own children and carrying out your obligations and responsibilities cannot be treated as a burden from such a perspective. Nonetheless, this is not to suggest that looking after persons who are falling ill is not a burden, but the obligations are best captured in an African proverb in Ndebele (spoken in Zimbabwe and South Africa) that says *Indlovu ayisindwa ngumboko wayo* (A Ndebele proverb that means that an elephant has never found its own proboscis too heavy to carry around), which means that an obligation is not a heavy burden for you to carry. Furthermore, African households are extremely complex; hence, the responsibility of *chengeta mwana wako* (looking after one's child) does not fall exclusively onto the elderly. Other siblings may also contribute as part of the extended family. Nevertheless, there might be light at the end of the dark tunnel where the elderly who need care take care of young children who have been orphaned by the ravages of HIV/AIDS.

Gurland and his associates suggest that seniors are likely to look after themselves much more carefully and manage their health more effectively because of a realization of the nature of their responsibilities. In that sense, the health of the elderly and the children are interconnected.

From a linguistic perspective there is also another important dimension that emanates from the HIV/AIDS research and the role of the elderly. For example, a lot of new terms have entered into local discourses, some of which are pejorative and stigmatize HIV/AIDS sufferers. If there is anything we have learnt from radical linguistic feminism, it is that it is indeed possible to change the various ways in which individuals react to daily issues by directly intervening and altering the meanings of words. There is thus a key role which public health communication founded on a nuanced understanding of the role of language in epidemics can play.

A contribution of public health communication (Djite 2007) towards enhancing communication in public health needs to be much more sophisticated and cannot depend exclusively on language, even if messages are framed in a manner which is congruent with the cultural and gender sensitivities of the receiving communities. A multimodal approach, which takes into account both the linguistic representation and visuals to enhance meanings and how the different semiotic systems transform one another, or what Iedema calls 'resemiotization' (Iedema 2003:30), is essential. Messages used in public health should combine visuals and language. It is not only a question of how the messages are framed (important though this might be), but how the visuals used with the message can render the messages more forceful.

Familial Decision Making During Troubled Times
In this special issue, McGadney *et al.*, explore how decision making is carried out in turbulent times, using Ghana as an example. They show the important roles played by senior women, particularly grandmothers. Grandmothers have been found to be essential for child survival, protecting the family from disintegration, again showing the importance of their role, with decision making an important part. The authors also demonstrate that the preservation of non-nuclear families has played an important role in turbulent times when

things are falling apart. Although this study is an important one, there are a number of critically important assumptions which need to be subjected to serious scrutiny especially if the 'model' is to be effectively extended to other African communities.

Feminist concepts emerged out of the assumption that a nuclear family can be universalized. This is not the case especially when taking different African countries into consideration. The concept of families which most gerontologists working in Africa make use of is based on the assumption that families are conjugally based. And yet, in other ethnic groups, families are organized around a core of brothers and sisters (Oyewumi 2006). The finding that senior women may play critical roles makes sense when it is assumed that families are both conjugally based and there is a gender hierarchy. This is not necessarily the case always. For example, amongst the Yoruba in Nigeria the 'family' is non-gendered. There are no single words to denote girl or boy (Oyewumi 2006). The main point of contention here is that such binary categories as male/female might not be directly appropriate for African contexts. Hence, there are categories which may be incomprehensible to Western scholarship. Categories such as male/daughters, female/husbands in Igbo societies and amongst Shona speakers in Zimbabwe when the brother's sister (*tete*) can be referred to as the male/female do not make sense in Western societies and yet these are the operative templates in these societies. If this argument is valid then the role of senior women has to be analyzed more carefully, because gender can be understood in radically different ways in African societies than is implied by the authors.

Conclusion
In this concluding piece, we situated the articles on aging in Africa within wider social, political and epistemological

contexts. I have also analyzed some discourses of aging in Africa and their potential impact on shaping the way aging can be framed. In the article, I have also shown the various ways in which aging research might contribute to other disciplines such as history. I have also argued for the need to develop nuanced understandings of notions such as time, gender, etc., in research in Africa since grandmothers are increasingly being seen as key role players in aging.

References
Apt, N. (1994). "Who is caring for the elderly" *Bold* 1(4), 5-10.
Apt, N. (2002). "Preface" in Makoni, S. and Stroeken K. (eds.) *Ageing in Africa: Sociolinguistic and Anthropological Approaches.* (pp.ix-xii). Hampshire: Ashgate.
Blaut, R. (1993). *The colonizer's model of the world: geographical diffusion and eurocentric history.* New York: Guilford Press.
Butler, J. (1990). "Performative acts and gender constitution" In S. E. Case (Ed.), *Performing feminisms: feminist critical theory and theatre* (pp. 270-282). Baltimore MD: Johns Hopkins University Press.
Clark, S., & Pierre, N. (2003). *Adult mortality in an era of HIV/AIDS in sub-Saharan Africa.* Available at http://www.un.org/esa/population/publications/adult mort/CLARK.paper3.pdf . Accessed on May 2, 2008.
Colson, E. (2007). "Biases, place, time and stance" In C. Lancaster, & K. Vickery (Eds.), *The tonga-speaking people of zambia and Zimbabwe* (pp. 307-345). New York:/Toronto: University Press of America.
Dervish, R., Makoni, S., & Stroeken, K. (2002). "African

gerontology: Critical models, future directions" In S. Makoni, & K. Stroeken (Eds.), *Ageing in Africa: Sociolinguistic and anthropological approaches* (pp. 227-285). Hampshire: Ashgate.

Djite, P. (2007). *The sociolinguistics of development in Africa.* Clevedon:Buffalo/Toronto: Multilingual Matters.

Foucault, M. (1971). "The discourse on language" (Trans. by Rupert Sawyer) *Social Science Information*, April 1971, pp. 7-30. Reprinted in: *The archaeology of knowledge and The discourse on language.* 1972. New York: Pantheon Books.

Gachuhi, J. M., & Kiemo, K. (2005). Available at www.helpage.org/Researchpublications. Accessed on April21, 2008.

Giles, H., Makoni, S., & Dailey, R. M. (2006). "Intergenerational communication beliefs" *Journal of Cross-Culture Communication* 20(30), 191-211.

Joseph, J. (2006). *Language and politics*. Edinburgh: Edinburgh University Press.

Hofmeyr, I. (1993). *'We spend our lives as a tale that is told': Oral historical narrative in a South African Chiefdom.* Portsmouth: Witswatersrand University Press.

Kress, G., & van Leeuwen, T. (1996). *Reading images: The grammar of visual design.* London: Routledge.

Iedema, R. (2003). "Multimodality, resemiotization: Extending the analysis of discourse as multi-semiotic practice" *Visual Communication* 2, 29-57.

Oakley, R. (2002). "Imprints of history and economy across the life course of an elderly Namaqualander: 1920-1996" In S. Makoni, & K. Stroeken (Eds.), *Ageing in Africa: Anthropological and sociolinguistic approaches* (pp. 67-89). Hampshire: Ashgate Publishing House.

Oyewumi, O. (2006). "Conceptualizing Gender in African Studies" In P. Zeleza (Ed.), The study of Africa: Disciplinary and Interdisciplinary Encounters. CODESRIA. 313-321.

Prah, K. (Ed.) (2000). *Africa in transformation: Political and economic transformation and socio-political responses in Africa. Volume 2: Political and Economic Reforms, Transformations and Gender Issues.* Addis Ababa: Organization for Social Science Research in East and Southern Africa.

Sagner, A. (2002). "Identity management and old age construction among Xhosa speakers in Urban South Africa: Complaint Discourse revisited" In S. Makoni, & K. Stroeken (Eds.), *Ageing in Africa: Anthropological and sociolinguistic approaches* (pp.43-67). Hampshire: Ashgate.

van der Guest (2002). "The toilet: dignity, privacy and care of elderly people in Kwahu, Ghana: approaches" In S. Makoni, & K. Stroeken (Eds.), *Ageing in Africa: Anthropological and sociolinguistic approaches* (pp. 227-245) Hampshire: Ashgate.

van Dongen, E. (2002). "Skeletons of the past, flesh and blood of the present remembrance and older people in a South African context" In S. Makoni, & K. Stroeken (Eds.), *Ageing in Africa: Anthropological and sociolinguistic approaches* (pp. 257-277). Hampshire: Ashgate.

Zeleza, P. (Ed.), (2006). *The study of Africa.* The Centre for the Development of Social Science Research.

XI

From Elderspeak to Gerontolinguistics
Sociolinguistic myths

> Nobody grows old merely by living a number of years. We grow old by deserting our ideals. Years may wrinkle the face, but to give up enthusiasm wrinkles the soul.
>
> – Ulman (1885)

Introduction

In this chapter, I adopt a critical gerontology sociolinguistic perspective, a critique inspired by critical theory, feminist theory, political economy, hermeneutics, and language ideology, to pose questions regarding why people age the way they do and how they experience and articulate the many dimensions of their social, political, economic, and linguistic lives. I am using the term *political economy* to refer to the complicated connections between politics, economy, and ideology that inform both implicit and explicit beliefs about language, culture, and society. From a sociolinguistic perspective, it is instructive that the use of a common language (e.g., English) in academic writing and notions of African aging promoted by international agencies (e.g., Aging in Africa) mask the underlying differences between the constructs of social aging in Africa and in Western contexts. If the use of English in writing research on Africa masks differences between aging in Africa and the Western world, the use of African languages and other labels (e.g., elderly, youth, male and female) masks the idiosyncratic and substantial differences in the ways that aging is individually experienced.

I am also interested in how aging is reflected in discourse, and can thus be treated as a discursive project itself (Rozanova, 2010). The discursive practices associated with aging result from an interplay between a number of factors and actions, including personal histories, social and economic class, and ethnicity. Importantly, the discursive practices associated with aging are neither predesigned nor preplanned. The discursive practices used by most people, irrespective of social status, formal educational levels, and age, cannot be preplanned. The discursive practices in such contexts is an "institutionalized assemblage of products of previous linguistic work" (Ross- Landi, 1983:46). The assemblage contains lots of material, including bits and pieces of language, phrases, and complete or elliptical stories. The assemblage is not a static entity but entails innovative and creative ways that social, linguistic, and other resources intersect in difficult contexts in postcolonial predatory economies. This creativity has been defined as "indefinite elaborability," which means that we "take" words as materials and produce new products from them. The "indefinite elaborability" arises because even in the field of nonlinguistic labor instruments are in continual evolution (Rossi-Landi, 1983: 47).

Elderly creativity or exploitation of the institutionalized assemblage is an invaluable strategy that the elderly deploy in order to survive in postcolonial predatory economies. Creativity is a serious activity, not a language game but a form of work, albeit linguistic work and not an activity because

> we either reject the Hegelian discovery of the anthropogenic character of work or, given that this character is also proper to language, we must admit that language itself has the character of work. Language is itself a form of work and not an activity... I speak of work rather than activity because word and messages, which are products, constitute the concrete social activity. (Rossi-Landi, 1983: 37).

Following Rossi-Landi, I deliberately speak of language as work rather than activity because words and messages, which are products, constitute the concrete social reality we must begin with by regarding languages as linguistic human work. Language from such a perspective is placed at the same level as other forms of work, and consists of products that are consequence of deliberate human intervention and manipulation of social contexts. The idea of language as work, or linguistic human work, is not unique to language in aging, but can be found in other types of language varieties such as child language and urban vernaculars. If language is work, linguistic work is also apparent in other varieties of language, notably child, youth, gendered, and other language varieties.

There is a substantial body of research that deals with language in aging in North American, European, and Australian communities. The applicability of this body of Euro-American scholarship to African contexts raises two partially contradictory perspectives. On the one hand, Euro-American research may be construed as inapplicable to African contexts because African contexts are sociolinguistically more complicated than Euro-American ones, a complexity that demands more sophisticated sociolinguistic approaches. On the other hand, Euro-American sociolinguistic frameworks may be construed as too sophisticated and unnecessarily complicated because from African sociolinguistic perspectives, sociolinguistic complexity is the norm and therefore does not require frameworks that are unduly complicated, a view well captured in the following quotation:

> The near absence of metalinguistic discourse such as language mixing, multilingualism and other terms widely used in western sociolinguistics takes place because heterogeneity is constitutive of linguistic practice. Language mixing, linguistic overlap, and plural linguistic practices are all part of daily life and do not for the most part evoke any special type of metadiscourse, they simply are reality, moreover, speakers are always baffled by the importance researchers give to the topic. (Canut, 2009: 87)

The strand of language and aging based on notions about "Elderese" in Euro- American contexts is different from the one I am proposing here. While most research into Elderese has focused on the various ways in which language addressed to the elderly is adapted so that it can accommodate imagined or real linguistic and cognitive differences of the elderly, the elderly are treated as passively engaged in conversations and not shaping those conversations. They are framed as spoken to, rather than active participants (Nussbaum et al., 2000). In this chapter I therefore deliberately turn the issues about Elderese on their head by focusing on the elderly as active agents, as opposed to passive conversationalists. Even though the primary thrust of this chapter is Africa, the examples that I cite are relevant to non-African situations as well, particularly postcolonial contexts such as Asia and Latin America, which in varying degrees have to address the social and political roles of elderly individuals.

Discourses about Aging in Sub- Saharan Africa

The general consensus among gerontologists in Africa seems to be that the African population is aging faster than in other continents and that Africans are living longer than they did in previous generations. If premature death from chronic conditions such as HIV/AIDS and malaria are factored out, the number of people aged sixty and older in Africa is predicted to double by 2050. Despite increasing survival to older ages in recent years, the life span of "frail" older people tends to be rather short, as the period of "old age" is still inherently fragile in many African communities (van der Geest, 2002).

Discourses regarding an increase in the number of elderly are framed as apocalyptic/alarmist by "merchants of doom," who predict strained social and health resources (Cohen, 1998) because African countries do not currently have social and health policies in place. Another important aspect of an increase in the number and proportion of the elderly relative to younger generations is the domination of the African political scene by older politicians, a form and type of political gerontocracy. In analyses of the impact of demographic changes, the relevance of political gerontocracy has rarely been systematically investigated because of the absence of a critical gerontology sensitive to political economy in Africa, even though a relatively large number of African leaders are advanced in age.

African terms for "old age" and the terms' relationship to chronological aging are complicated because, unlike in the West, what constitutes social aging varies considerably across different ethnic groups and African countries and may be partially influenced by the functional abilities of the socially old. For example, a young person chronologically accorded "a stool" (a prestigious position in Ghana) may be called "old" since receiving a stool is a mark of social status. Ironically, not everyone who is chronologically old is referred to as "old"; therefore, some people may be referred to as "old" even if they are chronologically young, because of their social status (Livingston, 2001). In such cases, seniority, rather than chronological age, confers old age status. The significance of relative age vis-à-vis absolute age (lived years/chronological age) becomes particularly apparent "when the two principles contradict each other so that an individual who is chronologically junior in years is accorded the privileges" of generational seniority (Keith, 1990). For example, a man aged fifty-five could be regarded as more senior than one seventy-five years or older because of the accomplishments of the former. In such contexts, seniority is not tied to chronology but is determined in part by social accomplishments. Therefore, in sub- Saharan Africa, the starting point should be recognizing the problematic nature of chronological aging, rather than taking it for granted as a given, uncontestable framework (Foner, 1984).

Even if chronological aging is used as a starting point, it is interesting that different generations may have radically different ideas about aging. For example, Giles et al. (2005) reported that the start age of "old age" varied between Ghanaian and American students. American students tend to regard aging as occurring earlier chronologically than West African students, even though life span in North America is longer than in West Africa. The differences in perception of when aging sets in underscores the importance of a contextually determined basis of what constitutes aging and when it occurs, since there is no universally agreed-upon determination.

Even though chronological aging is problematic, we cannot escape the power of chronology in social science research because chronology is a central feature of Western views about aging, and this chapter is written within the context of Western scholarship (even though it is a critique of that scholarship). There are a number of categories that define what we do as language scholars, even if we feel they cannot fully capture our experiences. We cannot escape the use of such categories as chronological aging because we are operating under the burden of Western scholarship. More important than the weight of the categories is that the categories we are using may constrain how we propose to analyze language in a social context. We are held captive by the metaphors of which we are critical. We therefore are partially appropriated by the instruments we seek to critique. By being appropriated by the instruments we seek to critique, I mean the tendency to view African gerontology through Western colonial lenses. We seek to negotiate and create space for African gerontology by developing local and critical approaches. Smith's (2002) argument, even though writing about Māori research in New Zealand and how Māori researchers seek to negotiate space for themselves, is applicable to African contexts:

> One of the challenges for Māaori researcher working in this context ... has been to retrieve some space—first, some space to convince Māaori people of the value of research for the Māaori, second, to convince the various, fragmented but powerful research communities of the need for greater Māori [...] which take into account, without being limited by, the legacies of previous research

and the parameters of both previous and current research. (Smith, 2002: 183)

One of the challenges of creating a space demands that the term "research" itself be rehabilitated because the term is intricately intertwined with European colonialism and imperialism. The term "research" is one of the "dirtiest" words in African social and cultural universes, at times provoking satirical poetry, such as that of Okot p'Bitek and his *Songs of Lawino*.

Traditional African Approaches to Aging

In this section I seek to analyze how some of the African terms used to refer to aging reflect orientations toward aging. One of the key terms used to refer to aging among the Akan of Ghana (who speak Twi) is *manyin*. *Manyin* is an active, rather than passive, state of being (van der Geest, 2002). It is a development process founded on the assumption that although an individual has reached a full state of being, she still has the capacity to develop further, even after old age. Because of this possibility, I suggest the use of a life-span perspective (which means a view of life founded on a philosophy of human existence that treats language analysis as a continuum from early to latter phases of life and is not restricted to specific phases such as childhood, youth, and aging).

Among the Akan of Ghana, older men refer to themselves and are referred to as *opanyin*, and older women are referred to as *aberewa*. Both terms connote a status of people who have met their social obligations. Even though both terms frame old age positively, the term *opanyin* is more prestigious than *aberewa*, perhaps reflecting the gendered nature of terms, even those used to refer to older people. Even though both *opanyin* and *aberewa* from Twi may be used to refer to socially aged persons, the language contains no strict equivalent to the English word "old." Therefore, one could assert that there is no aging in Africa if aging is viewed through Western prisms. In non- Western contexts, the meaning of "aging" and the terms used to describe aging are ambiguous and ambivalent. They are not equivalent to aging in Western communities.

The *opanyin*'s and *aberewa*'s language is characterized by abundant use of proverbs, stories, prayers, and songs. In public meetings, they excel through their eloquence, wit, astute and shrewd debating, creativity in the use of proverbs, and imaginativeness in the use of words (van der Geest, 2002). From a critical linguistic perspective, the use of proverbs is a form of linguistic ideology in which the values of a community are articulated, suggesting uniformity across context and language users. The individual idiosyncratic uses of proverbs are frequently overlooked. The unique ways in which an individual uses proverbs, when and in what discussion, is underestimated because of a general proclivity to conceptualize proverbs as independent of context and users. The tendency to view proverbs as independent of context ideologically creates an illusion of uniform meanings across contexts in both production and interpretation. In addition, even though proverbs are widely used, there is no consensus on how they are to be construed in African societies, even among the elderly who extensively use them. For example, in Ghana, there is disagreement even among the elderly about the meanings of proverbs such as *opanyin nni biribi a,owo, abatwe* (literally translated as, "If the elder has nothing, he has elbow"; see van der Geest, 2002). The multiplicity of ways in which proverbs are used and interpreted is indicative of the creativity and ingenuity of their use by individual elders.

In some contexts, the division is not between the old and the young, but between mature adults and frail older persons. Among the Ashanti, for example, one term, *pinyin*, is used to describe an adult, a respectable person, or an elder, and another term, *mmerer-ni*, refers to a frail old individual.

Another dimension that may be used to describe social aging is *subjective self-identification*. Subjective self-identification is multidimensional and is mediated by the old people's functional capabilities, which include a capacity to execute social functions like activities of daily living and appropriate language use. What constitutes activities of daily living and appropriate language use varies in Africa because of its diversity. For the pastoral Herero (residing largely in Botswana and Namibia), difficulties doing leatherwork, watering the cattle, fetching firewood, and building houses are major markers of aging. Among the !Kung hunter gatherers in Southern Africa, on the other hand, a man is labeled old at the very moment he does not have the physical strength to hunt anymore; women are considered old when they experience difficulties gathering bush food, sewing, and doing beadwork (Keith, 1990). For the !Kung women, old age is a gradual process, often marked by menopause or cessation of childbirth, rather than by diminished strength and loss of ability to perform strenuous work, as is the case with men (Cattell, 1992; Folta and Deck, 1987). The differences in how aging is defined in Africa in diverse contexts illustrate the degree to which functionality is context-specific. It is not functionality per se that is critical here, but the local standards for functionality that determine the beginning of old age. Indeed, capacities that are required in order to be viewed as a functional member of one society are not necessarily required in another. Many traditional and African indigenous models of old age should be able to take into account a combination of both inter-individual and intra-individual differences; consequently, it is plausible to propose that one may be old in one aspect but not in another. Only people who have achieved a senior age in all respects may be regarded as truly old. For example, one may be old but still have a capacity to use youth language because the latter is not specifically relevant to only the youth from a critical linguistic perspective.

Although Africans may not be intensely interested in chronological age in terms of numbers, most people are able to give an approximate age for *institutional* reasons, such as receiving pensions, which are available in all but three African countries. The use of chronological age is also a reflection of what the African elderly think the researcher wants to hear or know, and may, in some cases, be an approximate marker. Chronological aging in African contexts is not an emic view but a mediated socially reconstructed idea. An extreme example of how an elderly individual may self-categorize is apparent in the statement by the man labeled "the oldest man in the history of mankind." In some contexts, the elderly look forward to death and feel disappointed when it is delayed because death is not construed as the end of a life span, but marks a transition to another higher level of being. Paradoxically, in African aging, longevity is not necessarily a socially significant status in its own right since it deprives individuals of opportunities to move to another level of seniority that commands more respect.

Most elderly people are likely to be able to determine their age relative to certain historical incidents, wars, epidemics, droughts, burial of an important person, and their linear position relative to other age cohorts. Xhosa (spoken largely in South Africa) contains at least three categories: *abafana* (young men), *amadadona* (junior men), and *amadoda amadada* (old men). This "cultural calendar" seems to be more relevant to African social definitions of aging than chronological years. Therefore, in many African cultures, an individual's age is determined through localizing him or her within specific socially relevant time frames, not an abstract void frame of chronological age.

In societies that establish old age primarily in social terms, the onset of "late life" fluctuates widely. Meruans (a nomadic community in Kenya) equate old age with loss of physical strength; old age for them begins only between the ages of sixty- five and seventy. Among the Aziyo, a nomadic community in northern Tanzania and southern Kenya, the life stage of age (not elderhood) often begins between sixty and sixty- five (Fadiman, 1982; Gulliver, 1963; Spencer, 1965).

Van der Geest proposes distinctions between passive and active notions of generation (a.k.a. "historical generation"). The notion of generation illustrates the importance of construing aging in a relational manner, as opposed to reifying it into a separate and distinct entity. This tendency is apparent in the massive research into youth language, which avoids intergenerational perspectives. Intergenerational studies into the "young" and "old," therefore, serve as a corrective to the tendency to view studies into "youth" and other social groups, as if they are independent of society and exist autonomously outside of it. This is why the next section considers language and aging in the context of multigenerational families.

Multigenerational Families: "What Am I Supposed to Do, She Is Mine"

An increasing number of studies on aging in Africa focus on the relationship between grandmothers/grandfathers and their grandchildren, especially due to the premature deaths of the generation between these two groups (i.e., the adult children of the grandmothers/grandfathers) due to HIV/AIDS. In African townships, a majority of households are multigenerational and have been affected by HIV/AIDS. HIV/AIDS-affected households are typically female-headed, with grandmothers often acting as caregivers to adult daughters or sons dying from HIV/AIDS. Some of these households experience extreme poverty, and have little or no money. Grandmothers do their best to procure food and pay for essentials like medical treatment and school fees. In a longitudinal study carried out over six months, Ferreira et al. (2002) interviewed grandmothers and reported on the emotional and psychological effects of caring for children with HIV/AIDS. Excerpts from the study illustrate the difficult task of the caregiving process, which grandmothers accept because they regard it as a natural part of their role.

The following quotations capture the difficulties of caring for adult children with HIV/AIDS. One grandmother grieved about her relationship with her daughter, whose death was imminent: "She is not speaking to me; she is swearing at me and that bothers me very much" (Ferreira et al., 2002: 25). Yet another participant complained about the excessive consumption of alcohol by her daughter; however, other statements reflect her ability to cope with a hopeless situation despite her pain and sense of hopelessness: "My daughter is hurting so much that it has begun to affect me but what am I supposed to do, she is mine" (Ferreira et al., 2002: 26).

Aging, Gender, and Language

A substantial number of studies have investigated the nature of the relationship between gender and language. In most of these studies, women are defined and discussed in negative terms (Bagwasi and Sunderland, 2013). Grandmothers are, however, regarded in an honorable and respectful manner because of their increasingly important social roles. As a result, older African women may experience social contexts differently from younger women and may be portrayed more positively than younger women because of their increasingly powerful role, either due to age or widowhood. It is, however, instructive to note that the terms *women* and *men* used in Western scholarship do not always correspond with some African categories, which, at times, include possibilities of "female husbands, and male wife" (Amadiume, 1987). According to Amadiume, whether one is regarded as husband or wife depends on one's access to power. Individuals who had access to power were referred to as male, irrespective of their biological gender. Individuals who were in a subordinate role in a domestic context were defined as female, even if they were male. Hence the terms may be regarded as contradictory from a Western perspective—"male wife," "female husband."

Therefore, the role and status of women do not remain static (Bagwasi and Sunderland, 2013), and one of the major changes occurs after a husband's death. The Samia (women in Kenya) are required by custom to be remarried to one of the late husband's relatives. In order to resist the remarriage, the Samia women appeal to Christianity, as expressed in the quotation, "Praise the Lord and say no to men" (Cattell, 1992), during the funerals. Another strategy used to resist remarriage is the use of circumlocutions and oblique language only interpretable by them. The circumlocutions are an index of their ability to control their own language and shape a new identity (Cattell, 1992), reflecting the extent to which language and aging are influenced by social events, such as resistance to remarriage after the death of a husband.

In addition to widowhood, ethnic membership can play a role in how women negotiate aging. On the one hand, young women identify themselves by exploiting their ethnic membership; on the other hand, older women identify themselves on the basis of family relations and implied ethnic membership. The discourse of older women is marked by frequent complaints about the behavior of the youth, particularly their social and linguistic habits, which ostensibly undermine and deviate from tradition, real or imagined. Older women complain, "They talk to us like children," thereby ideologically exploiting tradition and power to reinforce their status, which they believe is being challenged. Functionally, the discursive trope is, at times, difficult to distinguish from complaining. Yet, van der Geest (2007) argued that characterizations of speech practices by the elderly as complaint discourse fail to take into account the target audiences of the discourses. He argued that since the elderly would like to project a positive image of themselves, they are unlikely to complain in public because to do so would be self-defeating. The complaint discourse is more likely to be used when addressing researchers than as a general discourse strategy. In some cases, the discourses that are used are a reflection of the interviewee's perspective of what they feel the researcher would like to be told.

In some ethnic groups (e.g., among the !Kung San people), complaining is not typical of aging. It is a "levelling discourse and reminds people of reciprocal obligations" and a "public exhortation to keep goods and services circulating" (van der Geest, 2007). The past is, therefore, used as both a better time and a source of legitimacy for the grandparents' power.

Language and Elderly Care in Institutional Settings
In this section I outline the complicated nature of the relationship between interactional styles and elderly care. Research has revealed three basic interaction styles in elder care institutions in which aged South African whites are cared for by black South African women: (1) controlling discourse, (2), infantilization, and (3) playful endearment. The discourse styles found in South African nursing homes are comparable to those used in radically different social environments, such as the United Kingdom (Makoni and Grainger, 2002).

An analysis of the discourse practices in institutional settings shows how care is interactional and accomplished from moment to moment, situation to situation, in a fascinating and unpredictable manner that creates a continuous drama of complementary and conflicting interpersonal relations. According to Marks (1994), the history of black South African nursing is marked by frequent attempts by black nurses to assert authority over white residents, while simultaneously upholding the principles of care and efficiency. The authority of black nurses is openly challenged by white residents because until after the end of the apartheid era, nursing was regarded as a form of black female labor. Controlling discourse is instructional talk characterized by the production of instructions such as "come," "go," "sit down." The objective of such instructional talk by black nurses is to regulate and control white residents.

The discourses used in nursing home must also be understood within a wider context that includes architectural design. Nursing homes are constructed so that senior nurses can monitor the practices of junior nurses. Lobbies are situated near the entrance, and the general ward is at the extreme end of the corridor. In the general ward, chairs are placed against the wall. Thus, the architectural design orients residents and nurses in very specific patterns that are not conducive to generating conversation. The South African nursing home facilities were architecturally constructed as a panopticon complex, particularly those that are still racially segregated. Power contestations in such nursing homes are typically between the older whites and black nurses, with the goal of both groups avoiding placement at the bottom of the power hierarchy.

Elderspeak and Urban Youth Vernaculars as Sociolinguistic Myths

An orthodox view may regard elderspeak as a language variety used by old, female, rural women in contrast to urban vernaculars spoken by young urban males. In this section, I challenge these assumptions from a critical feminist linguistic perspective by arguing that elderspeak and urban youth vernaculars are not binary opposites but rather are different sides of the same coin.

Massive urban-rural migration, the emergence of urban peri-settlements, and the existence of multigenerational households have led to intense interactions between the youth and the elderly, blurring the boundaries between the so-called urban youth vernaculars and elderspeak. The intense interactions between generations in multigenerational households are further consolidated by similar interactions in public spaces. These interactions have a substantial impact on language practices because of the extensive expansion of informal markets.

Even though urban vernaculars and elderspeak are different sides of the same coin, each speaker has a unique language variety because even though their backgrounds may be similar, no two people have identical networks.

Concluding Remarks
In this chapter, I have attempted to illustrate that the ethnic and political diversity of the sub-Saharan landscape renders it extremely difficult to talk about the language of aging in Africa. Aging and its discourses are not cross-culturally identical across continents, and not even across the African continent. Clearly, this argument has radical implications for research into language and aging, and for the so-called elderspeak, which is founded on uniformity. This chapter offers a counterargument to elderspeak, based on what I call *gerontolinguisitcs*, that is, the critical sociolinguistic analysis of the language of aging.

In this chapter, I have argued for the importance of considering how language and aging are actually experienced, since the onset of aging is understood differently in various contexts. I also have warned that aging intersects with gender, as well as with how families and institutions are constituted. The chapter warns of the dangers of examining the language of aging in isolation from its contextual use. Thus, using the African context, the chapter views how the language of aging changes in different societal contexts, in multigenerational families, in various institutions, with different gendered identities, and with different age groups. Gerontolinguistics offers a more nuanced critical approach to the study of the language of aging than traditional sociolinguistic analysis.

Bibliography
Amadiume, I. (1987). *Re-Inventing Africa: Male Daughters, Female Husbands*. London: ZED Books.
Bagwasi, M., and J. Sunderland,. (2013). "Language, Gender and Ageism in seTswana." In L. L. Atanga, S. E. Ellece, L. Litosseliti, and J. Sunderland (eds.), *Gender and Language in Sub- Saharan Africa: Tradition, Struggle and Change* (pp. 53–79). Philadelphia: John Benjamins.
Canut, C. (2009). "Discourse, Community, Identity: Processes of Linguistic Homogenization." In F. Mclaughlin (ed.), *The Languages of Urban Africa* (pp. 86–103). Maiden Lane, New York: Continuum Press.
Cattell, M. G. (1992). "'Praise the Lord and say no to men': Older Women Empowering Themselves in Samia, Kenya." *Journal of Cross-Cultural Gerontology* 7(4): 307–330.
Cohen, L. (1998). *There Is No Aging in India: Alzheimer's Disease, the Bad Family and Modern Things*. Berkeley: University of California Press.
Fadiman, J. (1982). *An Oral History of Tribal Warfare: The Meru of Mt.Kenya*. Anthens: Ohio University Press.
Ferreira, M., M. Keikelame, and Y. Mosaval. (2002). "Older Women as Carers for Children Affected by AIDS: A Study Towards Supporting the Carers." Report on Aging. University of Cape Town.

Folta, J. R., and E. S. Deck. (1987). "Elderly Black Widows in Rural Zimbabwe." *Journal of Cross-Cultural Gerontology* 2: 321–342.

Foner, N. (1984). *Ages in Conflict: A Cross-Cultural Perspective on Inequality between Old and Young.* New York: Columbia University Press.

Giles, H., S. Makoni, and R. Dailey. (2005). "Intergenerational Communication Beliefs across the Life Span: Comparative Data from Ghana and South Africa". *Journal of Cross-Cultural Gerontology* 20: 191–211.

Gulliver, P. H. (1963). *Social Change in an African Society.* London: Routledge.

Keith, J. (1990). "Age in Social and Cultural Context: Anthropological Perspectives." In R. H. Binstock and L. K. George (eds.), *Handbook of Aging and the Social Sciences* (3rd ed., pp. 91–111). San Diego, CA: Academic Press.

Livingston, J. (2001). "Physical Fitness and Economic Opportunity in the Bechuanaland Protectorate in the 1930's and 1940's." *Journal of Southern African Studies* 27(4): 793–811.

Makoni, S. B. (1998). "Conflict and Control in Inter-Cultural Communication: A Case Study of Compliance Gaining Strategies in Interactions between Black Nurses and White Residents in a Nursing Home in Cape Town." *Multilingua* 17 (2&3): 227–248.

Makoni, S. B., and K. Grainger. (2002). "Comparative Gerontolinguistics: Characterizing Discourses in Caring Institutions in South Africa and the United Kingdom." *Journal of Social Issues* 58(4): 805–824.

Marks, S. (1994). *Divided Sisterhood: Race, Class and Gender in the South African Nursing Profession.* New York: St. Martin's Press.

Nussbaum, J. F., et al. (2000). *Communication and Aging.*

Mahwah, NJ: Lawrence Erlbaum.
Rossi- Landi, F. (1983). *Language as Work and Trade: A Semiotic Homology for Linguistics and Economics*. South Hadley, MA: Bergen and Gravey Publishers.
Rozanova, J. (2010). "Discourses of Successful Aging in *The Globe & Mail*: Insights from Critical Gerontology." *Journal of Aging Studies* 24: 213–222.
Smith, L. (2002). *Decolonizing Methodologies: Research and Indigenous Peoples*. Dunedin, NZ: University of Otago Press.
van der Geest, S. (2002). "Respect and Reciprocity: Elderly Care in Rural Ghana." *Journal of Cross-Cultural Gerontology* 17(1): 3–31.
van der Geest, S. (2007). "It Is Tiresome Work: Love and Sex in the Life of an Elderly Kwahu Woman." In C. Oppong and I. K. Okokey (eds.), *Sex and Gender in an Era of AIDS: Ghana at the Turn of the Millennium* (pp. 211–232). Accra, Ghana: Sub-Sahara Publishers.

www.ingramcontent.com/pod-product-compliance
Lightning Source LLC
Chambersburg PA
CBHW071343290426
44108CB00014B/1427